-VOLUME One-

WE WERE EAGLES

THE EIGHTH AIR FORCE AT WAR

-VOLUME ONE-

WE WERE EAGLES

THE EIGHTH AIR FORCE AT WAR

JULY 1942 TO
NOVEMBER 1943

MARTIN W.
BOWMAN

AMBERLEY

First published 2014

Amberley Publishing
The Hill, Stroud
Gloucestershire, GL5 4EP

www.amberley-books.com

British Library Cataloguing in Publication Data.
A catalogue record for this book is available from the British Library.

ISBN 978 1 4456 3363 3 (hardback)
ISBN 978 1 4456 3375 6 (ebook)

Typeset in 11pt on 13pt Sabon.
Typesetting and Origination by Amberley Publishing.
Printed in the UK.

CONTENTS

CHAPTER 1

Yankee Doodle Goes to Town

'The British public have an erroneous belief, which has been fostered by effective RAF publicity, that the German war machine can be destroyed and the nation defeated by intensive bombing.'
American air attaché in London reporting to Washington in
April 1942.

Early in 1942, Blenheims were replaced on daylight operations by Bostons, much faster American bombers with a heavier bomb load, but at the same time fighters were carrying bombs or making attacks on shipping by cannon-fire. The really important daylight attacks of 1942 were long-range ones by Lancasters; these were essentially part of the great campaign of strategic bombing that began in the spring of 1942, when at last the striking force was large enough, and there were sufficiently few diversions, for the planned attack on German industry to be conducted with adequate resources.

'*Achtung, feindliche Flugzeuge!*'– *Jagdführer*, or Fighter Control, in Holland had picked up four three-plane elements heading across the North Sea. Immediately, Luftwaffe fighter units were alerted. German radar had picked up twelve US-built Boston medium bombers thundering low across the North Sea to four airfield targets in Holland. Six of the aircraft carried RAF crews, while American crews of the 15th Bomb Squadron (Light) manned the other half dozen. Significantly, it was 4 July 1942 – American Independence Day – and the first time

American airmen had flown in US-built bombers against a German target.

Being the first American airmen to fly a mission from England was probably the furthest thing from their minds when the officers and men of the 15th Light Bombardment Squadron aboard the P&O armed merchant cruiser HMS *Cathay* had docked in Britain on 14 May, at Newport, Wales. They were the first Army Air Force unit to arrive in the theatre since America had entered the war at the end of 1941. The USA had been dramatically shaken from its isolation, and was pitched headlong into the tumult of global war on 7 December when Japanese bombers operating from carriers in the Pacific Ocean carried out an unprovoked assault on Pearl Harbor and other military installations in Hawaii. Germany declared war on America the following day.

The 15th Bomb Squadron (Light) was symptomatic of America's almost total unpreparedness for war. It had no aircraft, although some of its personnel had worked on the Douglas A-20 Havoc (Boston) and a few had even flown them. Shipped to England as night fighters, the 15th was never part of the high-altitude, daylight, precision bombing offensive using heavy bombers that had been envisioned by American war planners. Its use was a hasty stopgap measure resorted to by AAF General Henry 'Hap' Arnold after promising British Prime Minister Winston Churchill on 23 May, 'We will be fighting with you on July 4th.' Arnold had in mind a scheduled B-17 Group for this job, but dire events interfered. On 4 June the Japanese initiated a major offensive in the Pacific, attacking Alaska and Midway Island. B-17s about to depart for England were immediately diverted to the American West Coast. With the turning-point Battle of Midway over, original orders sending the B-17s to England were reinstated, but the delay caused by the shuttle exercise made it impossible for any of the Fortress squadrons involved to fly a mission to Germany before mid-August. That left the 15th, the only AAF squadron in the 8th Air Force, to fulfil Arnold's promise to Churchill.

The 15th entrained for Grafton Underwood in Northamptonshire, the first of four bases it would occupy during its stay in England. The American squadron was given a warm welcome by the RAF CO, as Captain Bill Odell, a Midwesterner originally commissioned as an Anti-Aircraft Artillery Officer in 1938, recalls:

Beside him, US Brigadier General Ira C Eaker, representing the 8th Air Force, also greeted the newcomers, speaking with inspiration and pride when he said their arrival marked the first time in history that any American fighting unit set foot in England. 1st Lieutenant Philip Hennin, a pilot whose mother was active in the Burlington, Vermont 'Daughters of the American Revolution' chapter (an exclusive women's patriotic society restricted to female descendants of the men who fought in the War of Independence), glanced around at the blue-uniformed RAF officers present to catch any adverse reaction. Then he muttered, 'I wonder if General Braddock said something like that to his redcoat regiments that marched across Pennsylvania in 1775?' Hennin was known for his offbeat sense of humour and his rather dour outlook on life. General Eaker's closing comment, 'All those who come after you, by comparison, will be recruits,' was meant to be complimentary, but cool scepticism showed on Hennin's face.

Bill Odell said in an undertone, 'We aren't here for manoeuvres; this is for real. The general should have said 'replacements' not 'recruits.' Hennin then added a final remark: 'Anyway, that's the last we'll see of him.' He was to be proved wrong. In time, Eaker would visit the squadron again, along with the two highest-ranking American generals in the ETO, to make note of a memorable event.

The 15th Bomb Squadron had been despatched to England with the first influx of US troops in the UK to learn how to operate the airborne searchlight used by the RAF's Havoc (Douglas DB-7) night fighters. Airborne radar had replaced the airborne searchlight, and the Americans were moved around East Anglia. Frustration was creeping in. The 15th still had no aircraft and the men were becoming tired of quaint English village stone walls, vine-covered churches and warm beer. They liked the constant rejoinders – 'It's rationed you know' and 'There's a war on Yank!' – still less. The 15th were at the mercy of the RAF, and soon learned the meaning of wartime rationing. RAF cooks were running the mess, and the only palatable food for Americans used to peacetime fare was black bread and cheese. Everything else was slop. After a week or so, the American Mess Sergeant and cooks took over the kitchen and the food improved, but some rations defied their best efforts. On 4 June Lieutenant Cook went over to Swanton Morley for some first-hand experience of the RAF's way of doing things. Lieutenant Howard Cook was no happier with the state of affairs in the 15th than anyone else, and probably this led to his first big mistake when he tried to tell the RAF how to fly low!

While at Grafton Underwood, on Thursday 6 June, the 15th Squadron suffered two fatal accidents shortly after receiving its first DB-7 aircraft. The cause of the first accident was never discovered but the second was due to pilot error. Practising low-level flying, Lieutenant Raditsky flew the aircraft into a high-tension cable. One cable caught the aircraft at the junction of the metal and Plexiglas, shearing the entire nose glass covering section from the bombardier's compartment where Lieutenant Notorwitz was sitting. The pilot managed to avoid a crash, and brought the aircraft home safely. Jack Stone of the Engineering Office hurried to meet the aircraft, not knowing what to expect but certainly not prepared for the macabre sight that met his eyes.

> The Plexiglas had been sheared off and the decapitated body of the bombardier remained strapped in the seat. The force of the wind through the open compartment had whipped the body against the jagged edges of Plexiglas. The compartment was a horrible bloody mess and blood covered the sides of the plane from nose to tail.

On 7 June Captain Kegelman, acting squadron commander, was ordered to vacate the base to make room for the incoming 97th Bomb Group equipped with B-17s. Flights in training with the RAF were recalled and all flying activity was halted while the move to Molesworth, a new airfield constructed especially for US heavy bomber use, took place. No explanation was given for the sudden move, a mere 7 miles' distance. Much to their chagrin, the move to Podington put them within sight and sound of other bases, from which aircraft could be heard going on missions. While pilots in the 15th Squadron were awaiting radio equipment and aircraft to arrive from the States before anything else could be done, most of the ground crews were passing the time away at Molesworth, waiting for something to happen. By 25 June, by which time equipment had arrived, there was no place to store it and no aircraft either, as Kegelman, Crabtree, Odell, Cook and six other pilots and gunners, along with the Bostons, had started training under the direction of 226 Squadron.

Bill Odell recalls,

Senior Flight Leaders, Captains Kegelman, Crabtree and myself had been commissioned officers at least four years before our arriving in England, had flown the A-20 aircraft at least almost two years and each had over 1,000 hours flight time. Our junior pilots, like Lieutenants Hawel, Loehrl and Lynn, had completed flying school in December 1941. The only advantage we Yanks had was largely technical. We learned by flying in the RAF manner on the wing of battle-experienced pilots. There was much to learn. At the same time, the 226 pilots discovered we flew the Boston differently than they. In a subtle way we demonstrated a different technique when taking off in formation. While the RAF leader approached the end of the field still on the ground the US pilot wingmen would be airborne and flying alongside with their wheels drawing up into the wheel wells. The RAF mechanics were particularly grateful; damaged nose gear wheels and struts had become a major headache for them.

From the beginning, Wing Commander Lynn, CO, 226 Squadron, recognized that the senior ranking US pilots – Captains and 1st Lieutenants with up to two years flying the A-20 – knew and flew the Boston aircraft better than his own. Even the 2nd Lieutenants who had completed AAF flying schools in late December 1941 had more technical knowledge and mechanical aptitude than any newly trained RAF pilot being posted to his squadron. The training they had received and absorbed was consistent with that given RAF crews being readied for daylight sweeps or night intruder missions. They had recently conducted simulated attacks and live bombing runs on sunken ships near the coast or land targets on isolated spits of land. From the stepped-up frequency and types of formation flights employing minimum altitude approaches to coastlines so as to stay below radar detection and the use of evasive action at various altitudes over land to avoid enemy flak, there was little doubt that their RAF training was in its final phase. All they lacked was actual combat experience.

In that regard, Wing Commander Lynn had advised his superiors that aside from providing an initial baptism of fire, his ability to further the Americans' pre-battle education was limited. They had already participated in combat-related activities by flying with the host squadron aircraft, ranging far beyond the English coastlines on post-mission sea searches for downed RAF aircrews. Lynn believed the American aircrews placed in his custody to be fully familiar with the local topography and able to comply with all RAF flight procedures. They could be turned loose anytime and be perfectly confident of finding their way around in the dark.

On 4 June at Great Massingham ten officers in two groups, one under Cook and the other under Odell, left early in the morning to go to operational stations. Odell recalls,

I was also given ten sergeants, who hoped to make a show as aerial gunners. We arrived at West Raynham just at lunchtime, so booked our meals and went to a briefing of the Boston Squadron. Time had to be wasted, so we watched the installation of a power mount for the twin guns of the Boston. It seemed quite practical, since it had almost all advantages of a turret, yet none of the tremendous weight. I was anxious to see what results were obtained after practice firing.

The briefing took place in the ops Offices. The target was a 480 feet tower in the docks at Dunkirk. The route was almost direct using the tactics of sea level flight to foil the radio aircraft-detection system until about 13 minutes from the coast. At that point a 1,000-feet climb was to begin and drop four 500lb bombs at 10,000 feet. We watched the take-off and saw the English method much different than ours. Namely, their engines were run from ten to twenty minutes on the ground before flight. The members of this squadron were all Blenheim trained which might have accounted for such procedure. The Bostons were kept on the ground with all three wheels until a bounce forced the pilot to fly it. One new pilot took off with upper cowl flaps open and reported back to the Squadron CO that he thought for a long while it was the bomb load causing the different flight characteristics. They attempted to take off in formation but didn't seem to hold it very well and didn't become organised until after four–five minutes of flying. They had a much more open formation than we did.

We left the field for dinner after a talk with their Engineering Officer about engine trouble and booster coils as well as brake and landing gear problems. The average British pilot seemed to know very little about his ship. One Blenheim pilot didn't know how many cylinders there were in his motors! Their Engineering Officer seemed well trained but had trouble convincing the pilots of their errors. All through the meal Wing Commander Lynn (the CO) kept a close check on the flight by checking his watch. As soon as they left the target we left the mess. Back at 'Ops' we learned very shortly that only five of the six that went on the run would be back. Pilot Officer Skinner and crew ditched their ship and were all in the dinghy. Shortly the five showed up over the field, one circled and shot a red flare to show he was in trouble.

On 25 June after breakfast, the 15th Squadron contingent was driven to Swanton Morley. It was the night of the second 1,000-plane raid against Bremen, and the Boston squadron was to make a low-level dusk attack on two German night fighter airdromes. Odell recalls,

After the briefing we watched the take-off. The raid was a success though one flight bombed a dummy airdrome. Next day there was an air raid on Norwich, 18 miles distant that took a helluva pasting from Jerry. A couple of the rascals were stooging around overhead but luckily didn't drop a thing. Next day Norwich was closed to everyone. The Huns must have done a lot of no good. King's Lynn too was also out of bounds because of bombing. Someone saw a notice of a party at Watton, so I organized a group to go there. We were warmly welcomed and had a grand time discussing America with some Pilot Officers who were trained at Maxwell and Selma. Nothing much was doing for there were very few people circulating and the whole show folded up at 10:45. We drove home and piled into bed. Norwich was still smoking on Sunday, June 28th so we couldn't go there.

On Monday 29 June Captain Kegelman and Lieutenant Bell represented the USA when 226 Squadron flew an operational flight in the afternoon to the marshalling yards at Hazebroek. Kegelman was a skilled pilot and fighter leader who inspired trust and confidence in his men and was well liked. He, Bell, Sergeant 'Bennie' Cunningham and Technical Sergeant Robert Golay in DB-7 AL743, borrowed from 226 Squadron, flew as a member of the twelve-plane formation, led by Squadron Leader 'Shaw' Kennedy. Bombing from between 12,500 and 13,000 feet, the formation recorded two hits on the railway lines at the eastern end of the yard, and one or two were seen to burst on railway lines and sheds at the western end. The rest of the bombs fell on buildings to the south and north. No flak was encountered by the formation while over the target, and all the aircraft returned. Not so fortunate were the escorting Spitfires, who encountered German fighters en route to the target, claiming three destroyed for the loss of five of their own. Also providing cover for the first time on a 'Circus' raid were Hawker Typhoons.

Odell recorded,

The mission was just like manoeuvres because no flak at all was seen. All twelve planes returned and bacon and eggs was served to the crews. Immediately afterwards the beer began to be consumed. I took three officers and the two WAAF officers to their WAAF dance and remained to drive them home. I got into a grand discussion with a Scottish lieutenant and an English captain. We went thru the military history of the US, me taking the part of the South on the question of slavery. Comparatively, the dance was dull. I was surprised at the charming young women the Group Captain (Colonel in our air force) and the Mess Officer married. Though both were over 40 and 30 respectively, their wives were not over twenty. I danced with them as a matter of courtesy and even as a matter of choice. A hell of a way to celebrate an anniversary – dancing with someone else's wife but I can't say I was joyously happy. After the dance dwindled down I brought the WAAF and RAF officers home. It was later, about 1.30 a hell of a party was going on – always after a successful op and Bell and Keg were signing their names on the vaulted ceiling 22 feet up. The rest were pouring beer down each other's necks and playing madly all over the place. I went to bed – just dozing off when a couple of sports came in and up-ended my bed, piling me into the wall with mattress and blankets on top of me. I finally shoved it out from the wall just as the air raid alarm went off. I couldn't turn on the lights; the main switch was off. So tried to get organized in the dark just as the bombs started coming down. The windows rattled, the dull booming, hang out and dazed. Finally I got organized enough to get in bed but the bombs kept me awake for a while. The raid must have been at Norwich again although two of them hit Swanton Morley. It was a hectic night throughout.

Harry Castledine in 226 Squadron recalls,

The Americans were a really wild lot, but great fun. I was told they played cowboy and Indians in the woods around Bylaugh Hall with live ammo! At the All-Ranks dances you might think that they would win a jitterbug contest, but a lot depended on the partner and the WAAFs were not so experienced.

Leo Hawel, another American pilot, adds,

On July 1st Captain Kegelman put all nine American pilots' names in a hat. Six were marked with a 'yes' and three marked 'no'. I drew a 'yes' and later discovered I was one of six American pilots who would fly the famous 4th July raid over Holland. The six pilots drawn were Captains Kegelman, Crabtree and Odell and Lieutenants Lynn, Loerhl and myself.

On Thursday 2 July Generals Spaatz and Eaker arrived and Kegelman talked with them. The generals wanted the Americans to put on a 'Circus' without fighter escort. Odell wrote,

Just shows you how much our brass hats know or how they value the cost of men's lives … Spaatz, Eaker and Eisenhower met the crews going on the sortie on 4 July and shook hands with all of us. Not only were we surprised, but a little embarrassed by them coming to make such a big deal out of what aircrews of 226 Squadron considered to be just another mission not unlike many others to their credit. It seemed a little ironic that they had been pressed into taking part in an American Independence Day celebration commemorating the severance of ties between our two countries. Then it was off to dinner and the food did some good. At six o'clock we got our kit and at 6.30 we were briefed. Four flights were attacking four fighter airdromes at low-level in daylight.

Squadron Leader Shaw Kennedy was leading, with Kegelman and 2nd Lieutenant Jack Loehrl. Their target was De Kooy. The three Bostons flown by Flight Lieutenant Ronald A. 'Yogi' Yates-Earl, Pilot Officer C. F. 'Hank' Henning and Lieutenant Stan G. Lynn, were heading for Bergen Alkmaar. Three more, flown by Squadron Leader John Castle, Captain Martin Crabtree and Lieutenant Leo Hawel, headed for Valkenburg. The final three, flown by Flight Lieutenant A. B. Wheeler, Pilot Officer A 'Elkie' Eltringham and Captain Bill Odell, headed for Haamstede.

Odell, like the others, had been awakened at 5.15 and served coffee in the mess hall before going to the operations room. 'We turned in our papers and got packed for combat flight (concentrated food, water purifier, compass and French, Dutch and German money). More dope on the trip and then out to the airplane. Had no trouble but was a bit anxious on take off.' General Dwight D. Eisenhower, newly arrived in England to command the US Forces in the ETO, was to recall in his autobiography, *Crusade in Europe*, 'To mark our entry into the European fighting I took time to visit the crews immediately before the take-off and talked with the survivors after their return.'

The first of the Bostons had begun taking off at 7.09 hours. The rest of the formation, followed in the next five minutes. The first formation, led by New Zealander Flight Lieutenant 'Digger' Wheeler, reached Haamstede at just before eight o'clock. Behind Wheeler came Pilot Officer A. 'Elkie' Eltringham, followed by Captain Odell. Odell continues,

After getting in the air we settled down and flew right on the trees to the coast. Then we went down to the water. Nice ride until the other vic left us. Felt a little uneasy because there was a cloudless sky but no fighters appeared. Found land ahead and could spot the landmark of the lighthouse a long way off. Swung over the edge of the coast even lower than the leader and stayed right on the grass. I opened the bomb doors, yelled to Birleson and then it started. I fired all the guns for all I was worth and Birly dropped the bombs. I saw the hangar but that wasn't my dish. I saw Germans running all over the place but I put most of my shots over their heads. Our bombs were OK. I thought we would crash any moment for I never flew so reckless in my life. The next moment we were flashing past the coast and out to sea – the water behind us boiling from the bullets dropping into it all around. I kicked and pulled and jerked from side to side. I didn't look at the airspeed; I was trying to miss the waves. Over the target we were doing 265 but shortly after I opened up a bit. 'Digger' claims he shot his guns into a formation of troops lined up for an inspection – his bombs hit well where they should have. 'Elkie' was a bit behind but he got rid of his load. He got a broken radio antenna and a mashed in wing edge. I picked up a hole just above the pilot's step and a badly knocked up bomb door. We zigged and zagged while eight miles out and then closed up waiting for fighters. None came. We reached the coast and were the first ones home.

At Haamstede hits were achieved on administration buildings, a hangar and dispersal points. On their way across the airfield Wheeler's burst on his front guns had dispersed a parade of some 160 German aircrew in flying kit. The rear gunners on all three aircraft machine-gunned other targets as they swept across the field. As the formation left the target area, much smoke was seen over the south-eastern area of Haamstede.

At Bergen Alkmaar the three aircraft led by Yates-Earl in 'Y-Yorker' arrived at two minutes past eight. Difficulties in identifying the target caused the formation to attack at 100 feet in line astern, starting fires on hangars on the north side of the airfield. The Boston flown by Lieutenant Stan Lynn and his American crew was hit by flak after bombing, and crashed on the airfield killing all on board.

Another Boston, flown by Pilot Officer 'Hank' Henning, left the target area after bombing but was intercepted by a Messerschmitt Bf 109 of *Jagdgeschwader 1* 15 miles from the Dutch coast, and was shot down. The Bf 109 had taken off from Bergen Alkmaar during the attack and had chased the formation to the coast.

The formation attacking Valkenburg found themselves too far south after crossing the coast to turn correctly on to track for the airfield. Lieutenant Leo Hawel recalls,

> Our flight hit the Dutch coast south of the point we had planned and our course took us through the main part of The Hague. We were so low, I saw two young ladies eating breakfast right out of my side window. I recall flying under some telephone wires and had to lift my right wing to avoid a church tower. [Frank H. Donnelly, his bombardier-navigator, felt that he was 'looking up at a few honest burghers'.] The target came up very fast and we were briefed to open our bomb bay doors when the leader opened his and bomb on him. I instructed my gunners to fire with their machine guns and I did the same as we settled down for the bombing run.

As they ran in, Squadron Leader John Castle, leading the formation, found he was unable to open his bomb doors through an error in selection. On the run in to a target Boston pilots normally had the bomb doors selected to 'neutral' and then placed them to 'open' before dropping their bombs. Castle discovered too late that he was still selected to 'closed', and moving the door control had only placed the doors in 'neutral', so they failed to open. Captain Martin Crabtree and Leo Hawel waited in vain for the leader's bomb doors to open as the signal to drop their own bombs. Instead, the formation used their machine guns on airfield buildings and three dispersed Messerschmitt 109s, setting one on fire. All three aircraft were forced to bring their bombs back.

The formation attacking De Kooy also came in just off track and, finding itself unable to turn, was forced to fly through 3 miles of flak, which Squadron Leader Shaw Kennedy, the formation leader, was to describe later as the worst he had encountered in over sixty operational missions. The intense flak prevented all three Bostons from bombing. Kennedy machine-gunned ack-ack positions and personnel near the airfield. On the way home he attacked a 250-foot trawler with bombs and machine guns, the bombs unfortunately overshooting. He also attacked a second trawler with machine guns. Behind Kennedy, Lieutenant Jack Loehrl was hit by flak north of the airfield. Apparently, Loehrl made the fatal mistake of making a normal turn, allowing the flak gunners to anticipate his course. Loehrl crashed on the beach. He and his two gunners, Sergeants Wright and Whitham, were killed. Lieutenant Marshall Draper, the bombardier, survived and was taken prisoner.

The other wing ship – with Kegelman at the controls and crewed by Lieutenant R. M. Dorton, the navigator; Sergeant Bennie Cunningham, rear gunner; and Technical Sergeant R. L. Goley, dorsal gunner – was also badly hit. The starboard engine took a direct hit and burst into flames with the propeller flying off. Kegelman's right wing tip struck the ground, and the fuselage actually bounced on the surface of the airdrome, tearing a hole in the belly of the bomber. Golay recalls, 'We were flying so low over the target when I felt us take a hit and then saw a propeller go sailing by. My first thought was, I hope that isn't ours! Then I felt us hit the ground and the bottom oilcanning under my feet.'

Lifting the Boston back in to the air on one engine, Kegelman headed for the Channel. He was debating whether or not to set his crippled ship down on the sand dunes when, over the interphone, he heard his rear gunner exhorting him enthusiastically to 'give 'em hell, Captain'. Kegelman duly obliged. A flak tower on Den Helder airfield opened up and the young captain returned fire with his nose guns. He lifted the Boston over the tower and headed for England with the right engine on fire. The fire went out over the Channel and Kegelman continued home to Swanton Morley hugging the waves across the North Sea.

At Swanton Morley the first returning Boston, piloted by Kennedy, landed at 0814 hours. During the next forty minutes the others landed. The last to touch down was Kegelman, who, despite the loss of one engine, made a good landing and taxied to the control tower before shutting down. Inspection of his aircraft revealed scratch marks on the belly of his Boston where he had touched the ground. The experienced 226 Squadron crews were all of the same opinion that the flak encountered on the raid was the worst the squadron had ever experienced. Odell concludes,

All came back except Loehrl, Lynn and Henning. Loehrl was hit by a heavy shell and hit the ground right in the middle of the airdrome. 'He flew into a million pieces,' one gunner said. And I owed him £1 10s I felt like a thief! Lynn was following before the flight hit the target, but never came away from it. His wife was to have a baby in November. He really wasn't cut out for this game. At breakfast he was salting his food, trying to hold the salt spoon steady and yet throwing salt over his shoulders! I hoped he didn't crash. A Me109 that took off just ahead of him shot down Henning. He tried to get it, but it turned, got behind him and set one motor on fire. He crashed into the sea. General Eaker, General Duncan and Beaman were there at the start and finish and didn't look so happy at the finish. They must have thought it was a 'piece of cake' until three turned up shot down – two being American. Thusly, we celebrated Independence Day! Beirne Lay and some Major from HQ took down our names and addresses, as it would probably be recorded for the folks back home. A party started shortly after breakfast (10.15) and kept up till lockout. I have to admit that this was the first day in history when I had a scotch and soda before breakfast! Everyone went to bed after dinner. I went to Norwich with Hawel and Bell and bought a shirt. Norwich took a real pasting because it was in worse shape than it was last time I saw it. One factory was completely demolished. Good shooting on Jerry's part. There was a big party that evening but I wasn't in the mood to enjoy it. Shortly after the buffet supper, which was excellent, I went to bed.

Leo Hawel joined in the roaring party at Swanton Morley: 'When you lose a bunch of good boys, you *have* to get good and drunk; otherwise you'll get pretty browned-off with the whole set-up.' In the middle of Ambassador John C. Winant's Fourth of July party at the Court of St. James in London, Captain Harry C. Butcher, General Eisenhower's naval aide, was called to a side room in the J. Pierpoint Morgan mansion to take a phone call from General Charles L. Bolte. He passed the results of the first American raid to General Eisenhower. Of the four airfield targets, only one had been attacked successfully. Of the six American crews taking part, only one had engaged the Luftwaffe with good results.

General Ira C. Eaker, the theatre commander, later penned Kegelman in for a Distinguished Service Cross. He was promoted to Major and ordered stateside with his crew (after an 'agonizing' tour of duty in the USA helping to sell war bonds, he returned to the 15th Bomb Squadron).[1] Three others received the Distinguished Flying Cross. Of the RAF crews taking part, Flight Lieutenant Yates-Earl and his observer Pilot Officer Houghton were awarded the DFC, and his gunner, Sergeant Leaver, the DFM, for their part in the attack on Bergen Alkmaar. Next day, after reading the British newspapers and talking it over among themselves, the mood of the American ground crews changed. The maintenance men came to the inevitable conclusion that they could claim no credit; RAF ground crews had performed their work. The enlisted men did take over, though, after this.

On 5 July Captain Odell slept late, and after lunch went to the ops room to see the photos of the target they took from behind. Leo Hawel recalled that everybody was

feeling mighty rough – me included. There was quite a discussion as to the advisability of low-level raids. Our losses were the biggest the station had had in one operation. It all boiled down to this; In a high altitude bombing circus the chances of hitting your target are slim (in these Bostons) and you don't always have clear weather for them. In fact, it was very seldom you had a cloudless day. In low-level raids, you have the element of surprise and that's about all. Jerry wasn't surprised because off the coast he had many small boats called 'squealers', who radio warnings to the land. The squealers were tapping like hell just as soon as we crossed the coast of Holland and continued until we had made good.

The Americans continued with their training and were allocated twenty-three Boston IIIs from RAF stocks. The 15th recommened operations on 5 September 1942, when Major Griffiths led them against the heavily defended docks at Le Havre. Missions were flown using the normal box formation at 8,000 to 12,000 feet, bombing individually, the formation being covered by substantial Spitfire escort. On 11 September the 15th moved to Podington. Had joint USAAF–RAF plans to equip the 1st Pursuit Squadron (NF) with radar-equipped Beaufighters reached fruition, the fate of the 15th Squadron might have been different. However, the idea was postponed through lack of electronic equipment. At the end of September only twelve DB-7s were on hand, and the prospect of getting more Bostons was slim. Six pilots were transferred to wing HQ, and on 1 October Captain Bill Odell was posted to 8th Air Force HQ at High Wycombe. Only Howard Cook of the original cadre of pilots remained. On 8 November the 15th Light Bombardment Squadron was transferred to the 12th Air Force, moving to North Africa to take part in Operation 'Torch' on the 15th. Based at Youks-les-Bain, Tabessa, Algeria, the squadron arrived five days after the invasion, and was operational within a week. The 15th was later absorbed into the 47th Bomb Group in Africa and inactivated.

CHAPTER 2

Target: Germany; Act 1, Scene 1

'The British had no proof yet that their bombing had been any more effective than the German bombing of England. I thought they were asking the United States for a good deal when they wanted it to divest itself of all its bombers and devote a lot of production capacity to the construction of more bombers, thereby committing the US to the policy of reducing Germany by bombing, without affording sufficient proof that this was possible.'

General Raymond Lee, the US Military Attaché in London during a lunch at the Dorchester with assembled British officials and four Air Marshals.

Mid-afternoon on a grey day in February 1942, a Douglas airliner from Lisbon landed at a town in the west of England. The trip had been routine, but not uneventful. Two hours before, far out in the Bay of Biscay, a plane believed to be a German fighter had flashed past the transport not far ahead and slightly above. Failing to spot the DC-3, the unidentified aircraft had continued on its course toward the coast of France.

If the long-range marauder *was* German, the chances are it had been despatched specifically to intercept and destroy the plane carrying a party of seven American officers, led by a brigadier general, who were en route to England as the advance guard of an American bomber command. Lisbon, swarming with spies, had seen the Americans arrive from Bermuda on the previous day. The natural reaction of the Germans would have been to plot the course of the unarmed transport and intercept it at a point far from any possible Allied interference. If such was the case, they failed only by the thickness of a wing – their own wing – which screened the DC-3 from the view of the German pilot.

The seven officers who stepped out of the plane that day carried with them a directive signed by Lieutenant General H. H. Arnold, Chief of the Army Air Forces, and dated 31 January, fifty-five days after Pearl Harbor. The directive named Brigadier General Ira C. Eaker Bomber Commander in England and ordered him, among other things, to 'make the necessary preparation to insure competent and aggressive command and direction of our bomber units in England'.

It was a battered but still defiant Britain that greeted the Americans. The great German aerial Blitz was over; the danger of invasion seemed remote. But on the far fronts of the war things were not going well. The Libyan advance had turned into a retreat. In the Donets Basin, von Bock's steamroller was grinding its way slowly, but apparently irresistibly, toward Stalingrad. In the Pacific the Americans were making a last desperate stand on Bataan. The *Repulse* and the *Prince of Wales* had been sunk. Singapore, chief bastion of occidental power in the Far East, was tottering.

More significant still for these apostles of unborn air power from across the sea, shortly before their arrival, the *Gneisenau*, *Scharnhorst* and *Prinz Eugen*, supposedly immobilised at Brest, took advantage of the vile February weather to make a dash through the Channel for their home bases. The RAF and the Fleet Air Arm took suicidal chances in a gallant and vain attempt to stop them. Critics of air power – ignoring the fact that the German warships had also eluded surface vessels – made the most of the occasion. There were recriminations in parliament. It was a black week.

The Americans went to London. They had no time for sightseeing, but they were impressed by many things – by the bomb damage, neatly tidied but still an object lesson in the destructiveness of aerial bombardment; by the black-out; by the stringency of wartime diet; by the calm fortitude of the British people, who wore the war like an old coat, frayed around the edges, but still nothing of which to be ashamed.

The task facing the seven officers would have appalled anyone – as one RAF officer dryly put it – except Americans. Starting from scratch, they had to build an organisation which would – if their theories were sound, if their convictions were correct – eventually become a hammer that, used in conjunction with the RAF, would crack the iron skull of Nazi Germany.

It was a big job that they faced, but fortunately they had a big brother to help them – the Royal Air Force. The RAF was long past the immortal days of 'the few', to whom so much was owed. After two and a half war years of trial and error and successful experiment, with its Fighter Command guarding the skies by day, Bomber Command striking the enemy by night and Coastal Command sweeping the sea lanes, the RAF might easily have been excused for having a condescending attitude toward the advance guard of Americans, whose plans were so large and whose means were apparently so small.

However, they took no such attitude. From the start, their generosity and sympathetic interest were the keys that unlocked many problems.

'Tell us what you want,' they said. 'If we have it, it is yours.' They might have added, 'Whether or not we need it ourselves.'

There were some in the RAF – many, in fact – who took a dim view (to use their own expressive phrase) of the feasibility of daylight bombing over the fortress of Europe. They remembered, with acute and vivid pleasure, what had happened to the Luftwaffe's bombers over Britain on those autumn afternoons in 1940. They had tested the Germans' daylight defences themselves and found them uncomfortably strong. Nevertheless, if the Americans thought it could be done, they were all for helping them. The sooner the Americans could attain full partnership with the RAF in size and striking power, the better. That seemed to be the unspoken motto of the RAF in those early days. It has continued to be ever since.

Conferences with RAF and American Army officers began immediately. One of the first problems was to find a place where the Americans could hang their tin hats. This was solved eventually by the acquisition of an old abbey.

The story has been told of how the duty officer, on the first night of occupancy, was startled to hear bells beginning to ring all over the building. Investigation proved that each bedroom had a prim little card, relic of schoolgirl days, that read, 'Ring twice for mistress.'

The first combat units were preceded by Intelligence officers, who were sent to RAF operational stations and given every opportunity to study British methods. The first crew to return from the historic 1,000-plane raid on Cologne was interrogated by visiting US Army officers.

Work went on throughout the reluctant English spring. More personnel arrived, but barely enough to keep up with the demands. Airdromes had to be taken over from the British, and American modifications had to be planned; reports had to be sent back to Washington; everyone seemed to have colds in the head; at times the spadework looked endless.

There was always the uncertainty as to how the great machine they were building would function in actual combat. In April some of the staff officers went to inspect a B-17E that had been turned over to the British. They returned with the following gloomy conclusions:

British experts who made a joint study with the above officers condemned the B-17E so far as operations against western Europe are concerned on the following points: *(a)* defensive fire power is too weak to afford reasonable protection, the tail-gun position being cramped and the belly turret so awkward as to be useless; They plan to remove it and use the airplane on Coastal Command work; and *(b)* 4000-lb bombs cannot be installed and bomb loads in any case are small unless the bomb-bay fuel tanks are removed at the expense of range.

Such criticisms were not ignored, but neither were they allowed to shake the ultimate confidence of the planners in the planes that were going to have to do the job.

At the weekly Monday-night staff meetings, hundreds of other problems were discussed: the shortage of labour for airdrome construction, the problems of airdrome defence, of flying control, of transatlantic movement of aircraft, of security of information, of mud control on the sodden stations, of shortages of everything from vitamin pills to bulldozers. These meetings lasted far into the night, but in public little talking was done. The CG set the precedent at a gathering after a dinner given in his honour by the British. Called upon to speak, he rose and uttered twenty-three words: 'We won't do much talking until we've done more fighting. We hope that when we leave, you'll be glad we came. Thank you.'

Out in the field, early arrivals wrestled with as many problems as the staff officers at the 8th Bomber Command – and under far more trying physical conditions. Many of them were living under canvas. The English summer that year was not noted for its sweetness and light. These pioneers had to live on British rations – which were not to their liking. They soon made the acquaintance of those twin nightmares of station life – dispersal (the vast distances between key buildings dictated by the ever-present threat of aerial attack) and mud. As one engineer remarked, 'Where there's construction, there's mud; and where there's war, there's mud; and where there's construction *and* war, there's just plain hell.'

In May a light-bombardment squadron arrived. With it was Captain Charles C. Kegelman, destined within two months to become the first American aerial hero in the European Theatre of Operations. In other parts of the world the British were mopping up in Madagascar, and American air and naval power was winning the Battle of the Coral Sea. However, the Japs were pushing ahead in Burma, a German drive on the Kerch peninsula was gathering momentum, and the fall of Tobruk was only a month away. The war was still balanced on a knife-edge.

At the end of June the first American heavy-bombardment Group was on its way by air. Not without loss. Three B-17s were forced down on a Greenland icecap. One of the crews managed to survive 'by cutting off the blades of one twisted propeller with a hacksaw, then using that engine to furnish heat for the plane and power for the radio generator until a Navy flying boat, landing under extraordinarily hazardous conditions', rescued them. The other crews were also saved – one from a small island and the other from the sea. Two other Fortresses, caught by bad weather off Greenland, were forced down. Again, both crews were rescued.

The excitement that would normally have attended the arrival of this first Group was somewhat overshadowed by the decision, taken on 2 July, to have six crews of Captain Kegelman's light-bombardment squadron join six RAF crews in a daylight minimum-altitude sweep against airdromes in Holland. The planes to be used were RAF Bostons, but for the first time in the Second World War American airmen were to fly American-built bombers against the Germans. The fact that Americans and Britons should thus jointly celebrate America's Independence Day seemed a particularly happy omen.

The press enthusiastically hailed this debut of American airmen as the beginning of a new and gigantic air offensive. On the same day, at the headquarters of the 8th Bomber Command, the following notation was made: 'Arrival of aircraft: 1 B-17E.-Total: 1.'

By 1 August two heavy-bombardment Groups had arrived and were in a state of intensive training. Furthermore, certain target priorities had been established. The CG quoted from the directive as follows:

First the factories, sheds, docks and ports in which the enemy builds his *submarines* and from which he launches his submarine efforts. Next, his *aircraft factories* and other key munitions – manufacturing establishments. Third, his *lines of communication*. A subsidiary purpose of our early bombing operations will be to determine our capacity to destroy pin-point targets by daylight precision bombing and our ability to beat off fighter opposition and to evade antiaircraft opposition.

The first test came on 17 August. It was a critical day for the 8th Bomber Command, not because of the size of the effort – only twelve Fortresses were involved – but because so much was at stake. Pressure in the USA for action in the European Theatre had been mounting steadily. The British press had been hinting for some time that the American bombers were ready. Morale in the squadrons was wearing thin from repeated 'dry runs', bad weather and general impatience to get at the Hun. There were still plenty of sceptics who predicted dismal results from the first attempt at a daylight mission.

At 15.26 the first Fortress took off. Eleven others followed, the CG of the 8th Bomber Command riding in *Yankee Doodle*, lead ship of the second flight of six. The twelve Fortresses were carrying about 18 tons of bombs destined for the railway marshalling yards at Rouen – the city, somebody pointed out, where Joan of Arc had died for the liberation of France half a millennium before. The formation assembled over the field and climbed steadily to their attack level of 22,500 feet before disappearing in the bright clear sky in the direction of France.

For the next three hours, anxious ground crews, fellow airmen bitterly disappointed at being left behind and high-ranking Air Force officers – plus some thirty members of the British and American press – waited about as calmly as expectant fathers in the anteroom of a maternity ward. Shortly before 1900 hours, watchers on the control tower spotted a cluster of specks to the west of the airdrome. Eagerly they counted – for a tense moment there seemed to be only eleven. There was a sigh of relief as the twelfth appeared. Minutes later the big ships swept in to the runway, their names highlighted by the level rays of the sun: *Baby Doll*, *Peggy D*, *Big Stuff*, *Butcher Shop*, *Yankee Doodle*, *Berlin Sleeper*, *Johnny Reb*, *Birmingham-Blitzkrieg*, and the rest. Pilots and mechanics swarmed out to meet the crews. Quickly the word was passed around: all bombs dropped on or near the target, no casualties; good protection from escorting Spitfires; slight flak damage to one B-17; a few brief exchanges of fire with enemy fighters; mission successful.

Interrogation brought out additional information. Fighter cover by Spitfire squadrons had resulted in the loss of two RAF aircraft. The Germans lost two fighters for certain, five probables and four damaged. Two Spitfires chased an enemy fighter into the range of one Fortress and there was a short exchange of fire but no claims were allowed. One other gunner got a shot at an FW, but fighter opposition was generally light. Diversionary missions flown by six other Fortresses had apparently confused the German radio direction finders to such a degree that they concentrated most of their fighters in the wrong area. The attacking Forts were not even reported by Jerry over his radio until they had crossed the French coast and were well on their way to the target – at which point the enemy excitedly announced that 'twelve Lancasters' were heading inland. The only American casualties were suffered when one of the Forts on the diversionary sweep ran in to a flock of pigeons. The bombardier and navigator were 'slightly damaged'.

The combat crews were surprised that the mission had proved so easy. One of the pilots, describing his sensations, spoke for the rest of the airmen:

> When I was a little kid, I had a cousin and I used to hear him tell about the last war and how, when a bunch of men were asked to volunteer for a dangerous job, the whole damn line stepped forward, just like one person. I used to think that sure was fine, but I thought that if it was me I'd have been scared. And so on this show I expected to be scared, too.
>
> Well, sir, it was a funny thing. When we got over the Channel and sighted the French coast I kept thinking, 'Well, here it starts.' But nothing happened – just a little flak that never even touched us.' Then; as we got to the target and went into the bombing run, I thought, 'All right, there is where it starts.' But it didn't start there either; because we just dropped our load and turned around and headed back without being bothered by a single fighter. Some of the ships were, but ours wasn't.

In any case the first mission was far more successful than many had dared hope, Air Chief Marshal Harris, chief of British Bomber Command, sent an enthusiastic message to his American counterpart: '*Yankee Doodle* certainly went to town and can stick yet another well-deserved feather in his cap.' The American leader merely commented cautiously that 'the raid went exactly according to plan and we are well satisfied with the day's work'. He pointed out that one swallow did not make a summer so far as daylight attacks on Europe were concerned. This warning was almost lost in the surge of enthusiasm and confidence that resulted from the first all-American attack on Nazi-held Europe. An official squawk from the Vichy government was hailed as further proof of the effectiveness of the raid.

In the next four days the handful of Fortresses made three more attacks. The first was on 19 August, when they bombed the German fighter airdrome at Abbeville as part of the great combined operations that made up the Dieppe raid. Again the RAF sent congratulations. Of the thirty Focke-Wulf 190s based on that field, twenty were withdrawn to a base farther inland after the Forts paid a second visit to Abbeville some time later. On 20 August the railroad marshalling yards at Amiens were attacked, still without loss to our forces. The Germans were obviously puzzled as to how to handle the heavily armed bombers. Besides, the fighter escort continued to prove very effective.

However, the next day, when twelve B-17s set out to attack a target in the Low Countries, they were sixteen minutes late for their rendezvous time – and two were lost. They claimed four enemy fighters destroyed, nineteen probables, twenty damaged. The first 8th Bomber Command Fort lost in combat in the European Theatre of Operations went down over Flasselles, apparently under control but also under heavy attack from three FW 190s. Four men bailed out and their chutes were seen to open. The other B-17 was last seen near Beachy Head, struggling toward Dover. British Air-Sea Rescue launches went out to look for it, without success.

So the Forts were not invincible, after all. There must have been rejoicing in the Luftwaffe mess that night. Actually, the enemy fighters that day were observed to have yellow noses and bellies, reputedly the markings of Göring's crack fighter squadrons. Evidently the Germans were beginning to take the Fortresses seriously; still, they tried to hide from their people the fact that the Americans were invading the skies over Europe. There was no mention in the German press of American heavy bombers in action; the planes were always 'British', and since they flew so high that identification was almost impossible it was not hard to maintain the fiction – for the time being.

Twice during this period our light bombers went out to attack shipping and harbour installations on the French coast. Each time they returned without loss, but for the heavies the going was getting progressively tougher.

CHAPTER 3

'The Forts Fly High', 'Bruce Sanders'[1]

'Congratulations from all ranks of Bomber Command on the highly successful completion of the first all-American raid by the big fellows on German-occupied territory in Europe. Yankee Doodle certainly went to town and can stick yet another well-deserved feather in his cap.'

Air Marshal Sir Arthur Harris, Chief of RAF Bomber Command.

In the summer of 1941 the Berlin correspondent of the Italian newspaper *La Stampa* began giving his readers pep stories. One of them was to the effect that a Nazi fighter pilot had alone brought down no less than nine Flying Fortresses out of a squadron of twelve in one single engagement. Actually, for the day he mentioned, the Air Ministry stated the weather was so bad that not a single British bomber was operating.

However, that is by the way.

A year later the absurdity of the claim was manifest to the whole world. For, in the summer of 1942, the American Army Air Corps, based in Britain, began active cooperation with the RAF in attacking the strong points of the European mainland. The Flying Fortresses of the Americans flew high, by daylight, and their crews indulged in high-altitude precision bombing. Armed with ½-inch cannon, they were able to trounce soundly any fighter opposition that came up to deny them right of way. In proportion to the numbers of aircraft employed, and in view of the fact that the Fortresses were flying on offensive operations, it was the fighter defence that was defeated.

At first, the Forts flew with fighter protection, as when they roared over Rouen on the afternoon of 17 August and bombed the marshalling yards, with their commander-in-chief, Brigadier-General Ira C. Eaker, leading in an aircraft named *Yankee Doodle*.

It was a highly successful debut. Air Marshal Sir Arthur Harris, on behalf of Bomber Command, sent General Eaker the following message of congratulation: 'Congratulations from all ranks of Bomber Command on the highly successful completion of the first all-American raid by the big fellows on German-occupied territory in Europe. Yankee Doodle certainly went to town and can stick yet another well-deserved feather in his cap.'

Bomber Command was no longer alone on the offensive. The four-engined bombers of the American Air Force had joined in the invasion of the German-held skies. The Americans systematically went to work, testing out their aircraft and teaching their bomber crews the art of modern war. For two months the Forts flew into Europe and strafed military targets in the hinterland. At the end of that time the Office of War Information in Washington issued a considered statement to the American public on the performance of the Fortresses and other American warplanes. It was a frank statement, and it held many criticisms of some existing types of United States aircraft. However, of the heavy Boeing B-17s it had this to say:

The actual employment of the B-17 (the Flying Fortress) over Europe has exceeded even the fondest expectations of its American proponents. It has shown the B-17 capable of high-altitude day bombing of such precision that it astounded Allied observers. The public is already familiar with some of the B-17's feats, such as the recent flight over occupied Europe wherein gunners in a flight of B-17s engaged forty German fighters. Ten Focke-Wulfs were knocked down and eight more claimed as probables. All the B-17s returned to their British bases, although one had been hit by six cannon-shells and over two hundred machine-gun bullets. In the October 10th raid over France – the largest and most damaging raid ever staged over Europe – 115 Flying Fortresses and Liberators, B-24s, accompanied by Allied fighters, proved their ability to fight their way through to the target and back again against large and fierce opposition by the Nazi's newest and best Messerschmitts and Focke-Wulfs. We lost only four of our bombers, while over a hundred enemy planes were destroyed or damaged.

Possibly the Berlin correspondent of *La Stampa* rubbed his eyes when he read the announcement.

Two months later, in December, the Fortresses were probing deeper into Europe under the daylight skies of winter. The crews had learned much. The pilots of the Messerschmitts and Focke-Wulfs were still learning. On the afternoon of Sunday the 20th the Forts flew to Romilly-sur-Seine and attacked the German air depot there. They roared high over Paris, with Focke-Wulfs streaming after them and circling on their flanks, seeking an opening through which to dart with cannon spurting. Again the Nazi fighter pilots came off second best. The American bombers kept close ranks and the Focke-Wulfs were given little chance to demonstrate their killer propensities.

One of the Forts flying on that occasion was captained by Captain Allen Martini. His aircraft was already famous in its squadron as the *Dry Martini*, and his crew were known as the Cocktail Kids. They had been together as a combat crew for several months when they went on the pranging job to Romilly, and sitting hunched up over his cannon in the Fort's tail was a bright-eyed Filipino, Staff Sergeant Henry Mitchell. Mitchell was a man with a long score to settle with the Axis. His father was a major on the staff of General MacArthur during the Pacific battles, and it was believed that his wife and child were prisoners in the hands of the Japs. Henry himself was on a merchantman when the 'Wild Eagles' of Tokyo descended on Pearl Harbor. He enlisted for service in the American Air Force as soon as he got ashore.

That afternoon he showed the race-prejudiced Aryans of the Luftwaffe that the colour of a man's skin has little to do with his ability to shoot straight. His straight shooting was largely responsible for the safe return of the *Dry Martini*.

The Cocktail Kids and their Fortress comrades played the old year out to the tuneful rattle of their ½-inch cannon. On 30 December the Forts flew high over Lorient and gave the submarine pens a heavy strafing. On that occasion the Flying Fortress *Boom Town* got badly shot up, but returned to Britain's friendly shores covered in glory.[2]

Boom Town winged over the pens on schedule and the bombardier let go the bomb load. Over the Intercom the crew heard him shout excitedly, 'Bull's eye!' While the words were still in their ears, flak tore into the Fort's hull, and German fighters swooped down to attack.

The bombardier died at his post. Lieutenant W. M. Smith of Ashland, Wisconsin, the navigator, was wounded in the arm. The shell splinter passed out through his flight jacket, knocking him off his seat. As he lay prone, stunned for the moment, bullets from the fighters tore through the space where he had been sitting a moment before. Then an exploding shell ripped the base out of the ball-turret. Sergeant Green, the ball-turret gunner, had his oxygen mask destroyed, and his cases of spare ammunition were jammed so tightly against his side that he thought his leg had been torn off. Blinded by spurting oil and escaping cordite fumes, he stayed there, perched over space, covering his target area with his gun. In the tail-turret, Sergeant Krucher of Long Island was badly hit, but he remained sighting his gun as a Focke-Wulf swooped to finish off the mauled Fortress. Krucher waited until the FW 190 was closing up in his sights and then gave it a long burst. His shells ripped off half of one of the German's wings and the fighter went spiralling down. Staff Sergeant Stroud of Kansas, manning the right waist gun, covered another FW 190 that attacked from the front. Stroud coolly waited until he could see the German pilot's helmeted head in the Focke-Wulf's glasshouse.

'He came in at twelve o'clock,' Stroud said afterwards, explaining the angle at which he saw the German in his gunsight. 'As he banked and started in on our tail I let him have it. It looked as if part of the fuselage came off and he fell off towards the sea.'

Boom Town's pilot, Captain Clyde D. Walker of Tulsa, Oklahoma, headed out to sea as the enemy fighters came on in pairs, attacking furiously. The first blast of fire had broken the driving shaft of one engine, and another had been hit on the top cylinder, so that it had only emergency power left to struggle with as the pilot opened the throttle.

'The prop would run away when I advanced it a bit,' was how Walker explained the predicament in which he found himself. Oil pressure was dropping, and a shell splinter had made a large dent in a blade of a third engine. There was also a gaping hole in the nose of the aircraft, and the bomb-doors had been badly shot up. The de-icing system had been punctured, the radio equipment was badly damaged and the control cable had been knocked off the elevator. 'They missed the pilot and co-pilot,' Walker explained. 'That's all. And the co-pilot had a piece of flak in his parachute.'

Nevertheless, he did not give the order to bail out. If he could get Boom Town back across the Channel he was going to, despite wintry weather conditions and the worst the Nazi airmen could do.

Walker pushed his aircraft into a cloud bank and cleverly manoeuvred to evade another onslaught from the whirling Focke-Wulfs. Another Fort came close, to cover the staggering aircraft, but when Walker came out of the cloud formation he was alone and Boom Town was dropping at the rate of 2,000 feet a minute.

The crew were at their posts, facing looming disaster, ready to fight off any further attack that might mature, for they knew the Focke-Wulfs' liking for lame ducks. All, that is, except the bombardier and Sergeant Krucher, who had been relieved by Stroud.

'I had to get rough with Krucher,' Walker afterwards reported, 'to make him lie down. Stroud cut open his electric suit to give him first aid and when he put on the iodine Krucher didn't even let out a whimper.'

Just afterwards they sighted land.

'We were all looking for England,' Walker admitted.

We were looking for land so hard that when we saw some a little off to the right we started in. We thought it was England and started looking at the roads to see which side the cars were running on. We saw one bicycle. Green called on the intercom, 'That don't look like England to me!' Then all of a sudden we saw the sub pens we'd bombed before and we knew it was Brest.

The Fort was now down to some 600 feet and still losing height. The Americans were over the harbour before the merchant ships there could get up their balloon barrage. Walker headed out to sea again, and had great difficulty keeping the aircraft in the sky. The airscrew of his number two engine was still running away with itself and threatening to wreck the aircraft. The sea suddenly flashed up to engulf them. Desperately Walker hauled on the controls. The Fort bounced like a ball on the waves, rising 100 feet in the air. He gave the order to prepare for a crash-landing on the sea, and the crew began throwing overboard everything they could spare: ammunition, oxygen bottles, masks, parachutes and any loose equipment.

As the last drums of ammunition went out through the hatch, a couple of German fighters were sighted overhead.

Those Focke-Wulf pilots were themselves out of ammunition or they had taken enough punishment from the Flying Forts for one day; they did not attack. The lame duck bounced on out of their reach and finally clambered up in to the English sky, to make a safe landing and await the prospect of another lucky new year.

In the last half of 1942 the Forts went twenty-five times to bomb German-held Europe.

They started the new year in fine fettle, and within a few days the *Dry Martini* was in the news again. The Cocktail Kids took their bomber to Lille, with Major T. H. Taylor at the controls in place of the regular pilot, who was ill. The bombardier got his bombs away over the target, which was the Fives-Lille steel and locomotive works, but, as the bomber continued on over the target, an avenging Focke-Wulf came racing in to attack, weaving from side to side like a pugilist, all guns blazing. One of its cannon-shells tore through the cockpit and burst beside Major Taylor, killing him instantly.

The controls ran slack, the *Dry Martini*'s nose dipped and the aircraft began a sickening dive earthwards.

The co-pilot, wounded and dazed, lay beside Taylor. It looked as though nothing could save the high-spirited Cocktail Kids from total destruction. The commander of the flight, Brigadier-General H. S. Hansell, watching the episode from his station in the leading Fort, thought the *Dry Martini* was done for.

However, the B-17s are built to take punishment as well as administer it. The *Dry Martini*'s engines were still functioning, and the crew continued blazing back at the German fighters following it down in its apparent death dive.

The co-pilot, Second Lieutenant J. B. Boyle, who came from Teaneck, in New Jersey, suddenly came to and in a split second realised the desperate nature of the aircraft's plight. He hauled Taylor's body from in front of the controls and took the dead man's place. The *Dry Martini* flattened out and began climbing again to regain the formation of Fortresses. The FW 190s that had followed the American bomber down sheered off. The *Dry Martini* was in a sorry state, but under Boyle's careful handling got back to base.

General Hansell had some words of praise to offer.

'I was profoundly impressed,' he said,

with Lieutenant Boyle's skill and courage in flying a B-17 in good defensive formation at high altitude when he had been painfully wounded around the face and shot through the leg. Flying a B-17 in formation requires a great deal of physical effort at any time. I am still amazed that Lieutenant Boyle, despite the difficult conditions, could exert enough stamina to land his plane safely at its base. He and his crew deserve the highest credit.

Not long afterwards the Forts took off for their first assault on the German mainland. This attack was an outstanding success and marked the beginning of a new onslaught on the Reich's war potential. The episode brought words of congratulation once more from Sir Arthur Harris, who sent the following warm message to Brigadier-General Newton Longfellow, Commanding General of the 8th Bomber Command of the United States Army Air Corps:

Greetings and congratulations from Bomber Command to all who took part to-day in the first US raid on Germany. This well-planned and gallantly executed operation opens a campaign the Germans have long dreaded. To them it is yet another ominous sentence in the writing on the wall, the full import of which they cannot fail to grasp. To Bomber Command it is concrete and most welcome proof that we shall no longer be alone in carrying the war to German soil. Let us press past this milestone on the road to victory, assured that between us we can and will bust Germany wide open.

That was on 27 January. The next day General Longfellow replied. In his message to Sir Arthur Harris he said,

The entire personnel of the Eighth Bomber Command join me in an expression of thanks for your cordial message of greeting and congratulation upon the occasion of the first US raid on Germany. Our effort would have been impossible without the splendid co-operation and help, which has constantly been extended to us by the RAF since our arrival in this theatre. Our first raid was only the beginning. Men of the Eighth Bomber Command are eager to lend a hand to British Bomber Command in the business of bombing Germany.

In February the Forts went raiding again in to Germany. They made another particularly daring raid on Wilhelmshaven. On this occasion the *New York Times*' correspondent, Robert P. Post, went with them to get a first-hand account of the attack. He did not return.

A month later the Forts staged their memorable and daring raid on Vegesack. The night before the raid was scheduled, a well-known RAF bomber-pilot, Wing Commander N. J. Baird-Smith, was visiting an American Eighth Air Force bomber station. He chanced to remark that he had made forty-nine bombing raids in RAF aircraft and at once received an invitation 'to make it a golden wedding in a Flying Fortress'. He accepted the offer gratefully.

When he came back from Vegesack he had this to say:

As soon as we approached the enemy coast the fighters came up to have a look. They hung about, apparently waiting for an aircraft to stray out of the fold and I felt that they disliked the idea of coming near the American guns. In spite of pretty heavy flak our pilot got on to his target all right and made a good bombing run – straight and level. It was evident that the bombs of the preceding aircraft had found their mark, for the whole target was already obscured by thick smoke. You can judge a good deal about the crew of a bomber by its efficiency on the return journey. By this time they had been flying for quite a considerable time and with the obvious strain such close formation flying imposes they become tired. I can say, however, that the formation returned, as they had set out – closely packed and ready to do battle with anybody. The fighters were on the lookout for the lone aircraft homeward bound, possibly shot up by flak or disabled by fighters, thus being unable to keep with the main formations. There were plenty of fighters and they attacked until we were a considerable distance from the enemy coast. But these attacks became less and less aggressive as they saw the German coast receding; until just before they left us they were milling round in the hope that a Fortress would straggle. Our particular formation had all the answers ready. One more aggressive Ju 88, which came in too close was met by an intense volume of fire and blew up and I saw a FW 190 spinning out of control on its way down towards the sea. The meticulous planning of this operation, combined with the efficiency of the crews and leaders in carrying out this no mean task, seems to me to be the keynote to the successful bombing of Vegesack with such a small loss of aircraft to the USAAF.[3]

On that raid Lieutenant Jack Mathis, a young Texan, died as he sent his bombs whistling over the U-boat yards. As his formation approached the main target he was bent over his bombsight. Ack-ack stuff was flying up in a heavy curtain of exploding steel. Mathis's aircraft, the *Duchess*, was leading its particular group, and much of the success of the following bombardiers depended upon the young Texan's aim. The *Duchess* drew close to the target and Mathis pinpointed the spot where his bomb load would land. At that instant flak burst beneath him. His right arm was almost torn from his body. His right side was peppered with steel fragments. The force of the exploding shell threw him back fully 9 feet, to the lower hatch.

He did not lose consciousness. In great agony he crawled back to the bombsight, using his left hand to lever his mortally wounded body. He sighted, reached for the 'toggles off' switch and down went the *Duchess*'s load of bombs.

Over the intercom his crewmates heard him begin the customary 'Bombs away.'

'Bombs –,' he murmured faintly.

They heard no more. One of them went down to him. He was dead, his left hand outstretched to the bomb-bay door switch. As he died he had closed the doors.[4]

His was the eagerness to which General Longfellow referred. The attack on Vegesack brought congratulations from Mr Churchill, who sent the following message to Lieutenant-General Frank M. Andrews, Commanding General, European Theatre of Operations, US Army,[5] and to Major-General Eaker, Commanding General, US Army Eighth Air Force: 'All my compliments to you and your officers and men on your brilliant exploit of yesterday, the effectiveness of which the photographs already reveal.'

Lieutenant-General Andrews replied, 'The officers and men of the United States Forces in the British Isles appreciate and are deeply grateful for the interest and congratulations expressed in your message last night.'

Major-General Eaker's acknowledgement was:

The message received last night from you congratulating our air forces on the Vegesack raid was promptly transmitted to the combat crews, as I am sure you would want. It will give them a great lift to have this message from you. It has been of tremendous importance and value to our air forces in this theatre to know of your keen interest in their work. They join with me in realizing the paramount importance to us of your militant leadership. Again thanking you for your message and assuring you that we will repeat these efforts many times and on an ever-increasing scale.

The Vegesack raid was made on Thursday 18 March. Four days later the Forts went without fighter escort to raid Wilhelmshaven in daylight for the third time. Six days passed, and the Flying Fortress offensive swung to Rouen. Three days after that attack it was Rotterdam's turn. On this day, 31 March, Captain Clyde D. Walker, who brought *Boom Town* back from Lorient, was piloting *Boom Town Junior*.[6] The *Junior* made its bombing run with one engine dead and another giving only a third of its normal power. Nevertheless, the bombs went down accurately on the target, and Walker brought his aircraft and crew back to Britain.

Five days later the *Junior* was being eased through a fine-meshed net of flak by Walker as he made his bombing run over Antwerp. The Erla Aero Engine Works was the target. Staff Sergeant Krucher was again handling the tail-gun, and he had one eye on the enemy fighters and one on the Spitfires covering this probe into the outer shell of the German defence network.

'The group ahead of us got the worst attacks,' Krucher reported when he arrived back. 'At various times over the intercom, I heard reports of Fortresses in trouble. I saw an FW blow up after being hit by one of us – I don't know which. I was glad to see the Spit cover coming.'[7]

Only the day before, 4 April, the *Dry Martini*, with the Cocktail Kids doing their stuff, had gone with other Fortresses to the Renault works on the outskirts of Paris, and created an American Air Force record. Against a furious onslaught from the Focke-Wulf pack, the *Dry Martini*'s gunners had chalked up a score of ten definite kills. The Nazis were so stunned by the performance that their English-language broadcaster at Friesland went to the microphone and referred to Captain Martini as 'an outstanding example of American boastfulness'. The commentator went on to say that the Cocktail Kids' bombs fell not on the Renault works, but on a school. However, the Kids had seen the evidence on their own camera.

'That broadcast was good for my morale,' one of them laughed.

Not that the morale of the Forts' crews needed any stimulants. It was at its peak when, a fortnight later, a concentrated daylight attack was made on the Focke-Wulf plant at Bremen. The Forts cut through the fighter opposition like a hot knife through butter. The target was smothered with bombs, and more than half of the buildings comprising the large factory were destroyed or very heavily damaged.[8]

This was the occasion when Second Lieutenant L. C. Sugg and Captain Pervis E. Youree got back to base after the order to prepare to ditch had been given. The Fort's bombs went down on the Focke-Wulf plant, and Youree turned to meet a Focke-Wulf 190's headlong attack. Sugg was the co-pilot. His rudder pedals were shot away by the German fire, four hydraulic lines were knocked out and the control cables to three of the aircraft's four engines were cut. Two of the engines failed.

Youree could do nothing but leave the high-flying formation. As the Forts crossed the coast he went down almost to wave-top height. 'So low that we left a wake in the water,' were the words of one of the crew. However, try as he would he found control of the aircraft impossible. Reluctantly he gave the order to prepare to ditch. Before the aircraft could be abandoned, however, Sugg crawled under the catwalk, fumbled with the severed wires and cables, and found which cables controlled the engines. He stayed there and attended the engines by pulling on the cables.

The intercom system had been shot up, though. When he wanted to communicate with Youree, he had to leave the broken cables. This meant risking the aircraft. So Sugg devised a way out of the difficulty by tying the broken cables to a ring on some parachute harness and then stretching the harness to the cockpit. When he wanted to deliver a message he handed the parachute strap to Youree, who flew the Fort with his left hand and controlled the engines with his right.

It was a nightmare piece of flying, but the ingenious device saved the aircraft – and the crew.[9]

On 13 May the Forts put on their biggest show up to that time, when they flew, escorted, to bomb the aircraft works and repair shops at Méaulte. General Hansell went with them.

'The Allied fighter support was splendid,' he commented afterwards. 'It is my opinion that together we did a good job.' Colonel Stanley T. Wray of Birmingham, Alabama, the commander of one of the most famous groups of Fortresses,[10] known affectionately as 'Wray's Ragged Irregulars,' took his four-engined high-fliers through the hoops and over the hurdles at Méaulte. He, too, was impressed by the supporting fighter squadrons.

'Some FWs,' he said, 'came in six at a time from God knows where. But our cover was beautiful. I saw nine or ten Spits going up at one time to take out three FW's.'

The next day the record was broken by a still larger force of American bombers going out from Britain, this time in a four-pronged attack spread out over Europe, with the Forts concentrating on the U-boat base and marshalling yards at Kiel and on the General Motors plant at Antwerp.

Three days later the high-flying bombers swung round towards Bordeaux, and after a day's rest turned back to Kiel and added Flensburg to their visiting list. Over Kiel that day the Fortress in which Edward Lewis, one of the British 'Paramount News' cameramen, was travelling as a passenger was shot down. Another day's rest and then the Forts were raiding in daylight again over Wilhelmshaven. Emden was added to the day's calls.

The offensive was stepping up. The Americans were by this time well in their bombing stride. Major-General Follett Bradley, Inspector-General of the US Army Air Forces, went as an observer on the Wilhelmshaven raid. He journeyed in the Flying Fortress *Wham Bam*,[11] and when he returned he gave out this considered statement:

My impression is that the mission was extremely well planned. The methodical, painstaking seriousness with which this crowd of splendid young airmen go about their job convinced me, more than ever, that when adequate forces are available to hit Germany in six or eight places at once, the war will be brought to a speedy conclusion. I've never seen finer fighting spirit nor higher morale than is exemplified by the Eighth Air Force in this theatre.

The Fort crews were getting really tough, too, in their handling of the enemy. Seventy-four German planes were destroyed that day by the American gunners, for the loss of twelve US machines. That figure was a new record, the previous highest total being sixty-seven enemy aircraft destroyed during the 14 May raid over Kiel and other targets in occupied territory.

This raid also saw the *Dry Martini*'s record of ten enemy fighters destroyed by a single bomber beaten by the crew of a Fort piloted by Lieutenant R. H. Smith from Lamesa, in the Lone Star State. Smith and his crew, however, could not make it back to England. On the return journey, their badly shot-up aircraft was unable to keep aloft and they had to ditch it. The Americans spent thirty hours in their dinghies, concealed in thick mist, before being rescued by a British ship.

May was the Americans' record month. That month the Forts destroyed 355 enemy fighter aircraft, more than twice the previous highest monthly total. In addition, 70 per cent more bombs, by weight, were dropped than in any previous month.

On the debit side for the monthly account was an item of seventy-two bombers.

La Stampa failed to report these figures. Perhaps because it had other things to mention – such as the arrival of new squadrons of high-flying Forts over Italy from bases in North Africa. Or perhaps it had lost all interest in the Forts. Or even forgotten them.

Fascist memories are notoriously short.

CHAPTER 4

The Old One-Two

'June 22 – This was the date of our first engagement. Antwerp, where the Germans were building trucks and tanks; was our target. Our part was a minor one, more or less intended to keep their attention divided; while the main force went to Hüls. It was considered successful. We were hit hard by FW 190s and had our share of flak. The two other ships in my flight never returned; taking three of the men in my barracks down with them. Our tail gunner was killed by the only shot to enter our ship. He was a fine fellow.

June 25 – Today, Hamburg! Rather a wasted trip. A large formation dropping bombs through, a thick layer of clouds which obscured the target. The flak and the 190s were with us. One B-17 went down, taking more of my friends and our operations officer.

June 26 – Target, an airport in Paris, France. No. 1 engine cut out over Channel, so we turned back. Others went on in, but weather bad and only few bombed target.

June 28 – Big game, big formation this time. We made the Germans very well aware of our presence in Saint-Nazaire. Our bombs raised the submarine docks to heaven. We encountered clouds of flak and fighters. We left the fighter opposition shortly after bombing. Some time out from the target we picked up two German fighters that made repeated attacks on the tail of our ship. Had the rather unpleasant experience of seeing 20-mm cannon shells exploding close to our tail. No one was killed or badly injured. We stopped at an RAF base for the night. They treated us wonderfully.

June 29 – Flying today with Lt. L. All enlisted men in his crew are in hospital, with the exception of one man who is dead. The trip is without event. We go well into France looking for our target (an airport) which is hidden by clouds.

July 4 – Another Independence Day, quite unlike any other I can remember. A German aircraft factory deep within France got a look at some American fireworks in the form of several hundred 500-pound bombs. Our own crew went today as spares and had to return just short of France. Today we have been heavyhearted because Lt. B's crew did not return.

July 8 – No mission today. I received the award of the Air Medal for having successfully completed five combat missions.

A sergeant gunner's diary, covering the late June and early July attacks.

The author of the diary above was a member of Lieutenant Charles E. Hedlin's crew in the 533rd Bomb Squadron, 381st Bomb Group at Ridgewell. The tail gunner lost on 22 June was Staff Sergeant Arnold B. Lorick, who was killed when a 20-mm shell exploded in his face. The B-17 that went down on 25 June was 42-30027, piloted by 1st Lieutenant Robert K. Schrader. All ten crew, including Captain John H. Hamilton, the 533rd Bomb Squadron Operations Officer, who was flying in the co-pilot's seat, died. 'Lieutenant B', who did not return on 4 July, was Lieutenant Olef M. Ballinger and his crew, flying 42-29928. (Three men evaded, four were KIA and three were taken as PoWs.) The sergeant gunner did not return from the mission to Amiens-Glissy on 14 July when 1st Lieutenant Robert J. Holdem's crew was lost over the target. 42-30011 *Widget* also FTR. *Red Hot Riding Hood*, flown by Lieutenant Hedlin, lost No. 3 engine and crashed at Rattlesden airfield. Four men survived.

'*Achtung, feindliche Flugzeuge!*' It is probably about 1030 hours on 14 May when the Nazi *Jagdführer*, or Fighter Controller, of the Holland fighter defence area is given this warning of enemy aircraft approaching.

With half a dozen other *Jagdführers*, each allotted a coastal sector of *Festung Europa*, *Jagdführer* Holland is responsible for the day-fighter defence of Germany and its conquered territory. It is his job, using an intricate communications and radio-locator system, to deploy the fighters grouped at strategic points throughout his defence sector so that air attacks from England can best be met. *Jagdführer* Holland must have sworn a round Teutonic oath on this particular morning, for the approaching hostiles had crossed the North Sea so low they had eluded his radio-locator screen. Ground observers had picked them up as they neared the coast.

The *Jagdführer* alerts the Low Countries. Neighbouring defence sectors are notified that hostiles are abroad. For a while the defence network's flashes are sporadic. At 10.35 the hostiles are reported over the Dutch coast near Scheveningen: twelve twin-engine aircraft, very low, travelling east. They are spotted at Leyden, then over the outskirts of Amsterdam, at rooftop level. The quarry is flying too low and too fast to permit a planned interception by the fighters in the air. The *Jagdführer*, following the traced course of the intruders on his map, probably realises what their target is by this time; it is his business to know what points in his domain may attract the attention of enemy bombers. He knows, too, by now, that the intruders are American, that they are medium bombers, what bomb load they will be carrying and how fast they are travelling. That, too, is his business. The *Jagdführer* knows a lot, but he does not know how he can interrupt this operation with the few short minutes at his disposal. Minutes pass. The *Jagdführer* waits for the blow.

At 1100 hours *Jagdführer* Holland learns that the generating station at Ijmuiden, a town on the coast, has been attacked with delayed-action bombs. By 11.03 the hit-and-run raiders are reported across the coast once more. A minute later they have passed out to sea and are away. Then the bombs, having delayed fuses, start to explode.

It is an inauspicious start to 14 May. The efficient Nazi warning network is taken by surprise. This can happen in the best regulated of defence systems, as the *Jagdführer* well knows; his own fighter-bombers sometimes slip in unannounced at wave-top level to bomb the English Channel coast towns. However, on this occasion the Ijmuiden raid may be portentous. The day is fine and there are other targets in that area. *Jagdführer* Holland wonders whether it would not be a good idea to pull in a few of his fighter squadrons from the Belgian sector.

It is 1130 hours when *Jagdführer* north-west Germany receives a message from his radio-locator headquarters. The screen has picked up large hostiles, flying east over the North Sea. A minute later the locator stations have pinpointed the approaching planes on the map. *Jagdführer* north-west Germany, on the balcony of his plotting room, watches the enemy-bomber symbol being placed deep in the angle of the North Sea formed by the Danish peninsula and the Frisian Islands. Another flash – the symbol is moved. The general course is south-east. The enemy, moving fast, is still miles at sea. *Jagdführer* north-west Germany ponders his plan of battle.

Over his defence sector, comprising Denmark and the north-west corner of the Fatherland, are scattered scores of fighter bases. At each base Focke-Wulfs or Messerschmitts are stationed in groups of five, ten, or twenty. These are the *Jagdführer*'s pawns in the grim game to be played. With its four cannon firing explosive shells, and its two machine guns, each one of these fighters is a potent weapon. Nevertheless, each one has its limitations – a fighter's gas capacity limits its flying time under combat conditions to approximately an hour. The *Jagdführer* must remember this as he disposes his forces to meet the threat.

By 11.35 the airfields in the sector are alerted and the first fighters are airborne. At 11.45 the enemy formation has turned southward and is nearing the coast at the base of the Danish peninsula. What is their target? The *Jagdführer* studies the likely objectives – Flensburg, Kiel, Hamburg, Hanover. Perhaps a swing to the west, which would threaten Wilhelmshaven and Emden – or a turn to the east toward Lübeck and Wismar. This is the decision that must not be wrong.

The moments tick away. The plotters move about silently as they chart the course of the invading force. At 11.50 the first of the airborne fighter groups makes contact with the enemy. *Achtung, Dickeautos. Amerikanische* – Warning, American heavy bombers. The *Jagdführer* reaches a decision. The target will be Kiel. The important Germania and Deutsche Werke shipyards, not yet attacked by the Fortresses, are ideal objectives for the Americans and their precision bombing. Orders start pouring out over the telephone. Fighters roar into the air from stations 50, 100 and 200 miles away. Kiel is their common goal. When they are 5 miles above that port they will intercept the bombers – if the *Jagdführer* has guessed right.

To the south-west, *Jagdführer* Holland alerts his stations once again and makes ready, should the need arise, to defend the area left unprotected by his neighbour's moves. He will not have to wait long.

At 12.00 the hostiles, in 'great force,' are reported 10 miles south-west of Kiel. *Jagdführer* north-west Germany has a bad few moments. Are they going to bypass the target he has chosen and leave the bulk of his fighters waiting over Kiel? That will mean a chase, and waste of precious flying time. At 12.01 the hostiles have made a turn and are reported on a north-easterly course, almost over Kiel. The *Jagdführer* has guessed right; the main body of the fighters is in contact with their quarry now. The battle of Kiel is on.

At 12.06 comes word that the Germania yards and the Deutsche Werke have been bombed, with 'great destruction'. The bombers have swung north-west. Now they have turned back across the peninsula, 'heading for the safety of the open sea'. The fighters are hanging on, attacking the flanks of the retreating formation. Some of them, from the more distant stations, are beginning to run low on gas. Requests to land fill the air. *Jagdführer* north-west Germany now faces an uncomfortable period of waiting; the bulk of his forces will be immobilised as they are refuelled and rearmed on the ground. If there is another attack during that period – his thoughts turn to *Jagdführer* Holland and the idle squadrons in that sector…

Jagdführer Holland is having his own troubles. At 12.05, while Kiel is being bombed, his radio-locator stations report hostiles high off the English coast, flying south-east. This is a spear pointed at the heart of his defence sector.

Jagdführer Holland orders several squadrons into the air. *Jagdführer* France, covering the sector to the west, does likewise. They wait. At 12.14 *Jagdführer* north-west Germany inquires about possible assistance while his squadrons are refuelling. The answer he receives is short and to the point. At 12.18 the hostiles are reported over the coast east of Dunkirk, heading south-east: multi-engined bombers, escorted by fighters, flying very high. *Jagdführers* Holland and France both vector their airborne squadrons to intercept the interlopers and then try to figure which way the Forts are headed. At 12.30 the hostiles are over Ypres. Here they turn east. At 12.30 several of *Jagdführer*'s squadrons finally make contact with the intruders. Two minutes later *Jagdführer* Holland learns that approximately fifty Fortresses have bombed one of his most important stations – his fighter field at Courtrai. Hangars, shops, dispersal areas and runways have been hit. The raiders have turned north and headed for the coast.

At 12.40 the hostiles have left *Jagdführer* Holland's sector, crossing the coast between Ostend and Dunkirk. At 12.42 *Jagdführer* north-west Germany reports that the large body of hostiles that attacked Kiel have now passed out to sea on a westbound course, and that his fighters are gradually losing contact. By 12.55 most of the squadrons airborne to meet the Courtrai attack have been landed and are being refuelled. At 13.00 *Jagdführer* Holland's network reports large hostiles approaching the coast near Ostend. He calls on *Jagdführer* France for help. At 13.08 the hostiles cross the coast. It is another force of four-engined bombers with fighter support. The hostiles fly south-eastward toward Brussels. *Jagdführer* Holland vectors his squadrons toward Ghent. Some make contact and follow the hostiles as they turn abruptly north-eastward at Brussels. The *Jagdführer* knows now what is coming. He throws his entire available force into combat around the target at Antwerp. The Fortresses bomb the Ford and General Motors plants at 13.20. By 13.40 they are out across the coast once more, and ten minutes later the last fighter relinquishes contact and returns to base.

*Jagdführer*s north-west Germany, Holland and France, having been forced to meet four attacks in a morning, now sit down to add up their losses in men and machines. On the ground, other Nazis are totalling the death and destruction at the targets. The foregoing is a generalised picture of what probably happened among the directors of the Nazi day-fighter defence system on 14 May. On that day the 8th Bomber Command despatched well over 200 planes in four hours, attacking four targets, losing eleven bombers and claiming sixty-seven Nazi fighters as destroyed. It was the first American multiple attack. It is not an ideal example – early experiments seldom are – but, as the first, it deserves commemoration. Later multiple operations perfected the technique of delivering a rapid succession of attacks, confusing the enemy and dispersing his fighter strength.

14 May was not only the first day on which the American Bomber Command found itself with enough planes to initiate its multiple-attack technique, it was also a day of generally effective bombing. Ijmuiden was fair, Antwerp good, Courtrai good and Kiel, by far the largest raid, excellent. The 100-plus bombers that hit this latter target achieved a concentration which reminded the bombardment chiefs pleasantly of the assaults on Hamm, Vegesack and the Renault works. Destruction in the Germania shipyards was so widespread that the German radio stepped out of character long enough to admit that the American daylight raid had caused 'great damage' to the port, and that Liberators, accompanying the formations, dropped more than 25 tons of incendiaries – the first time this form of bomb had been dropped by American crews.

It was over Kiel that a twenty-three-year-old Cherokee Indian (Floyd Thompson from Durant, Oklahoma) known as Chief by his crew-mates proved that the early Americans can still take it. It was after the bomber had left Germany on the return trip that Chief finally broke in on the interphone from his place in the ball turret and confessed that his electric suit had stopped working and that, perhaps, his feet were frostbitten. Having been busy with enemy fighters, Chief hadn't wanted to bother the crew with his trouble until he thought the plane was out of danger.

Chief was removed from the ball turret and carried to the ship's radio compartment for first aid. The bombardier and the radio operator had removed his shoes and were rubbing his feet to restore the circulation when the warning, 'Fighters approaching', came over the interphone. Cautioning Chief to remain where he was, the other two left to man their guns.

When they returned some minutes later the only sign of Chief was his leather jacket. Chief, with feet so painful that he couldn't walk, had crawled barefooted back in to his turret, and resumed fighting. Beside his leather jacket, Chief had left his earphones – so that he would not be able to hear orders to leave his post. During the ensuing action, Chief fired so many bursts at attacking German fighters that he burned out one of his .50-calibre guns. When the fight was over, Chief crawled back to the radio compartment for further treatment.

Later, Chief waved aside tributes to his heroism: 'I just crawled back there because I got lonesome. My feet feel warmer without shoes, anyway. Shoes, they stop the circulation.'

Another 'first' was scored on 14 May when the Command's fast, twin-engined medium bombers executed their first mission in the attack on the generating plant at Ijmuiden. Flying over enemy territory at 50 feet, and climbing to 200 for their bombing, eleven of these B-26s reported their bombs had fallen fairly within the target area. The bombs were all fused for a delay to allow Dutch workers to escape from the bombed plant...

When the 322nd Bomb Group (Medium), commanded by Lieutenant Colonel Robert M. 'Moose' Stillman, arrived at Bury St Edmunds (Rougham) in March 1943, it had been decided to employ the Martin B-26 Marauder in low-level attacks against industrial targets in France and the Low Countries. The 322nd Bomb Group trained in low-level operations for eight weeks, and flew its first combat mission on 14 May. In four hours 8th Bomber Command attacked four targets, losing twelve B-17s and B-24s and claiming sixty-seven fighters shot down. The Marauders returned safely from their target, the PEN electricity-generating plant at Velsen near Ijmuiden on the Dutch coast, but when Stillman was called to a conference at HQ, Elveden Hall near Thetford, he was informed that reconnaissance photos of the plant had revealed no damage and that it was still in full operation. Stillman was informed that 8th Bomber Command wanted the target to be attacked again on 17 May. Stillman could not believe it and stated that to attack the same target so soon could mean enemy defences would be ready and waiting for them. General Newton L. Longfellow, 8th Bomber Command, was adamant that the attack should go ahead and although he sympathised with Colonel Stillman's point of view, Longfellow threatened Stillman with the loss of his command if he refused to obey orders. Upset at the thought of sending his crews back to the same target so soon after their harrowing first mission (where they suffered a number of casualties and lost Lieutenant Howell and his crew in a crash near the base), Stillman returned to Rougham, near Bury St Edmunds. The order for the mission arrived at 0036 hours on 17 May asking for a maximum-effort raid, flying the same route as three days before. Lieutenant Colonel Alfred Von Kolnitz, the 322nd Bomb Group's Chief Intelligence Officer, was alarmed that the same route was to be flown, as he expected heavy enemy opposition. He wrote a memo to Colonel Stillman, ending it, 'For God's sake, get fighter cover!'

The crews alerted for the mission were from the 450th and 452nd Squadrons, who with four exceptions had not flown the first mission. One of these was Colonel Stillman, who was determined to lead. The 322nd could field eleven B-26 Marauders for the mission, with the 452nd aircraft leading. Although the crews were confident of a second success, they all expected to meet stiff opposition, and many were convinced they would not return. Stillman was also convinced that the mission was going to be a disaster, but was determined to do his duty and ensure the target was knocked out this time. As he left the Intelligence Section after the mission briefing, Lieutenant Colonel von Kolnitz said, 'Cheerio.' Stillman answered, 'No, it's goodbye.' Trying to cheer him up, von Kolnitz said, 'I'll see you at 1 o'clock.' 'It's goodbye,' replied Stillman firmly.

At 1050 hours the Marauders began taking off. At 1147 hours, when they were 33 miles off the coast of Holland, Captain Stephens in the 452nd flight aborted due to power failure to the top turret and one engine not giving the correct boost. Off course, the remaining B-26s crossed the Dutch coast 25 miles from Noordwijk and headed toward Rozenburg Island in the Maas River Estuary, the most heavily defended area in the Netherlands. They were showered by 20 mm cannon shells. The lead aircraft took direct hits, which severed the flight controls and killed Lieutenant Resweber, Stillman's co-pilot. As a result of the loss of flying controls, the Marauder snap rolled and Stillman saw the ground coming up to meet him. His plane crashed upside down, but amazingly Stillman, Sergeant Freeman and Sergeant Willis were all pulled from the wreckage alive. The two sergeants survived the first mission and had now been lucky again.

The following flight, which was 2 miles to the south, also encountered heavy fire from the ground. Lieutenant Garrambone's aircraft was hit, he lost control and the aircraft crashed into the Maas

River. Garrambone and three of his crew survived. Believing that they were approaching the target area, pilots and navigators looked for the landmarks they had noted on the mission briefing. As they were way off course, there were none; they were flying somewhere between Delft and Rotterdam. Captain Converse now led the first flight and, taking evasive action to avoid flak, collided with Lieutenant Wolf's aircraft, which was leading the second element. Both B-26s went down, but four gunners survived from the two aircraft, one being Sergeant Thompson, the fourth veteran of 14 May. Debris hit *Chickersaw Chief*, causing the pilot, Lieutenant Wurst, to crash-land the B-26 in a field near Mieje. Sergeant Heski, the top turret gunner, lost a foot in the crash, but he was the only serious casualty. This left only Lieutenant F. H. Matthews and Lieutenant E. R. Norton of the third element of the lead flight in the air. Norton's co-pilot was his twin brother, J. A. Norton. These two aircraft joined the second flight to make a more effective force to bomb the target. Unfortunately, the second flight was as lost as the first and had no idea where the target lay. When they were 45 miles in to Holland the remaining aircraft decided to turn for home. Lieutenant Colonel William Purinton, who was leading the second flight, asked his navigator, Lieutenant Jeffries, for a heading. Jeffries answered, '270°,' followed by 'Hold it a minute, I think I see the target. Yes, there it is!'

Bomb doors were opened and Purinton's co-pilot, Lieutenant Kinney, sighted and dropped the bombs on what they thought was the target. (In reality it was the gasholder in the suburbs of Amsterdam.) All aircraft dropped their bombs when Kinney dropped his, but they were heading directly towards the 'real' target at Ijmuiden. There they encountered more heavy flak, and Purinton's plane was hit, but he managed to ditch 2 miles offshore. Jeffries was killed in the crash, and a German patrol boat picked up the rest of the crew. Lieutenant Jones's aircraft was the next to be shot down and crash. Lieutenant Aliamo was the only survivor. The Norton brothers, now flying at 250 mph to try and make it home, were shot down west of Ijmuiden. Their tail gunner, Sergeant Longworth, was the only survivor of their crew.

Only Lieutenant Matthews and Captain Jack Crane now remained, at some distance apart. They survived the coastal flak and raced for England. When the Marauders crossed the coast on their inbound flight,

26 FW 190s of II./JG1, on a combat alert from Woensdrecht, southern Holland, were vectored to meet them. At 12.18 they saw Matthews' and Crane's aircraft flying low and fast over the North Sea, and they attacked. Crane told the top turret gunner and engineer, Staff Sergeant George Williams, 'Come up front, George, there is something wrong with the rudder.' Williams checked the rudder cables and repaired a damaged section with some safety wire from the rear of the turret. As he returned to the turret the aircraft was peppered with bullets, and he saw the port engine in flames. He called to Crane but there was no reply. The plane started to lose altitude, levelled off and then dived in to the sea. (Williams and Sergeant Jesse Lewis, tail gunner, scrambled to safety out of the camera hatch, climbed in to a life raft and watched the Marauder sink in about forty-five seconds.) The time was 1224 hours, and they were 80 miles from England. They spent five days in the raft before being rescued and returned to England and to the 322nd Bomb Group. Lieutenant Matthews' B-26 was shot in to the sea at 1230 hours. There were no survivors. *Feldwebel* Niedereichholz of Stab II./JG1 and *Oberfeldwebel* Winkler of 4./JG3 were the victorious *Jagdflieger*. At Rougham, the estimated time for the Group's return was 1250 hours. On the control tower balcony, General Brady of 8th Bomber Command and other watchers were growing apprehensive. At 1305 hours an RAF listening post reported that it had intercepted a German radio transmission, which said that it had shot two bombers into the sea. By 1330 hours it was decided that no aircraft were still airborne and that a disaster had occurred, with all ten B-26s being lost.[1]

Later reconnaissance photos showed a disappointing amount of damage – suggesting that either the bombs had bounced out of the target area or that there had been a number of heroes on call to pull them outside the installations before they exploded. However this first rooftop raid could still be accounted an operational success, for the attack had been carried out according to plan. Another notable achievement of that day's activity was the brilliant support given the Antwerp and Courtrai attackers by the RAF Spitfire and the American Thunderbolt fighters. As a result, the enemy fighters 'seemed reluctant to attack' though Focke-Wulfs did attempt to bomb the formation attacking Antwerp.

Successes such as those of 14 May do not come by chance. Each step of this four-pronged attack had been planned weeks before. All bombing starts with the selection of targets; in the Anglo-American bombing offensive against Germany, the first selection is made by the Combined Chiefs of Staff. This body, knowing what forces will be available in each theatre of war, selects the categories of targets to be hit, i.e. submarine production may be given first priority, synthetic oil second and perhaps the enemy aircraft industry third place. The Chiefs of Staff also select the industrial areas most worthy of attention from the RAF's night bombers – thus it was decided that heavy industry in the Ruhr should be hit before the transportation and storage facilities of the port of Hamburg.

Then the Target Selection Committee, a group of military and economic experts who meet in London, with a blueprint of the enemy's industrial organisation before them, select the objectives needed to cripple the enemy's war potential in each category, and give each target, in turn, a priority rating.

With this information before him the Bomber Command chief decides what particular targets best suit the capabilities of his force. A Combined Operational Planning Committee – made up of representatives from the Fighter, Air Support and Bomber Commands and the Intelligence divisions of both the RAF and the American Air Force – after conferring with the CG and his staff, translates these decisions into a general plan of action. Given Kiel and Antwerp as the main targets, for example, and knowing the approximate force available, the Planning Committee laid out the routes, times and diversions, and decided on the details of the fighter cover to be supplied. Any necessary collaboration between the RAF and the AAF is also worked out at this time.

On a comparatively simple operation such as that of the 14 May attacks, these plans may comprise five or six pages of instructions and charts. Each plan, once it is completed and has been studied, amended and approved by the various commands involved, is given a code name and put on file – ready for instant use. When the weather is right and his force ready for a particular operation, the Chief of the Bomber Command takes the plan from his file. With the current disposition of the enemy defences, the weather report and certain other variables before him, the Bomber Commander adapts the basic plan to that day's operations. The command's Operations Officers then turn the plan into a detailed Combat Order, which is submitted to the Air Divisions for their corrections and suggestions. The amended version is despatched to the flying units.

With a force of more than 200 operational Forts available for the first time during the early days of May, the multiple attacks already planned and on file could now be launched. Another four-pronged assault, this time on French and Low Country targets, followed the Kiel-Courtrai-Antwerp-Ijmuiden operation. On 17 May, well over 100 Fortresses attacked two objectives – the sub-pen installations and the power station serving them – at the Lorient base, while two Groups of Liberators, operating as a separate operational unit for the first time, made a wide sea sweep to attack the submarine facilities at Bordeaux, and eleven medium bombers set out for objectives in Holland.

The operation was notable for an outstanding success and an equally outstanding failure: the Liberator flight produced some of the most spectacular navigation and bombing of the air war, and the B-26 attack on the Dutch targets resulted in the loss of all the ten planes attacking. Two lessons were learned that day: (1) that the Liberators operated more effectively when they flew by themselves and (2) that the fast medium bombers, flying at low altitudes, could not always depend on the element of surprise in heavily defended areas, but needed fighter support. The two Lorient strikes, one following the other along the same route at a fifteen-minute interval, apparently split the enemy fighter opposition. Losses were moderate – six Forts; the bombing was excellent; and claims of enemy fighters shot down were substantial. The Liberators, attacking a target 250 miles to the south twenty-four minutes later, met little fighter opposition. The multiple attacks were beginning to stretch the Nazi defences.

The months of May and June settled down to a grim exchange of blow for blow. Flensburg, Kiel, Wilhelmshaven, Emden, Bremen, the synthetic-rubber plant at Hüls, the submarine bases in Occupied France – these were hit, and hit hard. The Nazi defence command sought desperately for ways to stop the Fortress formations from reaching their targets. Air-to-air bombing increased; fighters armed with rocket guns were reported by returning crews. The Forts were not stopped.

The 8th Bomber Command celebrated its second 4 July in England by giving the Germans a demonstration of how a moderate-sized force of heavy day bombers could be used. Weather dictated the choice of three targets in Occupied France – the Gnôme & Rhône Aero Engine Factory at Le Mans, an aircraft factory at Nantes and the U-boat installations at La Pallice. Both factories, of course, were working hard for the Nazis.

Shortly after noon two strong forces of Forts flying parallel courses crossed the French coast, just east of the Cherbourg peninsula. As the German fighter force made hurried preparations to defend this area, a third force of some seventy Fortresses, having made a wide swing out to sea, appeared over the installations at La Pallice 200 miles to the south. This part of the operation bombed effectively, and returned without meeting any effective enemy opposition.

Meanwhile, the two main forces had reached Laval, 80 miles south of the Channel, at 12.30. Here the full force of the Nazi fighters converged upon them. At Laval, following the flight plan, one of the bomber forces swung left and hit Le Mans. The other force turned right and attacked Nantes to the south-east. This effectively split the Nazi fighter concentration. The Le Mans force withdrew north, picking up friendly fighter support at Argentan. The Nantes force continued from their target in a south-westerly direction, withdrawing out to sea and flying in a great semicircle back to England.

The German fighter force, dispersed to face the several prongs of this operation and held at bay by friendly fighters during the last part of the Le Mans withdrawal, was able to account for less than 3 per cent of the bombing force, despite its persistent and ferocious attacks. Returning crews claimed fifty-two Nazi fighters. The bombing against all three targets – a total of 542 tons being dropped – was exemplary.

On 4 July high-level precision bombing added a third development – tactical deception – to its already established reputation for accuracy and effective self-defence; it proved that, given sufficient force, the hand that guided the high-level daylight bomber could be quicker than the Nazi eye.

CHAPTER 5

The Log of the Liberators[1]

'The first of the Consolidated B-24 Liberator groups activated had been the 44th on 15 January 1941 at MacDill Field, Florida and the 93rd was created using personnel from the 44th. This Group also provided personnel for the 98th commanded by Colonel John Riley "Killer" Kane, the son of a Baptist preacher, from McGregor, Texas, which was dispatched to North Africa; and the 90th, which went to the South West Pacific. The 93rd would soon be commanded by Colonel Ted Timberlake, who "Tex" McCrary once described as a "broad-backed man who looked like a cross between Spencer Tracy and Bobby Jones". Born at Ford Hood, Virginia, one of four sons of a career Army artillery officer, who all graduated from West Point (three becoming general officers), Colonel Ted would take his group to the ETO [European Theatre of Operations] and the group soon became known as "Ted's Travelling Circus". But this was all in the future. A nucleus of the original personnel in the 44th, which was broken up and pocketed around the world like a gigantic game of pool, called themselves the "Eightballs".'

At noon on 17 May, the great sprawling French seaport of Bordeaux was relatively quiet. Far to the north, medium American bombers were slashing at the coast of Holland. Another 250 miles up the French coast, a furious air battle was raging between German fighters and strong formations of Fortresses, attacking their old objectives – submarines and installations – at Lorient. However, nothing was happening at Bordeaux. The Germans were not particularly vigilant. There were U-boats moored in the tideless basins and massive concrete shelters designed to protect them from air attack. Thirty or forty barrage balloons floated placidly in the air, a hazard for low-flying raiders. Bordeaux was a long way from England. American bombers had never attacked it. The fact that even at that moment they were hammering at Lorient made the German garrison at Bordeaux feel doubly secure. They had not even bothered to silence the German-controlled radio...

At 12.28 thirty-four Liberators – not a large force, but still the strongest Liberator formation yet seen in Western Europe – soared out of nowhere and dealt military targets in the harbour area of Bordeaux one of the most precise and devastating aerial blows of the war.

Actually, the Libs appeared out of the Bay of Biscay, where for hours they had been sweeping in a great 700-mile semicircle that had carried them far out into the Atlantic. Their landfall, timed to a matter of seconds, was a masterpiece of navigation. As the lead navigator, reserving most of his enthusiasm for the work of a fellow crew member, later described it,

> Suddenly through haze and mist we saw a break in the coastline. Although it wasn't very plain, it stood out well enough to be recognized as the estuary that curves crazily from the Bay of Biscay to Bordeaux, some thirty miles inland. When we reached our IP (initial point) on the bombing run a few minutes later, it was the bombardier's baby. He took over. It was the finest piece of precision bombing I ever hope to see. The locks collapsed, water gushed out of the basin into the river; there were hits on the bottleneck of the railroad yards, strikes on the aero-engine factory. It was beautiful!

The crews of the Libs had a right to be pleased. For the first time in seven months of sporadic operations in the ETO they had been given an assignment that called upon all their speed, range, and bomb-carrying capacity. They had carried it out successfully – and alone.

At 0900 hours that morning, two Groups of B-24s had assembled at 2,500 feet near Land's End. Four aircraft turned back with mechanical failures during the long overwater flight, and just before reaching the target one Liberator left formation with engine trouble and struggled to a crash-landing in Spain. This was the only bomber lost in the attack. Its crew was unhurt.

During the climb to altitude that began while the formations were still far out to sea, one Group began to lag behind because of lack of power in the lead ship. By deviating slightly from the prescribed course, the navigator managed to bring the Group to a landfall almost exactly at the ETA (estimated time of arrival).

A few flak bursts appeared over the target, but not enough to distract the bombardiers. Only one enemy fighter made a determined attack, and at 300 yards, under direct fire from three .50-calibre machine guns, he broke off and went down in a tight spin, with smoke pouring from his engine. He was claimed as a probable.

Two Americans were slightly wounded and one was lost in an accident so freakish that it was hard to believe. A waist gunner standing beside his open window somehow pulled the ripcord of his parachute. The billowing silk caught in the rush of wind, and snatched him out like a gigantic hand. Man and chute hit the tail assembly and disappeared over the Bay of Biscay. The parachute was observed to be badly torn…

Another 22,000 feet below, the harbour of Bordeaux was in confusion. Direct hits burst the great lock gates that kept the water level in Basin No. 1 from being affected by the rise and fall of tides in the river. Water gushed out in a colossal stream. A 480-yard pier, used exclusively by submarines, collapsed completely. Two U-boats, spotted there at the start of the attack, had vanished six hours later when the photo-reconnaissance plane flew over and took pictures. At least eight direct hits blasted the Matford aero-engine factory. Chemical works and railroad yards were hit. Damage to residential areas was negligible.

It was a sweet job and the crews of the Liberators were jubilant. They attributed much of the success of the mission to the use of only one type of bomber instead of the mixed formations in which the B-24s had usually flown at that time.

The fact that the two basic American heavy bombers performed better separately than together reflected discredit on neither ship. It was simply a matter of different speeds at different altitudes, causing certain obvious tactical difficulties. Most reasonable airmen were prepared to admit that there was not much that a Lib could do that a Fort was not capable of doing and vice versa. The main difference was one of appearance. Discrepancies in bomb load, range and armament were growing smaller as new bombers of both types incorporated various improvements that brought their performances closer together.

Nevertheless there still was, and always would be, an undeniable *esprit de corps* that set Fortress and Liberator men apart. Up to 17 May the sleek Fortresses had tended to overshadow their less photogenic sisters. This was inevitable in view of the disparity in numbers, and the Liberator crews wasted no time brooding about it. Still, they found particular satisfaction that day in doing a Liberator version of the American plan of high-altitude precision bombing, and doing it in so spectacular a fashion.

For seven months the Liberators of the 8th Bomber Command had been doing a variety of jobs, both odd and ordinary. Their debut over Lille on 9 October was not particularly brilliant. The abortive rate was high. However, they stood their baptism of fire well and to the people of Occupied France the name of the newcomer – an RAF idea – must have had a special significance.

For the next two months the Libs joined in the milk run down to the U-boat pens. There weren't many of them and, like their Fortress sisters, they were sorely pressed for replacements. They came back with the same battle damage from flak and fighters; their crews had equally harrowing combat stories to tell.

On 18 November over Lorient, a bullet from a Ju-88 entered the cockpit of a Liberator, smashing the pilot's arm and ricocheting off the control column in to the co-pilot's leg. At the same time the tunnel gunner was twice hit in the stomach; one bullet that had passed entirely through his body was found protruding from his hip by the navigator, who administered first aid. The gunner took the bloodstained bit of metal that was handed to him and put it in to his pocket, remarking that it would make a good souvenir.

The pilot, clinging to the controls with one hand despite the pain of his shattered arm, was lifted out of the cockpit and placed on the flight deck. The bombardier, who had had some flight training but had never been at the controls of a four-engined ship, took his place. He and the wounded co-pilot took turns flying the ship.

Near the English coast, visibility began to grow bad. The navigator took an Aldis lamp and flashed word to the other ships that they intended to land their wounded at the first available airdrome. Shortly afterward they left formation, climbed above the overcast and started hunting for a break in the clouds. The bombardier's flat, unemotional report told the rest of the story:

At about 6,000 feet we came into the clear over the overcast. I asked the engineer how much gasoline we had. He checked and said we had about an hour's supply. We decided to fly along for about forty-five minutes and look for an opening. We flew on a 65-degree heading that the navigator gave us. Just about the time this period was up we found an opening, came through and sighted the runways of an airdrome.

We had discussed the matter of landing while flying along. The co-pilot could not use the rudders and on the landing we were both on the wheel. I was using the rudders and working the brakes. We made a fast landing. I turned off the runway to the right as we came to the end of it. After landing we immediately called for an ambulance and rushed the three wounded to the hospital. The plane was not damaged on landing...

In October two squadrons of Liberators were sent to the south of England to work with British Coastal Command on anti-submarine patrol. By November, huge convoys were streaming south to supply the African armies. The 8th Bomber Command was already harassing the U-boats 'in the nest'. The Liberator squadrons were charged with responsibility for the second phase of the anti-U-boat campaign – killing them at sea.

In the harsh winter weather, the Libs went out on patrols that sometimes lasted nine or ten hours and covered hundreds of miles of steel-grey sea. Eyes grew weary searching for the telltale feather of a periscope or the shadowy outline of a U-boat hull. It was like looking for a pin in an acre of iron filings. The Liberator crews, stiff and cold, found consolation in the knowledge that they were a vital part of an immense net flung across the Bay of Biscay and half of the Atlantic, a net that was making efficient U-boat operations a mathematical impossibility.

Patrols were not always dull. One B-24 tangled with five Ju-88s far out in the bay, shot down two of them for certain, damaged one other and sailed home intact. Said the pilot happily, 'The Jerries must've thought we were one of those old British Liberators armed with .30-caliber machine guns, Brother, they were a surprised lot of Heinies!'

This was only the first odd job that the Liberators were called upon to do. In December, three squadrons of them were ordered to Africa, for a 'ten-day' period. Actually the ten days stretched out to three months, during which they lived in the desert on Spam and dehydrated cabbage, harassed Rommel's retreating rearguards, struck across the Mediterranean at Naples and the Sicilian airdromes, and made some good friends in the Ninth and Twelfth Air Forces.

The Liberators left behind in England struggled along with a force so attenuated that it was hardly visible to the naked eye. There were times when barely a dozen could be put in to the air. At one point they had to commandeer replacement crews intended for Fortresses. A fine large Briefing Room at one station – once the Group Intelligence Officer's pride and joy because it was so roomy – became a positive menace as the circle of chairs grew smaller and the unoccupied area increased.

When the wanderers returned from Africa in March, full of tall tales and with the Libyan sand still gritty on the floors of their ships, the confidence of the Liberator Wing soared again.

They went out with the Fortresses in what was – for them – considerable strength: eighteen, twenty, twenty-two planes. At Vegesack on 18 March they shared credit with the Forts for smashing the submarine-building yards. Only one Liberator was lost.

The Libs did not always get off so lightly. At Kiel on 14 May, flying lower than the Fortress formations and carrying incendiaries for the first time, they were singled out by enemy fighters for concentrated attack. Five B-24s out of seventeen were lost, the survivors destroying twenty-one German aircraft. The ferocity of the fighter attack and the violence of the evasive action taken by the big bombers are reflected in one pilot's account of the engagement:

> Then things began to happen. Three of them started at us. Our top turret gunner picked out the leader and let him have about fifty rounds from each gun. The co-pilot saw black smoke pour from the nacelle and the plane go into a spin.
>
> Despite the temperature of 20 degrees below zero Centigrade I was sweating like mad. I had on a pair of winter flying boots and nothing else except regular dress, which was wringing wet.
>
> Two more fighters came in from the nose. I could see them firing their cannons, so I pushed forward on the stick with all my might, We went down like a streamlined brick and they whizzed past us, barely missing the top of our wing, One of them took along several of our slugs with him, because our tracers were seen to go through his fuselage. When I pulled out of that dive, our top turret gunner was thrown from his turret, as was the tail gunner. All the other members of the crew were thrown about a bit: But the Jerries had missed us and that was the important thing.
>
> Just as we were approaching the target, four more fighters attacked us from dead ahead. One of their cannon shells hit our left wing. A moment later the co-pilot announced that the No. 3 engine was out.
>
> 'Want to feather it?' he asked.
>
> 'Hell, no!' I yelled.
>
> Feathering a propeller over enemy territory is like writing the boys at the mortuary for space on their slab. All of the fighters see that you are crippled and immediately set upon you for the kill.
>
> We had only three half hearted attacks from then on to the coast and those pilots must have been very green, or else I had become hardened to it all by that time. Off to our left, I saw one Me-109 do a slow roll and then head for home. His manoeuvre meant, 'Well, boys, it's all over for this time. See you soon.'

During the spring the Liberators began training for night operations. Personnel were sent to the RAF Operational Training Units to study the methods and technique of night flying. The American crews were not unfamiliar with night flying, but much had to be learned about differences in signal procedure, the tactics of night bombing and so forth. Again, the Liberators were being used experimentally. Whether those experiments would prove much or little, time and the course of the war would tell.

In June the Wing became non-operational; a new and very specialised training period set in. Combat crews had no idea what ultimate target they were pointing for, but it was obvious that it had nothing to do with high-altitude bombing. The big ships were sent roaring over the countryside in tight formation at treetop level. Low-altitude bombsights were installed. Armament modifications, designed to increase firepower forward, were speeded up. The Liberator men, pleased with their new hair-raising tactics, speculated feverishly as to the nature of their next assignment. One month later, much to the relief of harassed livestock in English meadows, the Liberators were no longer to be seen in the skies of Britain.

They would be seen in many places before they came back: over Rome in the first attack on the marshalling yards that tumbled Mussolini from his shaky pedestal; over Austria in the assault on the Messerschmitt factory at Wiener-Neustadt, one of the longest bombing missions of the war.

However, the climax of their mission came 1,350 miles from their home stations as the bomber flies. To attack this target, they flew from Africa, not from England. They were operating with the Ninth Air Force, not with the 8th Bomber Command. To the ground echelons left on the Liberator stations of Britain, three-fifths of the American force that struck the Romanian oil refineries at Ploesti on 1 August were 'our boys'.

Ten days later, at the station belonging to the oldest Liberator Group in the ETO, an eyewitness of the raid told how Lieutenant Colonel Addison E. Baker, commanding officer of that Group, led his last mission.[2] The Liberators took off across the Mediterranean after three weeks of rigorous and secret training in the desert, where a rough replica of the target had been built. Practice runs had been made until the timing of the whole attack was polished to the last split second. Crews were briefed with movies and lectures down to the last oil derrick in the target area.

With each plane carrying 3,100 gallons of gasoline and 5,000 lbs of delayed-action bombs, the bombers swept north and thundered over the coast of the Balkan Peninsula at 10,000 feet. It was a long trip, without the monotony of high-altitude approach. Once across the Danube, the formation came down to attack level. In the Romanian wheat fields only 200 feet below, the thundering engines caused wild excitement. Combat crews could see details with startling clarity. One girl in bright peasant costume flung her apron over her head in panic. An old couple fell on their knees and prayed. Some farmers threw stones and pitchforks. A man leading two horses beside a stream took one look and plunged headlong in to the water. Nor was all the excitement limited to people on the ground. No fewer than ten crews reported that as they crossed a river a girl was swimming in it. Opinion was unanimous that she was without benefit of bathing suit.

The plan was to sweep down on the oil refineries from the north, but two of the Groups, including Baker's, passed south of the target on their first approach. The leading Group made a wide circle, but Baker, spotting a refinery, turned and made a direct run for it.

By this time the defences were fully alert. Fighter planes were up. So low were the Liberators that more than once the fighters dove into the ground in frantic efforts to intercept them. As one crew member put it laconically, 'Those fighters used non-habit-forming tactics!'

Flak was more of a menace than fighters. Everything from machine guns hidden in haystacks to 88 mm cannon firing over open sights blasted at the Liberators. The guns in the big planes replied, waist gunners picking off riflemen, sending bursts of incendiaries in to oil storage tanks which exploded in sheets of flame.

Before the mission, Baker had stressed the absolute necessity of flying a tight formation in order to hit the relatively small target with the maximum number of bombs. 'If anything happens to the lead ship,' he said, 'pay no attention. Don't swerve. No matter what happens, keep straight.'

On the way in to the target a shell struck the right side of the cockpit of Baker's ship.[3] It probably killed the co-pilot and must have injured Baker, but he kept to his course. Fire broke out. Seconds later, just at the target, a heavier-calibre shell made a direct hit. Enveloped in flames, the Liberator shot over the target, dropped its bombs and crash-landed near the refinery it had helped to destroy. Colonel Baker is listed as Missing in Action.

In *Last of The Many*, Tex McCrary[4] wrote an account of Ploesti, which he called '*Operation Whopper*':

It's now American history, what happened on that raid, where fifty-three Libs were lost. But I'd like to tell you a few special stories. One is about Colonel Baker, the CO of the Circus who had said that he would lead his outfit to the target 'even if my plane falls apart.'

It was a good day, that Sunday, when the brown-green ships from the Eighth and the sand-pink ships of the Desert Ninth Air Force headed north across the Mediterranean. As they crossed the Balkans, they saw farmers in the fields even on Sunday and once they saw naked girls bathing in a river. 'Let's bail out here!' was the instant wisecrack that bounced around over the intercoms.

Baker's ship was in the lead as they went into the target. The flak was heavy and accurate.

Some of the boys said there were an awful lot of new guns around there – new earth around the gun emplacements. Baker's ship was hit, hit hard. Joe Tate[5] saw the whole thing:

'Baker was four hundred feet in front of me. He got hit three times: once far out on the wing, then at the roots of the wing and then finally square in the cockpit. His wing tanks and the bomb bay tank burst into a sheet of yellow flame. The Force was still sixty seconds from the target. The minute he was hit, he jettisoned his bombs – you can tell when the pilot drops them instead of the bombardier – they just dumped. But Baker kept on leading the Force into the target, like he said he would, aiming his ship for the narrow space between the towers of the cracking plants in the heart of the refinery we were headed for. I saw something coming down out of the nose-wheel hatch of Baker's ship – it was a man's legs. He dropped clear and came tumbling back over our props as his 'chute caught the air – came so close I could see that his legs were on fire. Baker kept his ship on course.

'But when we got right on top of the target, the devil himself couldn't have held that ship in formation any longer. Baker was flying pilot and Jerstad was co-pilot. The cockpit must have been a blast furnace. We could see the flames through the windows as the ship lost speed and we pulled up with it. The right wing started to crumple and drop off, but not before old Bake had taken us through the target. And then he pulled his ship up into a steep climb. God only knows how anybody inside could have been still alive, but something inside was pulling the ship up and up and out of the path of our Force. Three men fell out the back of her and then it fell off and crashed into a field.

'Baker could have saved himself if he had wanted to belly-land in a field before we got to the target, when he was first hit. Other ships had made belly landings. But Baker stuck.'

Seven of the ten men in Baker's ship had finished their tours of duty; they volunteered for the Ploesti job.

'Coming back was secondary...'

'Thundering down from the north,' continues *Target: Germany,*

another VIII Bomber Command Group led by Colonel Leon Johnson saw the delayed-action bombs of Baker's Group exploding in the target area. By going in at 500 feet or higher, Johnson could have lessened the danger from ground explosions, but mushrooming smoke would have made accurate bombing difficult. He took his Group in at 230 feet, the height of the tallest chimneys.

Casualties were heavy, but the target was completely wrecked. For his courage and leadership, Colonel Johnson received the nation's highest award, the Congressional Medal of Honor. He returned safely.

Near one of the targets, airmen saw the crew of a Liberator that had been shot down standing near their crumpled plane, waving their arms and cheering like maniacs. The surviving bombers raced away across the fields so low that some of them came back with corn stalks stuck in their bomb bays. Behind them on the horizon huge columns of smoke bore witness to the effectiveness of their work. 'I wouldn't give a million dollars for the experience of that raid,' a gunner said afterwards, 'and I wouldn't give ten cents for another like it!'

That was the story as told to members of Colonel Baker's Group at their deserted station somewhere in England. 'You can be proud of your boys,' the eyewitness said.

They were proud of them, of the ships they flew and of the job they did. The story would be remembered as long as there were Liberator men left to tell it. The Germans would remember it, too – five refineries hit, at least two of them completely smashed. The price paid in men and machines was high. It was no higher than expected. The crews that survived knew that the losses in planes would be made good with newer, better planes. They knew they could never replace the men.

CHAPTER 6

Twelve o'Clock High

'Not a soul was visible, nothing moved save the cows, nor was there any sound to break the great quiet. And yet Stovall, standing there solitary against the green landscape, was no longer alone. Nor, to him, was the suit he wore still blue. Rather it was olive drab, with major's leaves on the shoulders, as befitted the adjutant of a heavy-bombardment group. A gust of wind blew back the tall weeds behind the hardstand nearest him. But suddenly Stovall could no longer see the bent-back weeds through the quick tears that blurred his eyes and slid down the deep lines in his face. He made no move to brush them away. For behind the blur he could see, from within more clearly. On each empty hardstand there sat the ghost of a B-17, its four whirling propellers blasting the tall grass with the gale of its slip stream, its tyres bulging under the weight of tons of bombs and tons of the gasoline needed for a deep penetration.

'... There will be a briefing for a practice mission at eleven hundred this morning. Yes, practice. I've been sent down here to take over what has come to be known as a hard-luck group. I don't believe in hard luck. So we're going to find out what the trouble is. Maybe part of it's your flying. So we're going back to fundamentals. But I can tell you now one reason I think you're having hard luck. I saw it in your faces last night. I can see it there now ... You've been looking at a lot of air lately and you think you ought to have a rest. In short, you're sorry for yourselves. I haven't much patience with this what-

*are-we-fighting-for stuff. We're in a war – a shooting war. We've got
to fight and some of us have got to die. I'm not trying to tell you not
to be afraid. Fear is normal. But stop worrying about it and about
yourselves. Stop making plans, forget about going home. Consider
yourselves already dead. Once you accept that idea it won't be so
tough. If any man here can't buy that, if he rates himself as something
special, with a special kind of hide to be saved, then he'd better make
up his mind about it right now. I don't want him in this group. I'll be
in my office in five minutes. He can see me there.'*

> *Twelve o'Clock High!* by Beirne Lay, Jr, and Sy Bartlett.

In England in 1942, the USAAF high command believed in their own
mistaken prophecy that their B-17s and B-24s, heavily armed so as
not to need escort fighters, could, in broad daylight, penetrate even the
strongest defences and achieve the 'pickle barrel' bombing accuracy that
bombardiers had performed in the clear skies of Texas and the southern
states. In August 1942, Major General Ira C. Eaker, Commander of 8th
Bomber Command, which was activated in England on 22 February,
had just three operational B-17 Flying Fortress Groups – the 92nd,
97th and 301st. The 97th Bomb Group flew the first heavy bomber
mission, to Lille on 17 August.

By September, losses were on the increase. It was alarmingly obvious
that 8th Bomber Command's *raison d'être* was at stake. Tactics would
have to be drastically altered if the untried force was to continue to
function as an air force in its own right. The RAF, and even some in
the USAAF, were of the opinion that bombing in daylight was suicidal.
Eaker stuck to his guns, but to improve bombing accuracy he knew
that high-level bombing was no longer viable, at least if targets, mainly
U-boat pens in France, were to be hit at all. Even then, American bombs
would not penetrate the thick defensive shelters. Height, therefore,
would have to be sacrificed to permit lower and more accurate
bombing. This was an open invitation to the Luftwaffe fighters and the
German flak defences, both of which were formidable.

On 9 October, for the first time, over 100 B-17s and B-24s were
despatched. Their target was the vast steel and locomotive works at the
Compagnie de Fives in Lille. Also flying their first mission this day were

the 306th Bomb Group at Thurleigh, Bedfordshire, which, unlike the 92nd, 97th and 301st Bomb Groups, which flew B-17Es, was equipped with the improved B-17F. Colonel Charles 'Chip' B. Overacker, Jr, the CO, led twenty-three crews in a 369th Bomb Squadron Fortress piloted by Captain James A. Johnston. Each B-17 had a crew of nine, as a second waist gunner was not thought necessary. Two of the 306th Bomb Group B-17s aborted the mission before reaching the enemy coast. Nearing the target, flak enveloped the formation, and in the 306th, Colonel Overacker's Fortress was hit in the No. 2 engine and he was forced to relinquish the lead.

The 306th Bomb Group was intercepted by fighters of JG 26. *Snoozy II*, flown by Captain John W. Olson in the 367th Bomb Group, was shot down by 'Pips' Priller after raking the flight deck with cannon and machine-gun fire that left Olsen and his co-pilot, Lieutenant Joseph N. Gates, dead in their blood-spattered cockpit. First Lieutenant James M. Stewart's *Man o' War*, also in the 367th BS, went down to fighters over the target. Only sixty-nine bombers hit their primary targets, and many of the bombs failed to explode. The inexperienced 93rd Liberator Group and the 306th had placed many of their bombs outside the target area, killing a number of French civilians. Traffic control was bad, and some of the bombardiers never got the target in their bombsights. The B-17 gunners put in fighter claims for forty-eight destroyed, eighteen probably destroyed and four damaged, but when the heat of the Lille battle had died away their scores were whittled down to twenty-five, thirty-eight, forty-four, then finally twenty-one, twenty-one, fifteen (the Germans actually lost only one fighter). At the time the figures did much to compensate for the largely inaccurate bombing.

Beginning on 20 October 1942, the objective of all 8th BC heavies was 'the maximum destruction of the submarine bases in the Bay of Biscay'. Next day, sixty-six B-17s and twenty-four B-24s headed for the pens at Keroman, about 11 miles from Lorient, but thick cloud at their prescribed bombing altitude of 22,000 feet forced all except the fifteen Fortresses of the 97th Bomb Group to return to England. Three B-17s were shot down and six were badly damaged.

On 1 November Eaker's small force, strengthened by the inclusion for the first time of the 91st Bomb Group, attacked Brest without loss.

On 7 November, the Forts returned to the French port. Heavy cloud ruled out accurate bombing, and while in the target area the 306th Bomb Group was jumped by about twenty enemy fighters, although they failed to down any of the B-17s. Next day, thirty FW 190s made at least 200 attacks on the five B-17s of the 369th Squadron, which chose to make a second run on their target at Lille. Captain Richard D. Adams's B-17 was downed by flak.

Events now began to overtake the 306th Bomb Group and the other heavy bomb groups in 8th BC. For the raid on Saint-Nazaire, planned for 9 November, HQ decided that the forty-seven B-17s and B-24s would bomb from low level! Bombing accuracy had been so poor that Eaker directed the heavies to bomb from 7,000–8,000 feet! In theory, these heights were between the low and high flak. However, no one seemed to have taken into consideration the agonisingly slow speed of the Fortress at such low levels, which meant they would cross the target at 155 to 160 mph, if they were lucky! With no tail wind at this height, the B-17 crews would be at the mercy of flak guns for longer than before. At Thurleigh, Overacker reacted furiously to the Field Order. As soon as it appeared on the teletype machine at the base, he telephoned HQ, 8th BC, to protest. Overacker was promptly rebuked and told that nothing would change the decision. Overacker responded that if his crews had to fly the mission then so would he, and that he'd lead them! His four squadron commanders joined him on the mission, leading from the front also.

It was a disaster. The 306th Bomb Group trailed another group across Saint-Nazaire at the same altitude, and the German flak gunners had a simple task. In seconds, three Fortresses in the 306th Bomb Group were shot down in rapid succession by flak, with the loss of twenty-two crew. Several other B-17s, including Overacker's, which was very badly damaged, were in bad shape, and some barely made it home. On 17 November, the Forts returned to Saint-Nazaire, but 20 miles NW of the target the 306th Bomb Group, bringing up the rear of the formation, was hit by fifteen FW 190s. The Luftwaffe fighters caused mayhem and casualties. Captain Robert C. Williams in *Chennault's Poppy* was badly shot up and force-landed at Exeter. It never flew again. Next day, *Floozy* of 367th BS was shot down by a combination of flak and fighters over Saint-Nazaire, and crashed in the Bay of Biscay. Other B-17s returned to Thurleigh badly shot up, and with dead and dying on-board. Major Thurman Shuller, group surgeon, wrote later that 'the entire group was always emotionally jarred by the return home of the bodies of good friends'. As the situation worsened, it would become a morale problem.

On 23 November, the Fortresses returned to Saint-Nazaire. Bad weather and mechanical problems forced thirteen B-17s to abort, leaving forty-four B-17s in formation. On previous missions the B-17s had been intercepted from the rear, where enough guns could be brought to bear on enemy fighters. However, the frontal area of a B-17 offered very little in defensive firepower, so despite the dangers of very high closing speeds, intercepting from the front was now considered the best method of shooting them down. Egon Mayer, commander of III./JG2, who led the attacking fighters this day, is credited with developing the head-on attack, or from twelve o'clock high. Four B-17s were lost to head-on attacks, including 1st Lieutenant Clay Isbell's B-17 in the 306th Bomb Group, which was shot down on the bomb run. Isbell and six of his crew were trapped when the Fortress exploded.

On 25 November, the 306th Bomb Group was removed from the battle order. The group only resumed combat missions on 12 December. There then followed another week's rest from combat, missions resuming on the 19th with a long, unescorted mission to Romilly, 100 miles SE of Paris. The 367th 'Clay Pigeons' Bomb Squadron lost three B-17s and twenty-nine crew. This unlucky squadron's original complement of nine crews now numbered just three. Their nickname originated from an American war correspondent, who, writing in *The Saturday Evening Post*, said that the 367th Squadron reminded him of a bunch of clay pigeons. The name stuck![1]

Back at base, respiratory ailments were rife, and the enlisted men grumbled about unsanitary conditions and the poor food on offer. Every army has its complainers and backsliders, but feeling sorry for oneself is not a condition that can be tolerated for long, especially if higher command identifies that the condition is widespread and constitutes a serious morale problem.

On 3 January 1943, Saint-Nazaire claimed two more 306th Bomb Group B-17s in the target area. Navigators in the group were now in such short supply that some of the Group's B-17s flew without one. Major William Lanford, 368th Bomb Squadron CO, led the remaining B-17s back to England, where bad weather forced them to seek shelter in Cornwall. Three days later, on 6 January, they set off for Thurleigh, but the formation strayed south, over the Channel Isles, and the B-17s were bracketed by German flak. One B-17 was lost. It was not until 8 January that the formation finally made it back to Thurleigh. By then the 306th Bomb Group had a new CO.

On 4 January Eaker had set out for Thurleigh from 'Pinetree', his headquarters at RAF Bomber Command HQ, High Wycombe, on the green flanks of the rolling Buckinghamshire Chilterns, with his A-3 (Operations and Training), Colonel Frank A. Armstrong, Jr, and Lieutenant Colonel Beirne Lay, Jr, in tow. 'Things are not going well up there,' he told them. 'I think we ought to take a look around.' (Things obviously had not improved since Eaker's last visit to the 306th Bomb Group, on 14 November, when HM King George VI and top-ranking US officers toured Alconbury, Chelveston and Thurleigh.) Eaker's aide James Parton confirms in *Air Force Spoken Here*, his biography of Eaker, that he was unimpressed with Overacker's outfit, which, unlike the other two groups, appeared slovenly and undisciplined. Parton indicated as much to Overacker, and the royal visit then went 'pretty much like the others, but there was a notable absence of spit and polish'. Eaker told 'Tooey' Spaatz that he had better relieve Overacker, but the general waited six more weeks, by which time the 306th Bomb Group's bombing and loss record was the worst in 8th BC. Something had to be done.

Armstrong, a cool, tough, no-nonsense North Carolinian, was one of Eaker's original nineteen staff officers, and had been selected as the only regular officer of the group. At the end of July 1942, Armstrong had left 8th HQ to take command of the 97th Bomb Group. Colonel Cornelius Cousland was sacked for running a 'lackadaisical, loose-jointed, fun-loving, badly trained (especially in formation flying) outfit', which was 'in no sense ready for combat'. Armstrong's West Point training, his erect bearing and wind-tanned face – for the last fourteen of his thirty-nine years, most of his time had been spent in the cockpits of military aircraft – commanded the respect of those who served with him. Armstrong, who had served in the 3rd Attack Group, had worked closely with his RAF counterparts during the early formative days at High Wycombe. He worked his new crews hard and, with the help of officers like Major Paul W. Tibbets, he soon turned the 97th Bomb Group into a very effective outfit.

Beirne Lay, Jr, was another of the original six staff officers who accompanied Eaker to England early in February 1942. The red-headed Lay was a writer. He had penned the classic *I Wanted Wings*, which, in 1941, had been made into a successful movie by Paramount, and will be remembered as the movie that made Veronica Lake famous. It was written originally to tell what happens inside a boy who 'just has to fly'. Hence billed for 8th Bomber Command's first historian, Lay was to recall, 'I also filled in at first with the additional duties of Mess Officer and egg forager, PRO, aide and officially also a member of A-3 and Athletics Officer.'

At the main gate, General Eaker's Humber auto, flying the red flag with two white stars of a major general, was waved casually past by a sentry, who neither saluted nor checked the occupants' AGO cards. At group HQ, Eaker toured the base with Chip Overacker. The general was not impressed with what he saw. Eaker later recounted,

> As we visited hangars, shops and offices, I found similar attitudes as seen at the front gate. The men had a close attachment to their CO and he to them. But there was a lack of military proprietary and I could not help feel that this might be part of the problem that was being revealed in combat.

The 306th had lost nine Fortresses on its last three missions.

On their return to base HQ, Eaker relieved Colonel Overacker of command. 'Chip,' he said, 'You'd better get your things and come back with me.' The general then turned to Armstrong and announced, 'Frank, you're in command. I'll send your clothes down.' The purge did not stop there. Eaker summoned Major Lanford to his HQ on 17 January and relieved him of his post.[2] Two days later, Armstrong transferred Lieutenant Colonel Delmar Wilson, 306th Bomb Group deputy commander, and brought in as operations officer Major Claude Putnam, who, like Armstrong, was a veteran of the 97th Bomb Group's early days in England. As Russell A. Strong recounts in his book, *First over Germany, A History of the 306th Bomb Group*, the task of rebuilding the combat-decimated 306th was straightway undertaken by Armstrong. Within a few days he had begun to restore the fading morale. He also started preparations for an event which would forever tag the 306th with the proud slogan, 'First over Germany'.

On 27 January, Armstrong had the honour of leading the first American raid over Germany; eighteen B-17s of the 306th Bomb Group, on its sixteenth combat mission, headed five bomb groups, which bombed Wilhelmshaven. On 17 February, Armstrong was promoted to brigadier general and made deputy commander, 1st Wing. Command of the 306th Bomb Group passed to Claude Putnam. On 5 April, when the Fortresses were given the Erla VII aircraft and engine repair works at Mortsel near Antwerp as their objective, Armstrong returned to Thurleigh to fly as an observer with his former group. He climbed aboard Captain John M. Regan's *Dark Horse*, which also carried Lieutenant Colonel Jim Wilson, appointed 306th Bomb Group Executive Officer just three days earlier. The 368th BS flew Lead, the 423rd High and the 367th 'Clay Pigeons' flew Low. Altogether, 104 bombers were despatched.

One 306th Bomb Group B-17 turned back at 14.35, just before reaching the English coast, after a cylinder head broke and supercharger buckets blew off. A second turned back at the English coast at 14.36, because No. 4 engine went out and the aircraft could not keep up. Altogether, twenty-one Fortresses and Liberators turned back due to various mechanical problems before reaching the enemy coast, where, from then on, the 306th bore the brunt of head-on attacks that continued all the way to the target. The enemy fighters shot down four of the Thurleigh Group's B-17s. *Dark Horse* was hit by cannon fire from a FW 190 attacking head-on during the bomb run, but Wilson and Regan got the Fortress safely home, aided by Captain Robert Salitrnik, the lead navigator. Salitrnik had been critically wounded when he was hit in the leg by fragments from a can of .50-calibre ammunition, which exploded when hit by 20-mm fire from a FW 190 during a head-on attack. He received four pints of plasma on arrival at Thurleigh, and was out of shock the next day, but developed gas gangrene on 15 April and died on the 16th. General Armstrong, who, after Salitrnik was wounded, administered first aid to the navigator as he shared a walk-around oxygen bottle with Captain Regan, later received the DSC for this mission. Although his commendation said that Armstrong flew the aircraft, it was Regan who did all the flying.

According to Wilbur H. Morrison in *Fortress Without A Roof*, after 'Possum' Hansell left England in October 1943 to become the air member of the Joint Plans Committee of the Joint Chiefs of Staff in Washington DC, he discovered that Armstrong had told members of the 101st Combat Wing that General Hansell had supported suicidal missions, which led to high casualties. Armstrong gave the impression that, if he had been at the helm, he would have rejected missions against such heavily defended targets until 8th Bomber Command was stronger. In the Pacific war, Armstrong joined former 8th Air Force generals Curtis F. LeMay and Possum Hansell, being given command of 11th Bomber Command in August 1944; all took part in the final downfall of the Japanese Empire. Notably, Hansell and LeMay continued the same unescorted daylight precision bombing doctrine they had pursued whatever the odds in England. Brigadier General Frank Armstrong had assumed command of the 315th Bomb Wing (Very Heavy) on 18 November 1944, and he remained at its helm until January 1946.

In 1946, while many people's thoughts turned to peace, others were still thinking of war. Beirne Lay, who was working for MGM on *Above and Beyond*, another aviation film, received an interesting approach from Sy Bartlett, who as a major had been Gen Spaatz's aide. Bartlett was now working as a screenwriter at 20th Century Fox Studios, and he wanted Lay to co-write a book and screenplay about the air war called *Twelve O'Clock High*. The central character was 'General Frank Savage', who was modelled on none other than Brig. Gen. Frank Armstrong, with whom he had struck up a close friendship in the Second World War. At first Lay thought they did not have a chance with a book about the war, but Bartlett was so determined that he was ultimately persuaded. It was Lay who came up with the fictionalised

918th Bomb Group commanded by Savage, which he arrived at by taking the 306th Bomb Group and multiplying it by three.

In 1948, with the novel *Twelve O'Clock High* nearing publication, Louis D. 'Bud' Lighton, a producer at Fox, immediately became very interested in the possibility of a screenplay of the same name. Lighton sounded out studio head Darryl F. Zanuck, who promptly purchased the movie rights. The central theme in the movie version would be the gradual and ultimate destruction of General Savage, played superbly by Gregory Peck. Zanuck hired Henry King, an accomplished pilot, as the movie's director. King, Bartlett and Lay greatly refined the overlong script, which had already seen the removal of Savage's love interest, and together they pared it down to a highly polished final draft.

Twelve O'Clock High draws upon the 306th Bomb Group's troubled early combat history and its effect on the combat crews. Innovative and realistic pieces woven into the tapestry of the movie include the authentic action sequences, filmed in actual combat, while visual references, such as the targets 'smoked' on the ceiling of the briefing room, did happen in the 306th and 97th Bomb Groups and elsewhere. Allusions to real events and representations of actual wartime personnel abound. Savage's ship, *Piccadilly Lily*, was named after the 100th Bomb Group B-17 that Lieutenant Colonel Lay flew in as an observer on the Regensburg mission on 17 August 1943.

Some characterisations are amalgams of many actual personalities. Although he is not mentioned directly in the movie, Hauptmann Wolfgang-Ferdinand 'Wütz' Galland is named in Lay's novel as the 'credit-hogging Jerry fighter ace, Wütz Galland, who specialized in shooting down crippled Forts, after ordering other pilots away from the easy kill'.[3] Ben Gately, played by Hugh Marlowe, commanded the B-17 known as *The Leper Colony*, a Fortress crewed by misfits, backsliders and men known to be 'combat fatigued', or, as it was known, 'flak happy'. In the RAF, the term was more caustically termed LMF – Lack of Moral Fibre. Savage demotes Gately to the pariah ship to embarrass him and force him to reveal his true colours. It is Gately's chance to get back his self-respect and become the heroic figure Savage knows deep down that he is.

Casting veteran screen and stage actor Dean Jagger in the all-important role of Major Harvey Stovall, the 918th Bomb Group's

Ground Executive, was inspirational. Stovall transports the moviegoer through every facet of the story from the very outset, when he returns to Archbury in post-war England and by chance buys the very Toby jug that once adorned the mantelpiece over the fireplace in the officers' mess. In a nice, authentic touch, the jug is turned about face when a mission is to be flown.

The scene with Lieutenant Jesse Bishop is inspired by a true incident; the 918th Bomb Group co-pilot was awarded his Medal of Honor for doggedly getting his battered ship back to Archbury, staying at the controls for two hours after Lieutenant McKesson, his pilot, had been killed. In the script, McKesson, 'a beefy six-footer', is mortally wounded by a burst of enemy gunfire from fighters out of the sun from twelve o'clock high, which blows off the back of his head, exposing the brain. In the same attack, the top turret gunner slips through the flight deck hatch and falls to the floor, his right arm blown off at the shoulder, and is spouting blood all over himself and the inside of the aircraft. Lieutenant Heinz Zimmerman, Bishop's navigator, 'his coveralls spattered with the drying, dark stains of another man's blood', tries to give him a shot of morphine, but it is 40 below at 25,000 feet, so the needle bends and he cannot get it in. Next Zimmerman tries a tourniquet, but the arm is off too close to the shoulder so he bandages the pilot as best he can. Finally, Zimmerman, who knows that the critically wounded gunner will not survive the two hours back to base, puts a parachute on him and places the ripcord in his hand, before dumping him out of the nose hatch, praying that the French or the Germans will get him to hospital and save his life.

The actual incident occurred on 26 July 1943, during 'Blitz Week'. Among the ninety-two Fortresses that successfully attacked Hannover was a 92nd Bomb Group B-17, *Ruthie II*, piloted by Lieutenant Robert L. Campbell and his co-pilot, Flight Officer John C. Morgan, a 6-foot, red-haired Texan who had flown with the RCAF for seven months before transferring to the Eighth Air Force. The navigator, Keith J. Koske, wrote later,

We were on our way into the enemy coast, when we were attacked by a group of FW 190s. On their first pass I felt sure they had got us for there was a terrific explosion overhead and the ship rocked badly. A second later the top turret gunner, Staff Sergeant Tyre C. Weaver, fell through the hatch and slumped to the floor at the rear of my nose compartment. When I got to him I saw his left arm had been blown off at the shoulder and he was a mass of blood. I first tried to inject some morphine but the needle was bent and I could not get it in.

As things turned out it was best I didn't give him any morphine. My first thought was to try and stop his loss of blood. I tried to apply a tourniquet but it was impossible as the arm was off too close to the shoulder. I knew he had to have the right kind of medical treatment as soon as possible and we had almost four hours flying time ahead of us, so there was no alternative. I opened the escape hatch, adjusted his chute for him and placed the ripcord ring firmly in his right hand. He must have become excited and pulled the cord, opening the pilot's chute in the updraft. I managed to gather it together and tuck it under his right arm, got him into a crouched position with legs through the hatch, made certain again that his good arm was holding the chute folds together and toppled him out into space. I learned somewhat later from our ball turret gunner, James L. Ford that the chute opened okay. We were at 24,500 feet and 25 miles due west of Hannover and our only hope was that he was found and given medical attention immediately.

The bombardier, Asa J. Irwin, had been busy with the nose guns and when I got back up in the nose he was getting ready to toggle his bombs. The target area was one mass of smoke and we added our contribution. After we dropped our bombs we were kept busy with the nose guns. However, all our attacks were from the tail and we could do very little good. I had tried to use my interphone several times, but could get no answer. The last I remember hearing over it was shortly after the first attack when someone was complaining about not getting oxygen. Except for what I thought to be some violent evasive action we seemed to be flying okay.

It was two hours later when we were 15 minutes out from the enemy coast that I decided to go up and check with the pilot and have a look around. I found Lieutenant Campbell slumped down in his seat, a mass of blood and the back of his head blown off. This had happened 'two hours' before, on the first attack. A shell had entered from the right side, crossed in front of John Morgan and had hit Campbell in the head. Morgan was flying the plane with one hand, holding the half-dead pilot off with the other hand and he had been doing it for over two hours! (It was no mean feat; Campbell was a six-footer who weighed 185lb.) Morgan told me we had to get Campbell out of his seat as the plane couldn't be landed from the co-pilot's seat since the glass on that side was shattered so badly you could barely see out. We struggled for 30 minutes getting the fatally injured pilot out of his seat and down into the rear of the navigator's compartment, where the bombardier held him from slipping out of the open bomb doors. Morgan was operating the controls with one hand and helping me handle the pilot with the other.

The radio operator, waist and tail gunners were unable to lend assistance because they were unconscious through lack of oxygen, the lines having been shattered several hours earlier. Morgan's action was nothing short of miraculous. Not only had he flown the aircraft to the target and out again with no radio, no intercom and no hydraulic fluid, he had maintained formation the whole time, an incredible feat for a pilot flying one-handed.

Morgan brought *Ruthie II* in to land at RAF Foulsham, a few miles inland of the Norfolk coast, and put down safely. Campbell died one and half hours after they reached England. The other crew members survived, including Weaver, who had been put in a PoW camp after hospitalisation. On 18 December 1943, listeners to the BBC's evening news heard that Flight Officer (later 2nd Lieutenant) John C. Morgan (now with the 482nd Bomb Group) had received the Medal of Honor from General Eaker in a special ceremony at Eighth AF HQ, and heard him relive the moments of 26 July.

Back to *Twelve O'Clock High*. Returning to Archbury, Zimmerman tells Major Don Kaiser, group flight surgeon, that he has been holding down McKesson while Bishop flew the B-17 on his own. Equally, the navigator is concerned about the top turret gunner's right arm, which has been left in the blood-spattered B-17 after being shot off in the fighter attack. It is Kaiser who gets a blanket and climbs in to the nose to retrieve the limb. Later, after being blamed for a navigational error that results in the loss of seven of the group's B-17s and seventy men, Zimmerman commits suicide with his pearl-handled revolver. Bishop is lost on a mission to Oschersleben. ('Blitz Week' was resumed on the morning of 28 July 1943, when the 4th Wing had the dubious honour of flying the deepest penetration so far, to the fighter assembly plant at Oschersleben. Morgan, unlike Bishop, was shot down and taken prisoner on 6 March 1944 and he spent the rest of the war in Stalag Luft III.)

The leading players featured in *Twelve O'Clock High* are based on men such as generals Eaker and Armstrong, as well as group commanders and their crews generally, who not only shaped the future of the Eighth Air Force, but also affected the evolution of the 306th Bomb Group. The actual incident where General Eaker arrives at the guard post at Thurleigh, only to be waved through without the necessary military courtesies, is re-enacted for the cameras. Eaker is portrayed as 'Major General Patrick Pritchard'. Likeable, decent Colonel Keith Davenport, aka Chip Overacker, played by Gary Merrill, is popular with his crews, but he cannot prevent the high losses, delegate, nor impose the strong discipline needed to change things. He is replaced by the resolute taskmaster and West Pointer Frank Savage, aka Gregory Peck. Savage uncompromisingly sweeps in to office not so much like a new broom, but like a whirlwind. Gradually, he earns his crews' grudging respect, but not their devotion. He does not seek it. He requires only their obedience instilled by military discipline, both in the air and on the ground. Training, training and more training follow, until the 918th's poor formation flying is improved.

Savage knows that wallowing in self-pity and calling themselves the 'Hard Luck Group' is not going to help the air crews, least of all in placing bombs squarely on target, the reason for their entire being. In what is arguably the most memorable scene in the movie, in the briefing room Savage finally brings the crews to the reality of their situation with swift, sharp, shock treatment. He stuns his new charges (and the audience) with a well-directed bucket of ice-cold water more accurate than a bomb strike. It chills every spine in the room and in every theatre across the country. Savage fires from the hip and tells them straight, 'You're not going home. Consider yourselves already dead!'

The impact on the pale young faces has clearly found its mark. It is one of shell shock, much more powerful than a burst of flak, or a salvo of machine-gun fire in the cockpit.

In wartime every commander in the field has to constantly make unpopular life-or-death decisions among the ranks. In the Eighth AF and in RAF Bomber Command, those decisions needed to made more frequently and more consistently than in most other battlefronts. There is no room at the top for popularity contests. Respect and results are what count, as long as losses are not considered prohibitive over an extended period. Colonel, later General, Curtis E. LeMay, one-time commander of the 305th Bomb Group, Eighth Air Force, is indicative of this.

However, in the case of Frank Savage, we witness steady mental decline as battle fatigue overtakes and finally engulfs this remarkable leader of men. Ultimately, Savage allows the full weight of responsibility to fall squarely on his shoulders and his alone, much in the same way that events had overtaken Davenport. Savage continues to fly missions when it is not essential or required of him to do so. He insists on leading from the front as if he still has something to prove to his men. He begins to crack and then suffers the final painful mental breakdown at planeside prior to a mission. He is so wracked with mental fatigue that he cannot summon strength in his arms to lift himself up and in to the nose of his B-17. This final part of Frank Savage's persona is not based on General Armstrong at all, but the incident, as Lay confirmed, did happen to 'a very fine commander'. It seems that this 'very fine commander' was another regular officer, Brigadier General Newton Longfellow, one of Eaker's closest friends since they had served in the 3rd Aero Squadron in the Philippines in 1919. At the end of July 1942, the newly arrived Colonel Longfellow was put forward by Eaker for promotion to brigadier general. On 21 August, Eaker placed General Longfellow in command of the 1st Bomb Wing.[4]

On 24 August, seven days after the inaugural 8th Bomber Command mission to Rouen, Longfellow was aboard Major Paul Tibbets' B-17 (Armstrong's pilot on the momentous Rouen raid) when he led a dozen 97th Bomb Group B-17s to Le Trait. It was the new bomb wing commander's combat orientation flight. On the way home the formation was jumped from above by yellow-nosed Bf 109s, which, during an overhead pass, fired 20-mm cannon shells into Tibbets' cockpit, shattering the instrument panel and severely injuring Lieutenant Gene Lockhart, the co-pilot, in the left hand. The top turret gunner was also seriously injured. Tibbets, who was also wounded, wrote later,

Newt panicked. He started grabbing for the throttles and we had a critical situation. I told him to quit. He didn't even hear me. The only thing I could do was hit him with my right elbow. I was able to catch him under the chin, while he was leaning over and I knocked him flat on his fanny. He calmed down then and when he got back on his feet he spent the next half-hour ministering to the injured. Having done what he could for Lockhart's hand, he bandaged the head of the turret gunner who was lying on the floor unconscious. After lifting Lockhart out of his seat and making him as comfortable as possible on the floor, with a parachute pack for a pillow, Longfellow took over the co-pilot's duties to help me fly the plane.

When you have wounded aboard, you fire a Very pistol on final approach to the runway. Newt did that and as we rolled to a stop, ambulances moved in beside us to speed the injured men to the base hospital. All recovered in good time although there were some uneasy moments in the case of Lockhart, who had lost a large quantity of blood.

A ceremony was arranged soon after the mission so that General Spaatz could present the Purple Heart to those who were wounded. I was in that group but, quite frankly, I was embarrassed by all the fuss. My injuries consisted of a couple of punctures on my left wrist and several inside my left leg just above the knee. All were little more than skin-deep.

This event was as much for public relations as to honour the wounded, and General Eaker despatched Beime Lay, now on the staff of General Spaatz as public relations officer, to cover the ceremony. First his assignment met with many difficulties, as Lay explains:

I got nowhere for three days with Tib's subordinates because I couldn't get any okays to set things in motion. Tib was too busy to bother with me, snowed under as he was with more pressing demands. Finally, I got my dander up and accosted him in his office.

'Major Tibbets,' I said hotly, 'can you give me just five minutes?'

'I wish I had five minutes,' he growled.

'General Spaatz sent me down here to do a job. I need your okay to work out the details with your adjutant – set up an awards ceremony, drill the troops, write the citations and all that and...'

'Stop right there,' he cut in. 'I'm dealing every day with matters of life and death and I can't spare a man from the squadron for frills.'

'You may call this review ordered by Spaatz and Eaker a frill, but I should think you'd have enough interest in your squadron to give them their due.

'He sprang up and advanced toward me, face flushed, near breaking under the strain of fatigue.

'You have a lot of guts coming down here from your plush headquarters at Pinetree and telling me I don't really care about my squadron, because I don't have time for a PRO show!'

I immediately backed up. Apologizing for my choice of words, if I had implied that he really didn't care about his men. He calmed down enough for me to explain about how distasteful my job was to me and that I'd much prefer to change places with him. He called in his adjutant and gave the necessary orders.

Lay uses this incident in his novel, where 'Captain Reynolds, Public Relations, Bomber Command' has the same run-in, not with Tibbets, but with Lieutenant Jesse Bishop, after the latter's actions in the blood-soaked cockpit of his B-17 when the back of his pilot's head had been blown off, an action which earns Bishop the award of the Medal of Honor.

Lay got his parade, as Tibbets explains:

We wore our Class A uniforms and the press was invited. I was standing next to Lockhart and all the photographers were attracted to him because his left hand was heavily bandaged and splinted. As a result, I was prominently pictured in the newspapers around the world. We got a full page in *Life* magazine.

The 'jarring collision', as Lay later referred to the incident between them, did have a happy ending, as he explains: 'Later, we became great friends and collaborated on an MGM feature motion picture about his Hiroshima experience called *Above and Beyond*.'

Longfellow, who was given command of 8th Bomber Command on 1 December 1942, when Eaker moved to command 8th Air Force HQ, was, according to Geoffrey Perret in his book *Winged Victory*, 'perpetually overwrought, [he] struggled to overcome its [8th Bomber Command's] difficulties by shouting himself hoarse ... [His] nonstop ranting had earned him the nickname 'Screaming Eagle'. At the end of June [1943] he was sent home, a burned out wreck.'

Eaker had to replace his oldest friend (General Arnold held the opinion that his Bomber Commander was 'especially weak'). When he did, Eaker recommended Longfellow to the commander of Second Air Force, a training command, in the US. Eaker added, 'He is a tireless worker and despite the fact that we almost killed him off here working, or carrying the responsibility, for 24 hours a day, seven days a week, I believe he will spring back after a few weeks' rest and do a tremendous job.' Longfellow got the job but was reduced to his regular rank as colonel.

Twelve B-17s were used in the making of *Twelve O'Clock High*, which was filmed largely at Eglin AFB, Florida, and Ozark, Alabama, from February to 1 July 1949. All the Fortresses are in 91st Bomb Group markings, easily distinguished by the white Triangle A on the tail fins. Chief Technical Advisor Colonel John H. deRussy, USAF, formerly Operations Officer of the 305th Bomb Group, Eighth Air Force, at Chelveston, Northamptonshire, in the Second World War, personally led the formation flights, group landings and take-offs featured in the movie and filmed at Ozark. However, deRussy's superiors forbade him from also making the memorable belly-landing sequence, which was performed by veteran Hollywood stunt pilot Paul Mantz at Ozark early in May.

CHAPTER 7

Battles of the Bomb Groups

'*Under certain meteorological conditions and in given circumstances, an air battle of the sort which served to crack open Germany's inner structure takes on a fantastic quality beyond a Wellsian nightmare. Long trails of vapour stream back from each engine nacelle in four-plumed patterns across the five-mile sky. Through those patterns fighters weave their single wakes of vapour. Broadsides of rockets burst crimson and orange in the contrails, while the ground defences set to work building their umbrella of black-puffed flak. In this setting airmen fly and fight and some die and some live to come back again.*

Not unnaturally, the nightmarish quality of such a battle (although not all raids are in such circumstances) is reflected in the conduct of the participants. Too, the incredible speed at which events take place in the air is expressed in the reactions of the individuals: When bomber and fighter rush at each other at a combined speed of, say, 600 mph, the airmen involved will live or die by their reflexes, not their conscious thought and that makes for conduct varying in the extreme from the norm. Finally, there is the basic element of this warfare – the unstable, most volatile air itself.'

Air Gunner *by Sergeant Bud Hutton and Sergeant Andy Rooney*

The Luftwaffe revised its tactics, deciding that simultaneous attacks would produce more casualties than attacking in trail. The new tactics were tried on 23 January when the Americans attacked Lorient and five bombers were shot down. Four days later, on 27 January, 8th Bomber Command attacked Germany for the first time. Sixty-four B-17s and Liberators started the mission to the naval base at Wilhelmshaven on the north-west German coast, but, by the time the target was reached, only fifty-five Fortresses remained. The 306th Bomb Group led the mission with Colonel Frank A. Armstrong, the CO, in the lead ship. Crews reported being attacked by around fifty fighters, including some twin-engined types. *Jagdgeschwader 1* lost seven fighters and four pilots killed. Nine bombers were claimed shot down. In actuality, the Americans lost three ships. 'Everyone was sobered up by this raid and we're beginning to realize that war is no picnic,' wrote Captain Jim O'Brien of the 44th 'Flying Eightballs'. Combat losses were to be expected and, although not liked, were accepted as part of the game of war.

Losses were having an effect on morale at every bomb group and they were perhaps more noticeable in the Liberator squadrons, whose numbers were fewer than the B-17 groups. The 44th Bomb Group at Shipdham had not received any replacement crews until late March or April, so Colonel Leon W. Johnson's Group had a limited number of crews, as he recalled:

Every time we went out, while we might lose none, we might lose one or two. At dinner that night over at the club, there would be vacant seats. It was awfully hard. You didn't have to be very smart to figure out that if your force was going down all the time and you were doing the same number of missions and you were losing one and two and getting no replacements, your chances of surviving didn't look so good. As soon as the replacement crews started arriving, there were no problems at all. I don't mean to say that there were problems earlier, but you could see it in their eyes and their whole manner. Everybody did the calculations and they knew that their chances weren't very good. When the new crews came in, it changed completely.

It did not help either that the Fortress groups usually hogged the limelight when it came to publicity. To redress the balance, two war reporters for Eighth Air Force Public Relations, Major John M. Redding and Captain Harold Leyshon, paid a visit to Shipdham airfield in the wilds of Norfolk in the spring, where the crews of *Little Beaver* and *Suzy Q* in the 67th Squadron attracted their attention.[1]

There is a clearly understood working agreement between crew and pilots that permits maximum effectiveness with the least expenditure of work, time and effort. Only crews that gain such ability survive long, for the Nazis are quick to take advantage of any slip. But how does food affect these things? Surely food alone doesn't make the difference between a lost crew and a safe one? No, not food alone. Yet it is a fact that the losses in a large group of men will be smaller if they are properly fed. And the phrase, properly fed, deals with more than cooking alone.

The crews of the *Little Beaver* and the *Suzy Q* eat apart from the squadron mess. They have fostered a feeling of oneness among themselves to a point where they not only live together but they eat together, fight together and when the time comes, if it must, they will die together. Part of that feeling, that *esprit*, comes from their crew mess. The private mess they operate began because of the dislike of these men to 'foofaraw.' They didn't want to wear their blouses to dinner in the officers' mess. They came to England to fight a war.

When they landed as part of the early contingents of 1st Wing, they were ready to fight their way into the country. They alighted from their planes at an air-transport base with guns loaded at ready in their holsters. Lieutenant Chester Lucius Phillips, who through the subtle alchemy of nicknames is called George, phrases it thus: 'We thought the war was right here in England instead of two hours flying time across the Channel.'

These men wanted to grow beards and wear torn, comfortable uniforms like the men pictured at their posts in the Pacific. 'We didn't want to wear blouses and pinks and get all dolled up. To get away from that we just had to learn to cook, so we did,' Phillips explains it. In the Nissen hut where the crews of the *Little Beaver* and the *Suzy Q* await their dinner, there is a cheery odor of broiling pork. Through the pleasantly smoky atmosphere comes the crackle of spattering grease as the potatoes fry merrily on top of the little stove, behind the broiling meat. Coffee will be prepared later with Nescafe. The men are ready for their meal. And they are not wearing their blouses. It is important to them, this manner of eating.

Remote wartime airfields like Shipdham were notoriously difficult to reach in wartime Britain, and many correspondents found them disagreeable, but the American public back home clamoured for stories from the 'front'. They wanted news of their kinfolk, the doughboys, 'GI Joes' and the 'boy next door'.

Generally the multitude of American war correspondents who had descended on London were barred from flying on combat missions, though seasoned pressmen and women who flocked to the capital were feted and generally welcomed at headquarters and officers' clubs alike, and their stories found favour with all and sundry. Some were household names to a generation of Americans who tuned in to their favourite radio stations each night. Others would become equally familiar by the time the Allies crossed the Rhine. Invariably it was the Flying Fortress, made famous by William Wyler's *Memphis Belle*, that garnered all the Americans' attention at home, in the press and in the Eighth Air Force, and when permission was granted for eight members of the 'Writing 69th' or 'The Legion of the Doomed', as they called themselves, to fly on the mission on 26 February 1943, seven of them chose to fly on the Forts. Walter Cronkite of United Press flew in *S-For-Sugar*, flown by Captain Glenn Hagenbuch, the new CO of the 427th Squadron; and Homer Bigart of the *New York Herald Tribune* flew in *Ooold Soljer*, piloted by Captain Lewis Lyle of Pine Bluff, Arkansas; both were pilots in the 303rd. *Ooold Soljer* had flown General Eaker and his entourage to Casablanca in December 1942. Gladwin Hill of Associated Press went with Major Joseph Preston in the 305th. Andy Rooney, twenty-four, a graduate of Colgate University, lead correspondent of the *Stars and Stripes*, went with Lieutenant 'Wild Bill' Casey in *Banshee II* in the 306th at Thurleigh. Denton Scott of *Yank* magazine missed the mission, and the B-17 with William Wade of the International News Service (INS) turned back with engine trouble. Paul Manning of the Columbia Broadcasting System (CBS) flew in another Fortress. Harvard graduate Robert Perkins Post, a thirty-two-year old

New York Times war correspondent, asked to fly with the 'Eightballs' on the mission. His request was granted and he went in *Sad Sack*, flown by 1st lieutenants Robert H. McPhillamey of Sheridan, Wyoming, and Wilbur E. Wockenfuss who was from Watertown, Wisconsin.

All aircraft were in the air by 0815 hours. Paul Manning climbed aboard the B-17 to which he was assigned and went forward to the nose gun he was to operate. 'After take-off', says Manning,

> we climbed through the clouds and broke out into brilliant sunshine at 6,000 feet. Over the Channel, at 11,000 feet, all of us went on oxygen and kept a look-out for fighters as the German coast appeared. They did not attack until after we had passed over the Frisian Islands and were headed straight for our target.

Paul Manning could see a formation of B-24 Liberators having 'rough going'; two of them spiralled down, one with its engine on fire. 'Later I learned that this had been Bob Post's B-24.[2] The aircraft bearing Walter Cronkite, Bigart, Gladwin Hill and Andy Rooney, all returned to base safely.'

On landing after the mission, Paul Manning travelled immediately back to London and wrote up his account of the raid on Wilhelmshaven. One copy was for Edward R. Murrow, CBS Bureau Chief in London; two copies were for the American and British censors; and a fourth went to General Ira Eaker. Then Manning walked to the BBC studio, where he broadcast his account of this raid to CBS in New York for the entire CBS radio network. Both Cronkite and Hill filed their own stories, with UP and AP respectively. After that first mission, Manning went on flying missions with the Eighth Air Force for two reasons: 'First,' he said, 'the 8th Air Force was "The Big Story" in 1943 and also because General Ira Eaker, who read the transcripts of my broadcasts, expressed to me his wish that he would go on flying the B-17s and bringing into American living rooms my eye-witness accounts of American courage.' In his letter to Manning he wrote,

> It is important to the morale of these young men who risk their lives every time they go on a mission that they know people at home are

aware of the dangerous job they are doing in the skies over Germany ... I read the transcript of your last mission and it is remarkable reporting and exactly the sort of message I want the people at home to hear.[3]

One of the Liberators claimed shot down by I./JG1 was *Night Raider*, also called *Heavenly Hideaway*, in the 'Travelling Circus', flown by Captain Beattie H. 'Bud' Fleenor. The events that followed caught the attention of Corporal Carroll 'Cal' Stewart, a *Stars and Stripes* staff writer:

At the briefing, the Liberator known as *Night Raider* was tagged for one of the hot spots, an outside position on the next-to-the-last V-formation. That was nothing new: since early the previous October *Night Raider* had been a veteran of flight over enemy territory though never, despite its name, in a night raid. The skipper, Captain Bud Fleenor, 25, of Manhattan, Kansas, was at the wheel as usual. The Kansas State College alumnus tucked his long, gangly legs into the compartment while the engines warmed; beside him sat the co-pilot, 1st Lieutenant James J. Leary, 25, from Omaha, Nebraska. *Night Raider* went thundering down the runway and the take-off was uneventful; a few spurts of lead were fired into the thin air or into a cloud bank as the gunners warmed and tested the guns.

Then things began to go wrong. As the raiders reached the Dutch coast and enemy opposition began to appear, Sergeant Elmer J. Dawley, 19, the youngest of the crew, passed out in the high altitude: his oxygen mask was frozen. Staff Sergeant T. J. Kilmer, also 19, waist gunner went to investigate and found icicles on the kid's eyelashes. The effort to revive Dawley, plus oxygen trouble of his own, soon had Kilmer himself unconscious, clinging desperately to wire cables that control the tail assembly. The skipper and Leary managed to stay in formation.

Technical Sergeant Louis Szabo, 28, the 150lb waist gunner and engineer had an almost impossible task in trying to release Kilmer's grip, his own mask being torn from his face in the struggle. A few moments later Kilmer relaxed and lay there blacked out, unconscious.

1. Briefing Time. (*USAF*)

2. Pilots in the 4th Fighter Group being briefed at Debden. (*USAF*)

3. B-24D-90-CO 42-40738, *Fightin' Sam* (the squadron insignia), in the 566th Bomb Squadron, 389th Bomb Group, was originally commanded by Major Tom Conroy (back row, 2nd from left), the Squadron CO. Lt Harvey B. Mason (standing, 3rd from left) took over the B-24 and he and his crew failed to return on 5 December 1943. Nine of the crew were KIA and one was made PoW. Conroy was killed serving in the Korean War. (*Russ D. Hayes Collection*)

4. B-17F 42-30721, *Sweet And Lovely*, was assigned to the 482nd Bomb Group at Alconbury on 31 August 1943 before being transferred to the 533rd Bomb Squadron, 381st Bomb Group, at Ridgewell on 20 September 1943. It survived the war and was scrapped at RFC Altus in the USA on 4 October 1945. (*USAF*)

5. B-17F 42-30793, *Tom Paine*, was assigned to the 562nd Bomb Squadron, 388th Bomb Group, at Knettishall on 3 September 1943. It crashed at Ellough in Norfolk on return from a mission and was salvaged on 11 April 1944. (*USAF*)

Right **6.** B-17F 42-29524, *"Meat" Hound*, was assigned to the 423rd Bomb Squadron, 306th Bomb Group at Thurleigh on 2 March 1943 before being transferred to the 358th Bomb Squadron, 303rd Bomb Group, at Molesworth on 30 July 1943. It was badly hit on the raid on Oschersleben on 26 January 1944 and after the crew bailed out Jack Watson, the pilot, brought the ship home to crash land at Metfield in Suffolk. (*USAF*)

Below **7.** B-17F 42-31027, *Honey Chile II*, was assigned to the 569th Bomb Squadron, 390th Bomb Group at Framlingham and was transferred to 214 Squadron RAF at Sculthorpe, Norfolk on 21 January 1944. It was written off on 13 November 1946. (*USAF*)

8. B-17F 42-3259. (*USAF*)

9. B-17F *The Fast Worker* in the 359th Bomb Squadron, 303rd Bomb Group. (*USAF*)

10. B-17F 41-24412 *Flying Flit Gun* was assigned to the 340th Bomb Squadron, 97th Bomb Group at Polebrook in August 1942 and went with the Group to North Africa and flew missions from Italy in 1943–44. (*USAF*)

11. A B-17F taking off. (*USAF*)

14. B-17Fs in the 322nd Bomb Squadron, 91st Bomb Group, stepped up in formation head for their target. (*USAF*)

Opposite top: **12.** B-17F 42-29536 *Mary Ruth – Memories Of Mobile* was assigned to the 401st Bomb Squadron in the 91st Bomb Group at Bassingbourn on 19 April 1943. It went MIA on the raid on Hüls on 22 June 1943. (*USAF*)

Opposite bottom: 13. Two camouflaged B-17Fs in the 322nd Bomb Squadron, 91st Bomb Group en route to the target. Nearest Fortress is 41-24453 LG-O *Mizpah*, which FTR with 2nd Lieutenant Everett L. Kenner's crew on 17 August 1943. Behind is 41-24497 LG-P *Frisco Jinny* which was renamed *Mizpah II* and was lost on 6 September 1943 when it was ditched in the Channel by Lieutenant William R. Cox. All ten crew were picked up. (*USAF*)

15. Another image of the 322nd Bomb Squadron, 91st Bomb Group, en route to their target. (*USAF*)

Opposite: 16. B-17E 41-9020 *Phyllis* was assigned to the 340th Bomb Squadron, 97th Bomb Group, at Polebrook in March 1942. It collided with 41-9051 and was repaired before going to the 92nd Bomb Group at Bovingdon that August. It then joined the 303 Bomb Group at Molesworth on 1 May 1943 and was painted in bright colours and used as a formation ship. As *Tugboat Annie* it was used as a hack by Group HQ. (*USAF*)

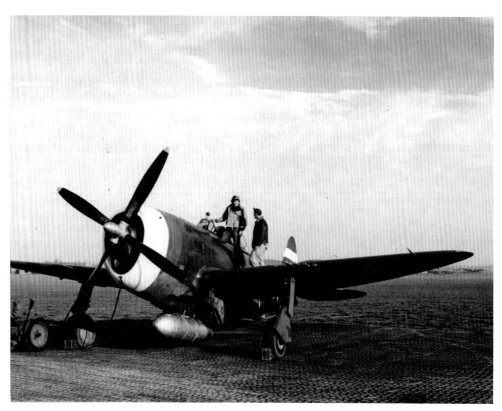

17. P-47C Thunderbolt with drop tank. (*USAF*)

18. P-47D in the 78th Fighter Group coming into land. (*USAF*)

19. P-38 Lightning N2-K *Betty* in the 383rd Fighter Squadron, 364th Fighter Group at Honington, Suffolk. Lightnings in the 55th and 20th Fighter Groups flew their first escort missions for the 'Big Friends' in October 1943. (*USAF*)

20. P-38 Lightning at its airfield with dawn breaking. (*USAF*)

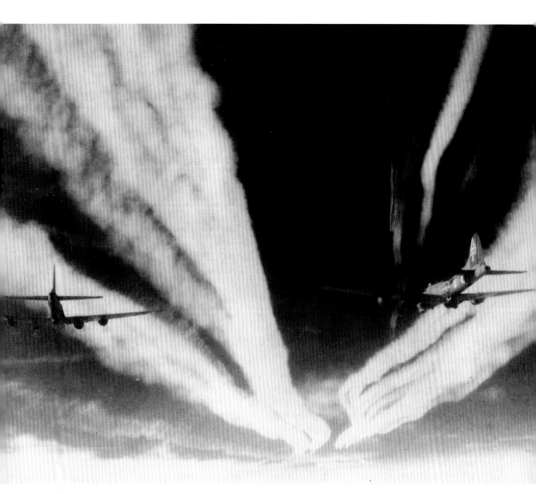

21. Contrails. (*USAF*)

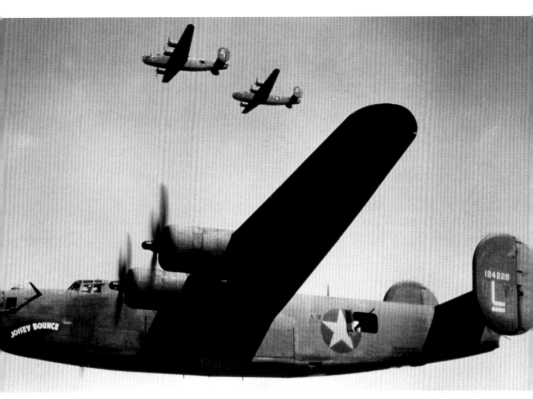

22. B-24Ds in the 93rd Bomb Group over Norfolk in late August 1943 after their return from North Africa where 'Ted's Travelling Circus' were part of the Liberator force that bombed Ploesti and targets in Italy. Nearest aircraft is B-24D 41-24228 *Joisey Bounce*. This aircraft was lost on 13 November 1943. The top aircraft is 41-23729 *Shoot Luke*, which was lost with Lieutenant Charles R. Hutchins' crew on 18 October 1943, 'C', the leading aircraft in the vic, is 41-23722 *Bomerang*, which returned to the ZOI in May 1944. (*USAF*)

23. B-24D 41-23754, *Teggie Ann*, in the 409th Bomb Squadron, 93rd Bomb Group, which was interned in Turkey following a raid from North Africa on 28 August 1943. (*USAF*)

24619 A

25. Post-attack reconnaissance photo of the Columbia Aquila refinery at Ploesti showing the distillation and cracking plant completely smashed. (*USAF*)

Opposite: 24. B-24Ds at low level over the burning pyres at the Ploesti oilfields on 1 August 1943. (USAF)

55231

26. and 27. Wrecked refinery equipment at Ploesti. Despite the great sacrifice, the Liberators had only destroyed 42 per cent of the plant's refining capacity and 40 per cent of its cracking capacity. Most of the refineries were repaired and within a month were operating at pre-mission capacity again. This led to repeated attempts to destroy the plants and the USAAF would lose in excess of 200 more bombers and over 2,000 further aircrew in raids on the Ploesti refineries before the end of the war in Europe. (*USAF*)

28. 'White V', Columbia Aquila, burning from bombs dropped by seventeen B-24Ds of the 44th Bomb Group, 'Flying Eightballs', led by Colonel Leon Johnson. 'White V' was put out of operation for eleven months. Another nineteen B-24Ds of the 44th Bomb Group, led by Major Posey, wrecked 'Blue Target', the Creditul Minier Brazi. (*USAF*)

29. B-24D-55-CO 42-40402, *The Sandman*, of the 345th Bomb Squadron, 98th Bomb Group, is silhouetted against the burning pyre of 'White IV' at Ploesti as 1st Lieutenant Robert W. Sternfels, the pilot, banks in vain to avoid a balloon cable which subsequently wrapped itself around the No. 3 engine propeller. Amazingly *The Sandman* continued flying, cleared the target and made it back. (*USAF*)

30. A B-24D of the 98th Bomb Group roars over the Astra Romana refinery, the most modern and the largest at Ploesti, amid smoke and flame. The 'Pyramiders' suffered the highest casualties of all five Liberator groups, losing twenty-one of the thirty-eight B-24Ds that started out from North Africa. At least nine were destroyed by the blasts from the delayed-action bombs dropped by the 376th Bomb Group. (*USAF*)

24620

31. and 32. B-24D Liberators pass low near the burning Ploesti oil refineries. (*USAF*)

C-246.

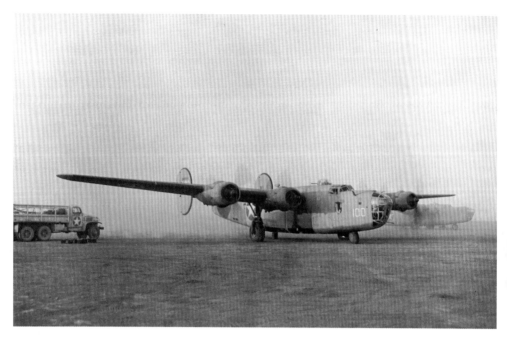

33. B-24D-85-C0 42-40664 *Teggie Ann* of the 515th Bomb Squadron, 376th Bomb Group; this plane carried Brigadier General Uzal G. Ent, CO, 9th Bomber Command, and Col Keith K. Compton, CO, 376th Bomb Group, to Ploesti and back. Colonel Compton and General Ent had the command of this vital mission unexpectedly thrust upon them after the loss of the original lead aircraft. *Teggie Ann*, originally named *Honey Chile*, crash-landed at Melfi, Italy, returning from a raid on Foggia on 16 August 1943. (*USAF*)

34. 9th Air Force B-24Ds lined up in the Libyan Desert at Benghazi before the attack on Ploesti. The nearest aircraft is *Brewery Wagon* in the 376th Bomb Group, which was shot down on the raid. (*USAF*)

35. A B-24D which returned from a raid on Emden on 11 December 1943 with its nose badly damaged and wire wrapped around the top of the turret. (*USAF*)

26468

36. Smashed turret on a B-24 Liberator once occupied by 'Available Jones'. (*USAF*)

37. The final mission is painted on the nose of the *Memphis Belle* in the 91st Bomb Group at Bassingbourn. (*USAF*)

38. Sergeant Casimer A. Nastal of Detroit, right waist gunner on the *Memphis Belle*. (*USAF*)

39. Major William Wyler, the famous Hollywood director, was sent to England late in 1942 to make a documentary about 8th Air Force operations, principally for American cinema audiences. Filming for the morale-boosting documentary began early in 1943 after bad weather had delayed its start. One Fortress which caught Wyler's lens more than most, probably because of its emotive and eye-catching name, was the *Memphis Belle* (B-17F-10-BO 41-24485), piloted by Captain Robert K. Morgan. During crew training at Walla Walla, Washington, he had met Miss Margaret Polk of Memphis, Tennessee, who was visiting her sister in Walla Walla. The romance between the pilot and the Memphis girl flourished for a time, but war was no respecter of tradition, and Morgan and Margaret later married other partners. However, the *Belle* would become legendary. The crew flew the twenty-fifth and final mission of their tour on 17 May 1943, to Lorient, and it was duly recorded (using a 'stand-in' B-17F) in 16 mm colour and used with great effect in the documentary. Everyone, it seemed, wanted to meet the famous ten men of the *Memphis Belle*. On 26 May they were introduced to HRH King George VI and Queen Elizabeth at Bassingbourn, and on 13 June Generals Devers and Eaker paid them a visit and then bade them a Stateside farewell to take part in a bond tour of the USA. (*USAF*)

40. Three of the crew of the *Memphis Belle*. (*USAF*)

41. The *Memphis Belle* after arrival in the US to begin a War Bond drive. (*USAF*)

79287 A.

43. Battle damage. (*USAF*)

Opposite: **42.** B-17F 42-29921 *Oklahoma Okie* was assigned to the 324th Bomb Squadron in the 91st Bomb Group at Bassingbourn on 23 May 1943. It went MIA on the mission to Cognac on 23 March 1944 when it crashed at Salaces, near Lesperon, 15 miles north of Dax, near Bordeaux. (*USAF*)

44. and 45. Two images of Stalag Luft One, Barth. (*Ross Greening*)

As they approached the target, flak was puffing all around; cannon hits were heard; and shrapnel was spraying the fuselage everywhere. Enemy fighters had already made an estimated thirty passes at the *Raider* and even when the flak was heaviest they continued to attack. Then the *Raider* began its run; its yawning bomb-bay doors wide open. Wilhelmshaven rocked under the bursts: 2nd Lieutenant George A. Pinner, 25, the bombardier, had pinpointed his mark. But trouble mounted fast as this B-24 limped back toward England, its big belly empty. The supercharger was knocked out, ack-ack fire was intense and German fighters were still submitting them to deadly attack – even a destroyer lying thousands of feet below in a Dutch harbour sent up a barrage of flak and hot lead.

The *Night Raider* made its way doggedly into the clear, high over the Zuider Zee. The sister ships that had led the attack were now disappearing, far out on the horizon. The skipper knew the *Raider* couldn't possibly catch them up, not with the supercharger out and one engine dead, the result of enemy cannon fire. The radio, too, was dead, so it was impossible to call for help. Staff Sergeant Robert P. Jungbluth, 24, the fair-headed radio operator, from Arlington, Nebraska, left his position on the flight deck to administer first aid to Kilmer, whose face was now purple. Others who saw him thought that he was dead but 'Jung' fixed an oxygen supply on him and worked hard with artificial respiration and finally Kilmer showed signs of life.

By now the *Raider* was losing altitude as one of the remaining three engines began to vibrate and cough. Jung left the reviving Kilmer and worked on Dawley, the tunnel gunner who had been unconscious since first reaching the Dutch coast. Ellis left the nose to go to the rear and lend a hand. 'Big Jung saved the lives of those two fellows, all right,' the North Carolinian testified later. Then the skipper sent word for Ellis to hurry back to his gun in the nose because more trouble was brewing. Jungbluth took over one of the waist guns and Szabo was on the other.

Suddenly twenty German fighters appeared, FW 190s and Me 109s, Me 110s and Ju 88s; they had been lurking in the sky in the hope of picking up a straggler and this was their chance. Peeling out of the bright sunlight, they came in a vicious running attack that was to last for forty minutes. *Night Raider* had taken care of enemy fighters before – one, two or three at a time – but this was different. Captain Fleenor eyed a large friendly cloud in the distance, perhaps a half-hour away at the speed they were travelling. It was their only hope – and a slim hope at that.

The guns of Sergeant Edward M. Bates, 22, the curly-haired 175lb tail gunner, had long been silent – they had frozen up tight after he had poured only eight volleys into the Huns on the way to the target. He was bluffing now, training the sights on the MEs and FWs as they came in. One Ju 88 sat out there, about 200 yards off our tail, for several minutes. 'I could have shut my eyes and hit him if my guns had been working,' he complained from a hospital bed, where his hands and face, frozen early in the flight, were being treated. One Jerry planted a 20mm shell inside the rear turret, barely missing him and causing the hydraulic fluid to spurt from the turret mechanism in numerous places. 1st Lieutenant Earle E. Ellis, 25, navigator and Pinner were pulling their triggers on everything that came into sight and up in the top turret Staff Sergeant Ronald L. Nelson, 31, was shooting round 360° – he didn't even have time to 'follow through on the shots'. Later he said, 'I was shooting over 2 o'clock for a Me 110 when an Me 109 came in from 11:30, putting a 20mm into one engine. If he'd been any lower he'd have sure hit Captain Fleenor and Lieutenant Leary and if he'd been any higher he'd have hit me!'

Dawley picked off a Me 110. Big Jung hadn't been on Kilmer's waist gun long when he sent one Me 109 plunging in flames into the sea and Szabo bagged another off the starboard side. Besides the three knocked down for certain, there were three 'probables'. 'A FW 190 came toward us,' Szabo recounted later. 'His wings were pure red and I could almost see the lead coming point-blank. I froze onto the trigger. His left wing dropped off and he went hell bent into the water. But he'd fired first and he hit Jung and me. I knew Jung was hurt worse than I was because I looked up and saw part of his arm hanging above the window – then looked around and saw his side intact. The 20mm blast had ripped his arm from his body! The shrapnel had hit us both.' Kilmer began to administer morphine and sulfa to Big Jung, the Staff Sergeant who'd saved his life a few minutes earlier. 'When I got to look around, I realized I was injured pretty bad' said Jung later from his hospital bed. 'We'd been expecting the end for so long that we figured things couldn't be much worse.'

All the while there was no respite for Ellis, Pinner and Nelson and their guns blazed steadily. Nelson, from the circular top turret, was covering the dead spots', where *Night Raider*'s fifties had been silenced – there wasn't even a split-second time for intercom orders or questions. The skipper knew his boys in the back were 'catching hell' but he also knew that the big cloud formation was much nearer now. Ammunition was getting low: Szabo's gun had only three shells left when he was hit. Dawley's parachute was hit and began to blaze. Then suddenly, Fleenor put the *Raider* into a dive and they disappeared into the cloud. There was no gunfire: visibility was almost nil. 'Four Jerries followed us in,' one crewman related, 'but that was the last we saw of them.'

Night Raider was still some distance from England, however and gaping holes as big as a fist were draining precious gasoline. Ellis, the navigator, gave the skipper a course to steer. Nelson went out on the catwalk, checked the remaining gasoline and diverted it to the two good motors. None of the fuel gauges was working and one engine was cut and feathered. Pinner went back and helped adjust Mae West life preservers, because a dunking in the North Sea seemed imminent. As Szabo said afterwards, 'I figured Jung and I wouldn't have a chance if we were forced down at sea.' Big Jung himself said later, 'I guess everyone took time to pray.' Bates climbed out of the tail turret to stand guard with a waist gun. 'How are you doin' Lou?' he asked. 'OK,' was the reply from Szabo. And Jung recalled, 'When Bates shouted, "There's land!" I knew that our prayers had been answered!' Both the skipper and Pinner had been in the rear helping Kilmer, who was doing a superb job of administering first aid. Dawley had taken over Szabo's gun. Ellis' uncanny navigation had steered Fleenor and Leary straight for the nearest landing field and England's friendly coastline fields stretched out below. Emerging from the cloud at 1,500 feet, the *Raider*'s two engines struggled and strained to climb to 5,000 feet. 'Just as we reached the coast,' Fleenor explained later, 'our two remaining engines petered out – we were out of gas.'

'The wounded didn't know that the undercarriage had been shot out, that the hydraulic system was knocked out, that the tyres were punctured and that a forced crash-landing was inevitable. The skipper sent word round that he'd 'have to crack 'er down'. Ellis and Pinner went back-ship again to arrange the wounded in such fashion as to lighten the shock. Dawley held Szabo in his lap to cushion his side and Kilmer lay down with one arm around Jung's body and used his free arm as a brace. But the shock never came. Skilfully the skipper set the *Raider* down [at Ludham, Norfolk]. Said Ellis, 'It was a smoother landing than when we had wheels!'

The ground crew chiefs handed the skipper his report on *Night Raider*'s wounds.[4] One ground crew man muttered, 'This one shouldn't have come back.' But it had and so had the crew and death had been cheated into taking a holiday.'[5]

In London, Margot Post waited for news of her husband.

CHAPTER 8

'Phyllis Had the Stuff', Charles W. Paine

'Then I looked out at the right wing and saw it was shot to hell. There were holes everywhere. A lot of them were 20-mm cannon holes. They tear a hole in the skin you could shove a sheep through. The entire wing was just a damn bunch of holes.'
Lieutenant Charles W. Paine, writing in *Air Force*, January 1943.

At 5 a.m. on October 2 1942, I was awakened at a Nissen hut in one of our bomber stations in England.[1] It was dark and for a moment I didn't know quite where I was. The hut was so small that I could reach out on either side of me and touch the other officers in their beds. I wondered what I was doing awake at that hour. Then I remembered that the day before I had been assigned as pilot of a B-17 on a bombing operation over Occupied France. At the moment I didn't know the exact location of the objective but I had been told that it was a munitions plant that was now making goods of war for the Nazis.

I dressed quickly and gulped down the tea that was brought me. After that I went to the Intelligence Office where they gave me the exact location of the objective. My navigator, Lieutenant Thompson, of St. Louis, and my bombardier, Lieutenant Komarek, of Muskegon, Michigan, were there and I then met them for the first time. We learned that the objective was the Potez plant at Meaulte, in Occupied France.

Very shortly after we got the news that the operation wouldn't take off as planned, but we were to stand by. There was a good possibility that we'd get 'on with it' – as the RAF says – before the day was out.

We stalled around until about noon, while I got acquainted with my crew. I had never met any of them before. They had worked together, but I was a stranger to them. We were polite about the whole thing but we wanted to know more about each other. As CO of a B-17 that was going to take off on an operation over enemy territory, I wanted to know more about them. They'd flown together as a crew and called each other by their first names. A good crew does that. In the air you're all out on the same party. You have to know what each member of a crew will do under any situation of the thousand and one that may come on you without warning.

But I didn't know them, so I went through the motions of inspecting the ship. I discovered her name was *Phyllis*. It was because of a picture on her front end. It was a picture of a swell girl, but no one in the crew could quite agree as to whose girl it was. The rear gunner, Technical Sergeant Taucher, a coal miner in normal life, said it was because 'Phyllis' was two of the crewmembers' girl. That remark caused indignation among the rest and the thing has never finally been settled. The ship, so far as I could see, was just called *Phyllis* because she was Phyllis.

I went through the usual routine of checking the ship and seeing that everything aboard – including the guns – was okay. They were. I've never seen a sweeter functioning aircraft than *Phyllis* when we took off. She had a good crew and I hope that I – the pilot and the captain – am in their class.

One thing I found in our favour was that two of the crew – myself and Lieutenant Long, the co-pilot – were lawyers and that Lieutenant Komarek, the bombardier, was in his last year of law before he got in the Air Forces. Lawyers are often looked down upon, but I can only say that my co-pilot and my bombardier were damn good airmen. The rest of the boys did okay, too, in spite of being commercial artists, truck drivers, statisticians and other assorted trades.

In the middle of the afternoon, the signal for our take-off came. As is usual at these moments, I was so scared I could hardly walk. Somehow, though, I managed to make it.

Phyllis was a long way from her home in Seattle, but she was magnificent. That was what our ground crew did for us. The guys who'd like to fly, but who take out their yearning by seeing that everything is right before the take off.

We were in the Vee of Vees all the way to the target. The main formation was in Vees and we who were in the 'rear guard' were in echelon of Vees, from left to right, inside the rear wings of the main formation. Our ship was 'Tail-end Charlie.' We were the rearmost left hand ship in the formation and hence the last to bomb.[2]

We hit scattered heavy (high altitude) 'flak' on our way in, but it was slight and did no harm. We got well over our targets, in formation and unmolested, when I heard the bombardier yell through the interphone, 'Bomb doors open! – Left! – Right a bit! – Right hard! – Right, damn it! Right!'

I kept trying to follow his directions. It was tough because we were in the slip-streams of the ships ahead and it took a lot of rudder to keep Phyllis on the course he wanted. At last he said 'Okay!' Bombs away! Button her up!', which meant for me to get the bomb doors closed. Then he said 'HIT-HIT-HIT on target!' It sounded fine.

The bombing part was easy. We'd got over the target and dropped them on the nose – by the grace of Lieutenant Komarek. All we had to do now was get back.

But that's when they started to pour it on. The open bomb doors had slowed us down a lot and we were behind the formation. The Germans' strategy was obviously to pick on the last ship and shoot it down.

Most of the others got no attention at all from them. And I might say I think it would be a lot better if the last ships in a formation were to slow down momentarily and let 'Tail-end Charlie' get his bomb doors closed and catch up before they high-tail it for home. You can get a lot of inter-protection from even two other B-17s. And we certainly needed it right then.

But there we were. Behind the others, pulling between 47 and 50 inches of mercury – a hell of a lot at that altitude – and trying to catch up, meanwhile taking evasive action. The flak was really being poured on. Heavy flak. I saw it below me, in front and then above me. We were bracketed and I knew that when it came next, they'd have us. They did. We started getting hits and plenty of them. I could feel the ship buck and shudder each time they hit us. And I might say, incidentally, that one of the boys in the other ships saw them hit and destroy one of their own pursuits, a Me 109G.

Things were happening fast and it's a little hard to get them in their proper order. I'm trying to tell what occurred in about five seconds, but it's going to take a hell of a lot longer than that to do it. I was talking about their pursuits. I forgot to say that I had seen a dog fight – or what looked like one – ahead and above me. Just a flash of it. That was when we were on the target.

Then came the flak, as I've said before. And then the hits. But after that came something worse, the flak suddenly stopped cold and I knew we were in for it. That's the toughest moment of a bombing raid – the few seconds between the time the flak stops and the enemy pursuit comes at you. I found time to be scared but not for long.

Just then all the gunners in the crew started calling through the interphone: 'Enemy aircraft at three o'clock, Lieutenant! … At five o'clock' … At nine o'clock! …'

Sergeant Taucher, the rear gunner, was more specific. He yelled: 'Hell, Lieutenant, they're coming in! From behind! There's a jillion of 'em! They look like pigeons!'

I said 'Give 'em hell boy!' or something like that.

He said, 'I can't. My guns are jammed. I'm trying to clear 'em!'

'Keep swinging them around so it looks like you're firing', I said.

'Okay Skipper!' Then, 'I've got one gun cleared now.' He started firing.

He told me later that once he got his guns going he didn't take his finger off the trigger from the time their formation started to come in until the last ship of it had gone out. They were employing two tactics that were new to me – and damned effective. When they peeled off to attack, they came in so close together that by the time one ship had shot us up and banked away, the next in line had his sights on us.

The other dodge they used was to pretend to come in on one of the other ships and then do a twenty-degree turn and shoot hell out of us. And while Taucher said their fire came mostly from a range of about 1,200 yards, he also said that they were so close when they finished firing that he could see their faces. Mostly they came from the rear, but at least one of them got up under us from in front, stalled and as it fell off, raked us the length of Phyllis' belly. I could feel his hits banging into her.

As a matter of fact, I could feel the effect of all their fire. It was rather like sitting in the boiler of a hot water heater that was being rolled down a steep hill.

I began to realise that things were getting tough. There was an explosion behind me as a 20-mm cannon shell banged into us just behind the upper turret and exploded; and I kept thinking, 'What if it hit the flares?' If it hit the flares and ignited them I knew we'd go up like a rocket.

Then I looked out at the right wing and saw it was shot to hell. There were holes everywhere. A lot of them were 20-mm cannon holes. They tear a hole in the skin you could shove a sheep through. The entire wing was just a damn bunch of holes.

I looked at Lieutenant Long, the co-pilot. That was a treat. There he was with his wheel shoved clear over to the right in a desperate looking right-hand turn which seemed, at the time, very funny because my control wheel was centered. I started to laugh and then decided there wasn't anything to laugh about. The position of his wheel meant his aileron control cables had been shot away. That wasn't funny at all.

About that time several other unpleasant things happened all at once. First, the waist gunner, Sergeant Peterson, yelled through the interphone: 'Lieutenant, there's a bunch of control wires slapping me in the puss,' which meant that the tail surface controls were being shot up. Second, the right-hand outboard engine 'ran away' and the engine controls were messed up so we couldn't shut it off. Third, the left-hand inboard engine quit. And fourth, the ship went into a steep climb which I couldn't control.

I forgot to say that the whole left-hand oxygen system had gone out with the first burst of flak and that I was trying to get the ship down to 20,000 feet to keep half my crew from passing out. I forgot to tell about this before because things were happening too fast to tell them all at once. Behind me there was a pretty nice little piece of drama going on that I couldn't see. My radio gunner, Sergeant Bouthellier, passed out from lack of oxygen and the radio operator, Parcells, seeing him lying by his gun, abandoned his own oxygen mask and put the emergency bottle over his face. Sergeant Bouthellier revived, just in time to see Sergeant Parcells pass out himself. He, in turn, took the emergency bottle off his own face and revived Parcells. After that, on the verge of going out again, Bouthellier called though the interphone to tell me that the oxygen supply line was damaged. With Lieutenant Long's help I managed to put the ship into a steep dive and levelled out at 20,000 feet. At this altitude, everyone could keep going without oxygen.

To return to the fourth unpleasant thing that happened – when *Phyllis* went into a steep climb I simply couldn't hold her level. There was something wrong with the controls. I had my knees against the wheel and the stabilizer control was in the full-down position. The control column kept trying to push me through the back of my seat. I motioned to Lieutenant Long to help me and between the two of us we managed to get it forward and assume normal level flight.

Then I started to think. The enemy fighters were still shooting us up, we had had a long way to go to reach England and safety, we were minus two engines and it took almost full left aileron to hold that damaged right wing up. It was clearly time to bail out of that aircraft. It seemed a funny idea, but I decided it was the only thing to do. So I yelled into the interphone: 'Prepare to ditch!'

Then I started to call the roll. Everyone answered 'Okay Skipper!' except the top gunner, Sergeant Coburn. Sergeant Peterson was badly hurt, but he answered, 'Okay, Skipper' and even had time to ask me if I was wounded. He said, 'How's the ship, Lieutenant?' I said 'Okay'. He said, 'On second thought, what I really want to know is "How are you?"'

I might say right here that it was the finest bomber crew that ever took off. The whole gang was right on the nose. Everyone did the job every inch of the way. I'm the one who is telling the story, because I was the guy in command. But there were nine other men in *Phyllis* and any of them could tell you a better story of what happened. *Phyllis* had it all right; but so did her gang.

But to get back to what happened. I gave the order to prepare to 'ditch' ship, with visions of a German prison camp in my mind. But just about that time Sergeant Coburn, the top gunner, slid out of the top turret and fell to a position between me and co-pilot Long. Coburn's face was a mess. He was coughing blood and I thought he'd been wounded in the chest. It later proved that he wasn't, but he was clearly in no condition to bail out of an airplane.

Things were tough right then. They were still shooting at us and the coast of France was a long way away. Our target had been about 60 miles inland and with our reduced speed – two engines out of action – it would take us quite a while to get to the coast. I felt a little sick inside. I yelled through the interphone that anyone who wanted to could ditch right then and there. But no one wanted to. Phyllis was still 'airborne' as the British say and I guess by this time they trusted her. Meanwhile, the enemy pursuits kept pouring lead into us and there's no evasive action worth a damn you can take when you are shot up the way we were.

Lieutenant Long left his controls and went back to give first-aid to Sergeant Coburn. Immediately, I had the problem on my hands of keeping Phyllis from climbing through the ceiling. The damned stick just wouldn't stay forward and I kept on gaining altitude. I called for help through the interphone and I'm sure that everyone on that ship thought I was injured. Lieutenant Komarek tried to get up through the hatch to help me; but he couldn't because Lieutenant Long and Sergeant Coburn were on the door in the floor through which he'd have to come. I didn't dare throttle the engines, either, for fear we'd just quit flying. Phyllis, at this point, had a stalling speed of about 160 mph, in spite of her ambitious climbing tendencies. So I just fought her.

Meanwhile, Coburn was doing his best to bleed to death. Throughout, however, he never lost consciousness and he kept making funny remarks.

Finally, the radio operator, Sergeant Parcells, came forward and took over the first aiding of Coburn, allowing Lieutenant Long to crawl back into the co-pilot's seat. Between us we got Phyllis under control.

We were over the Channel by that time and some British Spitfires took us in tow. The Jerry pursuit stuff gave up and departed for home. We went into a dive from 20,000 feet for anywhere on the coast of England.

The runaway engine gave us a lot of trouble. The electrical system was shot to hell and we couldn't shut it off. Long tinkered with the fuel valve but no soap. I was afraid to tinker with the fuel valves. Finally, we gave up. Phyllis was still flying and I didn't want to ask her too many questions.

We made a wheels up landing at the first aerodrome [RAF Gatwick – now London Gatwick Airport] we saw in England. We could only make left-hand turns because both Long and I knew that if we ever got that shot up right wing down we could never pick it up again.

I buzzed the field once and scraped a chimney or two of some buildings at the end of the runway. I knew we were going to have to crash-land because the hydraulics were shot and I couldn't get the wheels down. Besides, I didn't want to land *Phyllis* normally at 160 mph. She'd have coasted clear across England.

So we belly-landed her. The wrong way of the runway and cross-wind. It was a damned fine landing – marred only by the fact that Coburn, the wounded man, kept making remarks about how tired he was of flying. Sarcastic remarks. I promised him that I'd put him on the ground and was lucky enough to do it in good shape. We all walked away from that landing. Belly-landing a B-17 is an art and both Long and I agree we have mastered it. Sergeant Coburn agrees, too.

And next time anyone tells you a Fortress can't take it, give them the works. As one of the boys said after we got back: '*Phyllis* had the stuff.' God rest her soul.

Oh yes, Komarek, the bombardier, got sick after we landed. But he was considerate about it. He took off his flying helmet and used it as a receptacle so the kids that dismantled *Phyllis* wouldn't have to clean up after him. We all laughed like hell about that.[3]

Major William Wyler, a Jew from Alsace who was the famous Hollywood director of *Mrs Miniver* (1941), was sent to England late in 1942 to make a documentary about Eighth Air Force operations, principally for American cinema audiences. Wyler was given a great deal of help by General Eaker, Chief of 8th Bomber Command, and his subordinate staff, not least Lieutenant Colonel Beirne Lay, Jr, a Hollywood screen writer with *I Wanted Wings* among his list of credits.

In William Wyler's files there are two film outlines, one called *Rendez-VoUS*, which was to be a joint US/RAF film story; and another draft script from Beirne Lay's Eighth Air Force Film Unit, dated 11 October 1942 and revised 23 November 1942, which was titled *Phyllis Was a Fortress*. This was linked to an article published a few days after the date of the draft script – on Monday, 19 October 1942 – by *TIME* magazine, called 'Phyllis the Fortress'. On 4 November, Wyler wrote to the Assistant Chief of Staff, Eighth Air Force:

> Among the Film Unit's plans for future production is a film based on the experiences of Lieutenant Charles Paine and crew of B-17F (*Phyllis*) on the bombing mission to the Potez factory at Meaulte, Occupied France on 3 October 1942. The scenario for such a film is now in preparation and when in satisfactory form will be submitted to the Command for approval. Actual production can begin as soon as adequate equipment and personnel become available.

It seems that Wyler was still looking around for projects but, whether it was the difficulties in recreating the entire *Phyllis* incident or his failure in stopping the crew being transferred to the Twelfth Air Force, it was never made.[4]

Wyler headed for Bassingbourn and was given more help by Colonel Stanley T. Wray, Commanding Officer of the 91st Bomb Group. *Memphis Belle* caught Wyler's lens more than most, probably because of its emotive and eye-catching name. Filming for the morale-boosting documentary began early in 1943 after bad weather had delayed its start. On occasion, additional scenes were shot at other bases, and ground shots were inter-spliced with real live action over the Continent. Dangers were many. Lieutenant Harold Tannenbaum, one of Wyler's original cameramen, and four other combat photographers were lost aboard B-17s that failed to return from raids over the Continent. In the spring of 1943 several B-17s at Bassingbourn were running neck and neck for the honour of being the first to complete twenty-five missions (a combat tour for the crews). Those lucky to survive the fatigue, flak, fighters and possible mental breakdown were given a certificate and admitted to the 'Lucky Bastard Club'; this at a time when the average survival rate amounted to no more than a handful of missions. More importantly, they could go home. The crew of *Memphis Belle* did go home, too; the story became a movie, and the rest, as they say, is history.

CHAPTER 9

Twenty-Five Missions:
The Story of the *Memphis Belle*

'The "Memphis Belle:" a Boeing B-17, has been retired from active service in the European theatre after 25 successful bombing missions. With its distinguished crew, which has remained intact since its formation 10 months ago, the ship has been returned to the United States for another – and no less important – mission. At my direction, Captain Robert K. Morgan, the pilot, his crew and his ship are making a tour of Army Air Forces training establishments in all parts of the United States. There are three principal reasons for this tour: First, that combat crews in those units now being trained for the European theatre may be guided in their training to achieve combat skill, team-work, mutual confidence and fighting spirit. Second, that student pilots, bombardiers, navigators and gunners may profit by the experience and knowledge of the men of the Memphis Belle. Third, that battle conditions now existing in Europe and the magnificent achievements of the United States Eighth Air Force in mastering these conditions may be represented properly to AAF personnel and the public. I consider it important that the message of these men be given mass circulation, therefore I have had each member of the crew interviewed by an officer of the Army Air Forces and their stories, told in their own words, published in this booklet. I commend the contents of this booklet to the thoughtful reading of all AAF personnel and especially those officers and enlisted men being prepared for duty in the European theatre. Here are factual accounts of aerial warfare

over Germany and the occupied countries. Here is an appraisal of the enemy we are fighting. Here is the advice of men who have taken the war to the enemy. We must not fail to make the most of the experience of men who have pioneered the American task in Europe.'

H. H. Arnold, Commanding General, Army Air Forces.

The following booklet was authored by Ben J. Grant, who had been a Washington correspondent for many years and now worked for the Associated Press, so he was experienced in fast interviewing and writing. His first session with the crew in Washington was 'too disorganised, too repetitive, too diffuse' for what he needed, so a subsequent interview with the crew in a Nashville hotel room over a day and a half formed the basis of the booklet. The whole process – the conference in Washington, the flight back to New York, the flight to Nashville, the flight to Washington to write the interviews and other elements of the booklet, the coordinating, the flight to Dayton, the printing and the flight back to new York – all took just one week.[1]

In September 1942 a new Flying Fortress was delivered at Bangor, Maine, to a crew of ten eager American lads headed by Robert K. Morgan, a lanky 24-year-old AAF pilot from Asheville, North Carolina. Proudly, the boys climbed aboard, flew their ship to Memphis, Tenn., christened her *Memphis Belle* in honour of Morgan's fiancée, Miss Margaret Polk of Memphis and then headed across the Atlantic to join the US Eighth Air Force in England.[2]

Morgan had told them it was rough where they were going. There would be no room in the *Memphis Belle* for fellows who couldn't take it. The boys said they were ready. They took it. Between November 7 and May 17, they flew the *Memphis Belle* over Hitler's Europe twenty-five times. Bombardier Vincent B. Evans dropped more than 60 tons of bombs on targets in Germany, France and Belgium. They blasted the Focke-Wulf plant at Bremen, locks at St. Nazaire and Brest, docks and shipbuilding installations at Wilhelmshaven, railway yards at Rouen, submarine pens and power houses of Lorient and airplane works at Antwerp. They shot down eight enemy fighters, probably got five others and damaged at least a dozen.

The *Memphis Belle* flew through all the flak that Hitler could send up to them. She slugged it out with Goering's Messerschmitts and Focke-Wulfs. She was riddled by machine gun and cannon fire. Once she returned to base with most of her tail shot away. German guns destroyed a wing and five engines. Her fuselage was shot to pieces. But the *Memphis Belle* kept going back.

The longest period she was out of commission at any one time was five days, when transportation difficulties delayed a wing change. When the tail was destroyed the Air Service Command had her ready to go again in two days.

Only one member of the crew received an injury. And that, says Staff Sergeant John P. Quinlan, the victim, 'was just a pin scratch on the leg.'

The *Memphis Belle* crew has been decorated 51 times. Each of the 10 has received the Distinguished Flying Cross, the Air Medal and three Oak Leaf Clusters. The 51st award was Sergeant Quinlan's Purple Heart.

The ship's 25 missions follow:

November 7	Brest, France
November 9	St. Nazaire, France
November 17	St. Nazaire
December 6	Lille, France
January 3	St. Nazaire
January 13	Lille
January 23	Lorient, France
February 4	Emden, Germany
February 14	Hamm, Germany
February 16	St. Nazaire
February 26	Wilhelmshaven, Germany
February 27	Brest
March 6	Lorient
March 12	Rouen, France
March 13	Abbeville, France
March 22	Wilhelmshaven
March 28	Rouen
April 5	Antwerp, Belgium

April 16   Lorient
April 17   Bremen, Germany
May 1   St. Nazaire
May 4   Antwerp
May 15   Wilhelmshaven
May 17   Lorient

The flight time on these missions ranged from three hours and 50 minutes on December 6 to nine hours and 30 minutes on May 1. The total sortie time for the 25 missions was 148 hours and 50 minutes. Approximately 20,000 combat miles were flown.

Today, the battle-scarred *Memphis Belle* is back home with her remarkable crew, the same crew to a man that was organised 10 months ago in Maine. The *Belle* is the first bomber to be retired from active service and flown back from the Eighth Air Force.

Still flying the *Memphis Belle*, the crew is touring the United States to tell their story to the boys in training establishments Student bomber pilots, navigators, bombardiers and gunners are learning from the members of this crew the things they picked up the hard way.

The succeeding pages of this booklet tell the stories, in their own words, of the boys of the *Memphis Belle*. Here is what they saw, learned and did in the world's toughest theatre of aerial combat. There are important lessons in these stories. Let us learn and apply them.

Captain Robert K. Morgan, Pilot

He is the officer in charge of the ship and is called 'chief' by his crewmen, who swear by him, declare he is the best in the business. Typical is the observation of Sergeant Quinlan, 'Thousands of times I have seen him make that ship do the impossible.' Morgan is 24, tall, competent, comes from Asheville, North Carolina, was an industrial engineer before going in the Army in April, 1941.

HIS STORY

IF you want in just one word how we were able to go through the hell of Europe 25 times and get back home without a casualty, I'll give it to you. The word is TEAMWORK. Until you have been over there, you can't know how essential that is.

We had 10 men working together, each ready and able to help out anybody else who might need him.

Take just one example of what I am talking about. If it weren't for the tail gunner using the interphone to keep me posted on the formation behind, the top gunner reporting to me what he can see, the ball turret gunner telling me what he can see, it would be almost impossible for me to fly the airplane in combat. I can't get up and look around. Those fellows are my eyes.

In the same connection, every man in a bomber-crew should know something about every other man's job. Aside from the value of having someone to take over in case of emergency, understanding the other jobs and knowing each other's problems develops teamwork. It also promotes confidence in each other and enables us to anticipate each other's needs for help.

I would like to make one suggestion to improve the training of bomber pilots. Cut down on transition training – landings and take-offs – and emphasise high altitude flying and formation flying. I could have used a lot more of that.

Now a few tips:

Before taking off on a mission, the pilot should check the airplane over from one end to the other. I mean that literally. He should check even the smallest details and never be satisfied with anybody else's word that everything is okeh.

He should consult with the navigator and get the course well in mind so that he can anticipate turns, can have some idea where the heaviest flak is going to be, etc.

Heavy flying equipment is cumbersome and a bomber pilot doesn't need it. It never gets very cold in the cockpit and anyway the pilot is so busy he could sweat at 35 below. I wear heavy underwear, a regular uniform and coveralls and that's enough.

Keep your formation. I can't emphasise that too strongly. At first the idea seemed to be to get the bombs out and then go hell-bent for home. But we have learned how important it is that the formation be maintained. There have been cases when we turned a formation nearly around to pick up a man who was straggling.

The Germans always try to break up the formation and then jump the stragglers. If we concentrate our fire power by keeping the formation, the only thing they can do is to slug it out with us. They don't like that.

We like having fighter escort. We wanted P-38s but couldn't get them. The best escort we ever had was the P-47. If they'll give us fighter protection, they'll get a lot of stragglers back home that otherwise won't make it.

As for German tricks, here's one to watch for: they are painting Focke-Wulfs with white stripes like our P-47's. It's hard to tell them apart at a distance. Also the Germans have a camouflage color that is very effective when they get up in the sun.

If you aren't careful, you won't see them and they'll be on you before you know it.

The Germans are learning some things about the Americans. They used to say that we couldn't carry out daylight raids over Europe because our losses would be too great. They also said we couldn't hit pinpoint targets. We have proved them wrong on both counts.

American morale in England is good and is getting better every day. Morale is always good when results are good. Also, we were well provided for and the British were damned nice to us.

THERE are many incidents that I could tell you about, but here is one that stands out most vividly in my memory.

On January 23, our mission was a raid on the submarine installations at Lorient. One of the other groups went over the target first. Through the flak, fighters were beginning to attack us. Because ours was the smallest of the four groups, they concentrated on us and for about 22 minutes they gave us hell.

Most of the attacks were from the front. One Focke-Wulf 190, attacking straight in from 12 o'clock, was heading right into us. One of us would have to move. The usual procedure would be to dive. I couldn't do that, because another group was below us, so I pulled her straight up. The shells that were intended for our nose got our tail.

I didn't know what had happened until Sergeant Quinlan started giving it to me play by play.

'Chief, the tail is hit, the whole back end is shot off,' I heard him say. 'Chief, it's blazing! The whole tail is leaving the planet.'

There was a silence then. I asked for a report. Nothing happened.

Finally, I heard Quinlan's voice again, 'Chief, it's still on fire! There goes another piece!'

Another silence for a minute and then Quinlan said, 'Chief, the fire has gone out.' I don't need to tell you that that was the sweetest music I had ever heard.

I climbed up to look back and see what had happened. It looked like we had no tail at all. I got back in the cockpit and flew for two hours back to the base. It was tough flying and tougher than that to set her down. The elevators were damaged so badly that the controls jammed.

But somehow we managed to get down safely. That was a close call.

Captain James A. Verinis, Co-Pilot

Captain Verinis went over with the *Memphis Belle* as co-pilot, but during much of the time he was overseas he flew another B-17 as first pilot. Captain Morgan leans heavily on him, insists that he be called the 'other pilot,' not co-pilot. He is 25, short, dark, soft-spoken, comes from New Haven, Conn., was a business administration student at the University of Connecticut before entering the service in July, 1941.

HIS STORY

TO begin with, let me say to the fellows who go over as co-pilots that they probably won't be co-pilots long. The chances are that if they are good they will get their own ships. So don't get the idea that you are going to fight the war as a co-pilot. You should be prepared to take over your own ship and crew any minute you are called upon to do so.

But while you are co-pilot, you have very definite responsibilities. Captain Morgan and I had it pretty well worked out. As co-pilot, you should do everything you possibly can do to relieve the pilot. The pilot has tremendous responsibilities and I consider it the co-pilot's job to relieve him of all the worries that he can.

There is no question about the need for a co-pilot in the B-17. The strength of one man is not sufficient to kick it around in combat. Usually, the co-pilot will do at least half the flying, but the pilot takes over in actual combat.

But even in combat, when the pilot is flying the ship, the co-pilot should keep his hands on the wheel and his feet on the rudders. In that way he is ready, when needed, to apply pressure in the direction the pilot indicates.

If the co-pilot sees something that the pilot doesn't or can't see, he should notify the pilot or take the controls himself. It has been my observation that there is too much of a tendency to leave everything to the pilot. It's too much for one man. He can't see everything and the co-pilot should help him watch.

I consider the training I had fairly thorough, but I did need more high altitude and formation flying. There is too much transition flying. There are fellows coming over with 500 to 600 hours in the B-17. A lot of that is wasted. After completing my tour, I have only about 450 hours.

If you are going over, talk to somebody who has had combat experience. The fellows who have been through it can tell you a lot about dodging fighters.

Here's something else important: learn to judge exactly when you are in position to be hit. And don't forget that pursuit planes have fixed guns and they've got to be pointed at you before they can hit you. You don't have to run all over the sky to dodge them if you'll just learn the positions that keep you out of their aim.

The Germans have some tricks they use on us, but they are all perfectly obvious if you keep on the alert. For instance, they will pretend to be shot down. They will shoot out a jet of black smoke and peel off. But if you watch you'll see them come right back. They seldom fool anybody.

THE worst scare I ever had was in a raid on Hamm March 3. I was flying my own plane that day. There were 16 planes in our formation and we ran into about 100 fighters. We were caught 150 miles inland. We came out of a haze and discovered that our 16 planes were alone, because all our others had gone to the secondary target.

They got four of the 16 and I want to tell you that we were lucky to get back with 12. It was a running fight for an hour and 20 minutes. They literally swarmed on us just after we dropped our bombs. They were down and up, side and over. Boy, it was a sight.

NOW that the boys know they have only 25 raids to go before they get a let-up, morale is good. As long as they have a goal, as long as they know there is a stopping place, they're okeh. If they felt they had to go on indefinitely, the spirit wouldn't be so good.

Don't misunderstand me. It's no picnic over there. If anything, the missions are getting tougher. These daylight raids on the Ruhr valley must be hell. I've never been over the Ruhr myself.

But the boys know that their equipment is good. They know that our bombers surpass anything that anybody else has. Our P-47 will tangle with a Focke-Wulf any day. And our pilots and crews are good.

Here's another thing that helps the spirit of the boys: the food and housing are excellent and conditions generally outside combat are better than in any other theater. There is no danger at the base. The tension is off when you get back from a mission.

Just keep sending the B-17s over there and our boys will be all right.

Captain Vincent B. Evans, Bombardier

A genial Texan, 23-years-old, one of the two married members of the crew. From five miles up in the substratosphere, precision bombing is a fine art. The Eighth Air Force knows him as one of the best. Before going in the Army in January 1942, he operated a fleet of trucks in Fort Worth.

HIS STORY

AMERICAN bombing skill and equipment are the best the world has ever seen. There is no question about that. They all marvel at the results we get from high altitude bombing. And I am convinced that the German war machine will be destroyed by daylight, precision bombing from high altitudes.

When you go after one specific small target – not a whole plant, but one building in a plant – find your target and put your bombs right on it, you are doing some real bombing. There's no guesswork about it. And that's what the Americans are doing day after day.

As for my job as bombardier, I wouldn't trade with anybody. Of course, I would like to be a pilot too, but if I had it to do over again I would sign up for bombardier training. It's the greatest thrill in the world to see your bombs hit the target.

I would like to see our schools place more emphasis on high altitude bombing training. Also, our training should concentrate more on pilot-bombardier teams, teaching them to work together and less on individual training. Bombing problems should be given real problems, like bombing Denver from Seattle. That would be a great help to the boys in preparing them for combat.

Student bombardiers should be given more practice in photographic and map reading. I didn't get any of that in school. They should be given more pilotage navigation training. Every member of a B-17 crew should learn other duties besides his own. The four officers should be able to interchange.

A fellow who doesn't finish near the top of his class shouldn't get discouraged. The fact that a man leads his class in school doesn't mean that he will be the best bombardier or pilot. You just can't tell until you try him in combat.

(At this point Captain Evans was asked to relate his experience in the St. Nazaire raid of January 3. For that performance he was awarded the Air Medal.)

It was a building that we were after that day. It was a small target, but very important and we were glad of the opportunity to lead the Eighth Bomber Command. As we turned to make a run on the target, which I knew by its relation to other buildings, we ran into a strong wind, which we hadn't anticipated. That caused the plane to go wide on the IP and we almost went over Nantes. It also caused our ground speed to drop to 85 or 90 mph. There we were sitting up there like clay pigeons. I told Captain Morgan and Major C. E. Putnam, who was riding as co-pilot and wing leader that it was going to be a long run. They said let's settle down on it. We were anxious to get it right. We had a 2½-minute run. The usual one was about 55 seconds. We were really sweating out the last few seconds of that run. The flak was terrific. I could see the flashes of the anti-aircraft fire through my bombsight and occasionally a fighter crossing underneath. I could hear flak slapping the side of the ship like kicking the door of a Model-T Ford. Later we discovered that we had a lot of holes in the ship and a tire was blown to hell. Captain Morgan asked me when the hell I was going to drop the bombs. I told him to take it easy. I put my cross hairs where I knew the target to be, although I couldn't make it out at that distance. The second I released the bombs; I knew they were going to be good. The bombardier can usually tell. They were squarely on the target.

(Captain Evans put it modestly. Actually, photographs showed that the mean point of impact was only 10 or 15 feet off the center of the target, a torpedo shed.)

The new Automatic Flight Control Equipment will be a means of shortening the bombing run. When we went over, they hadn't perfected AFCE. Bob (Captain Morgan) and I worked so well together.

Now that AFCE has been perfected, I certainly would recommend it to other crews. We have tried it and found it to work very well.

Here's a tip that will help: When you first turn on the target, take out the big corrections by talking the pilot over, using the interphone, before clutching in. Then you will have only minor corrections to make.

Bombardiers would do well to spend a lot of time in the bombsight vault talking to enlisted men. I figure that I have learned 30 per cent of my knowledge of the bombsight from commissioned officers, 30 per cent from actual experience and 40 per cent from enlisted men in the bomb-sight vault. These master sergeants can really put you wise to a lot of things.

I believe in dropping on the leader. It is the only way to keep the formation closed for maximum fire power. Of course, it puts the monkey on the lead bombardier's back. It makes me nervous to think about it.

Captain Charles B. Leighton, Navigator

Quiet, likeable Captain Leighton has never been lost in European skies, tough as long-range navigation is in aerial combat. He calls it luck. His fellows on the *Memphis Belle* credit it to skill and alertness. Declared Sergeant Hanson, 'He has never made a mistake.' He is 24 years old, comes from East Lansing,

Michigan, was a chemistry student at Ohio Wesleyan before entering the Army January 20 1942.

HIS STORY

We usually have three hours between the briefing and the take-off. During that time the navigator is busy as hell. He must make sure that he fully understands weather conditions, including any anticipated changes. He must check on any flak areas on or anywhere near the route so that he can avoid them. He must be thoroughly familiar with the formation that is going on the mission.

After briefing, he consults with the pilot. In fact, it is a very good idea to go over the route with the pilot and the whole crew before take-off. Otherwise, some of them won't be able to keep up with where they are and that is a great handicap.

It is especially important for the navigator to talk to the radio operator and to make sure that all the radio equipment is ready.

I think the navigator should brief the pilot on how to get back in the event something happens to the navigator. I have tried drawing the route on a small map for the pilot. I think it's a good idea, but every precaution should be taken not to let a map get out and it must be destroyed if the ship goes down.

I SHOULD have had more gunnery training. The first moving target I fired at was a Focke-Wulf.

I could have used more practice in navigation. It would be good training to take a navigation student up, let him play checkers or something for a few minutes and then have him try to figure out where he is. Without practice of that kind, you might have a hard time finding yourself after a fight.

There are two conditions that might cause a navigator trouble:

First, poor weather when he can't see the ground. Second, a fight that takes him out to sea, causing him to lose all his landmarks.

This leads me to this important advice: Train yourself to write down your compass heading and to continue your navigation work even through a stiff fight.

I like being a navigator. Of course, I would like to get up and walk around a little sometimes, but I can't. I have to work like the devil all the time. But there is nothing like the satisfaction a navigator gets when he hits his ETA (estimated time of arrival) right on the head.

When you are the lead navigator, the whole formation depends upon you. The responsibility is frightening sometimes. It really keeps you on the ball. Actually, though, you should be just as alert if you are the navigator of any of the other ships in the formation. You might lose your lead ship or you might get separated from the formation.

There are some things to watch for. The Germans will sometimes send out beams exactly like ours to throw you off. Once some of our ships were fooled by these false beams and the Germans brought them over Brest, which looks like the English coast. Then German fighters dropped on them and got three of our planes.

Another German trick is to stay just out of range and play around, trying to get us to use up our ammunition.

You get scared sometimes, but usually any feeling of fright or tenseness leaves you when you start mixing it up. The worst scare I ever had, I think, was in our second mission over St. Nazaire. We were at 10,000 feet. Looking out the window all the way down the run I could see the bursts following us, one after another. It was only a minute or so, but it seemed like 15 years. When we heard 'bombs away,' we ducked. It wasn't a second too soon.

From experiences like that, I have learned that it is important to keep your eyes off the flak. It helps a lot.

I also got scared the time I ran out of ammunition. We were away down past Paris. It doesn't bother me if I can shoot back. But looking down those barrels and not having anything to shoot is no fun.

Technical Sergeant Harold P. Loch, Engineer and Top Turret Gunner

Having slugged it out with Hitler's fighters from a B-17 top turret, he now wants to be a fighter pilot. Sergeant Loch is 23 years old, comes from Green Bay, Wisconsin, used to be a stevedore and has been in the Army since November 1941.

HIS STORY

The engineer of a B-17 doesn't have much ground work. I think he should have more, at least enough to keep his hand in. It is important that he know his engines, that he knows every gauge, switch and fuse. Fuses are especially important to him, because they sometimes blow out and he must know where they are.

Every man on the B-17 should be able to assemble his gun blindfolded. He ought to be able to fix it quickly if it goes out while he is in the air.

The biggest part of the attacks come from the nose. German fighters will come from away behind, slip up to the side just out of range and gradually get closer. If you don't watch closely, they'll nose right into you before you know it.

Sometimes one plane will fly along in line with you dipping his wings to attract attention while a lot of other planes sneak in on you from the other side. You have got to be on the alert all the time.

When you shoot at him and he peels off, don't worry about whether you got him. It doesn't pay to watch him. While you are doing that, another one might sneak up on you. Just use common sense. That's all it takes.

The upper turret is a good position. You can see any plane that is in position to do damage to you. Also, from there you can let the ball turret gunner know when a plane is coming in and from what position so that he can take a crack at him.

We had good teamwork on our ship. I think that is the main reason we were able to complete our 25 missions without a casualty. It doesn't pay any dividends to have trouble in the crew. All of ours were good boys and we worked together and had confidence in each other.

Before going over, bomber crews should get used to high altitude flying. It gets cold up there and gunners should get accustomed to it. The first time most of the fellows see an electric suit is after they get over there.

We had a lot of excitement. I'll never forget our March raid on Rouen. We flew over the French coast, feinted and flew back across the Channel. We knew the Jerries would get wise some time and they did. They jumped us over the Channel, 30 or 40 of them. They attacked from every position.

Then just after we dropped our bombs, more fighters came from out of nowhere. Our tail got hit. We weren't bothered much more until we got almost to the Channel. Then six of them jumped us, circled around our tail from seven o'clock to five o'clock and went to work on us. Shells were bursting everywhere. Finally, the foremost fighter began to smoke. He turned away and the rest followed him.

We hear they get an Iron Cross when they shoot down a B-17. They are a pretty determined bunch.

When you cross into enemy territory, you have a tense, expectant feeling. You never know just what you are getting into. But get busy and then you are okeh.

Technical Sergeant Robert J. Hanson, Radio Operator

Sergeant Hanson was a construction worker in Spokane, Washington, before joining the Army in September 1941. He is 23 years old, married.

HIS STORY

IF you are in a new combat crew, you would do yourself a favor to sit down and have a good bull session with men who have been through it. Talking to them, hearing what they did and how they did it, you can pick up things it would take you a long time to learn for yourself.

Also, you should get accustomed to talking over your interphone. Learn not to talk in an excited, high-pitched voice. A little noise on the interphone going over always helps, because everybody is nervous. When you are in combat, use the interphone to keep the rest of the crew informed about what you can see. In a fight, the interphone is one of the most important things on your ship.

You will find that Jerry is fond of putting out false signals and false beams to confuse you. You have to be careful.

There should be others on the crew besides the radio operator who can take code. There is always a chance that somebody will be hit and it may be the radio operator. The ball turret gunner or the tail gunner should be able to take messages by blinker code if the radio operator can't see them.

Practice wearing your helmet before you go over. If it doesn't fit, get it fixed. You probably won't be able to get it fixed over there. At best our helmets aren't satisfactory. The wind whistles in and if you pull them tight they hurt your eardrums. The British helmet is far superior to ours.

WE have been in some pretty tight spots. There was the time that six Focke-Wulfs appeared from nowhere and all six cut loose on us. We could see cannon shells bursting around us and had to slug it out with them. One of the fighters started smoking and went down. We headed in the direction of another and after that they left us alone.

The radio operator's position is a good one, but it's a rough place to ride. In the Lorient raid, when we got the tail shot off, Captain Morgan put the ship into a terrific dive and we dropped two or three thousand feet. It pretty nearly threw me out of the airplane. I hit the roof. I thought we were going down and wondered if I should bail out. Then he pulled up again and I landed on my back. I had an ammunition box and a frequency meter on top of me. I didn't know what was going on.

Captain Morgan didn't have time to tell us and I couldn't have heard him if he had.

American morale in England is very high and the boys are really on the ball. The fellows would enjoy more current magazines. About the only one we got was Readers Digest. By the way, the Red Cross does a swell job. If it weren't for them, we couldn't have gone to London because we wouldn't have had any place to stay.

Staff Sergeant John P. Quinlan, Tail Gunner

Captain Morgan calls him the 'horseshoe of the outfit.' He has had more close calls than anybody else on the crew. Short, stocky, 24, comes from Yonkers, New York, worked for a carpet company before joining the Army December 9, 1941. He, too, wants to be a fighter pilot.

HIS STORY

I like being a tail gunner. It's my own private little office back there. I sit down all the time and when I get a chance I relax. I get a lot of good shots too. The tail gunner is in a good spot to help the pilot by telling him over the interphone what's coming up from behind. But he should be careful to call out only the ones that are attacking. If he calls everything he sees — one at five o'clock, one at seven o'clock, one at six o'clock — he'll get the pilot so confused he won't know what's going on. He should call out only the ones that are after him.

Don't be afraid to use your ammunition, but don't waste it. That is the best advice I can give.

You've got to be alert all the time. You never can tell what will happen. The time they shot my guns out and hit my leg, I hadn't expected any trouble at all. I thought that mission would be a cinch. It was a short raid and we were going to dip in and pop out again. Just after bombs away, I thought I saw flak. It wasn't, it was fighters.

A fighter will climb until he thinks he can give it to you, then he'll dive on you. That's what this one did. I looked up just in time to see his belly. It always gives you a funny sensation to see the big black crosses on the wings. I could hardly miss him. I got him. He burst into flames. I guess I was gloating over the one I got. Then I saw the other one. It looked like he had four blowtorches in his wings. All of a sudden, it sounded like somebody hit the tail with a sledgehammer. It got my guns and me.

But the one I got the biggest bang out of was the Lorient raid. Captain Morgan went up, then down. I lost equilibrium. I didn't know whether to jump or stay there, I didn't know what was going on. That was the time the horizontal stabilizer got on fire. I guess it was the wind that put it out.

Staff Sergeant Casimer A. Nastal, Waist Gunner

He is the baby of the crew. At 19, he has two confirmed fighter kills to his credit, thinks he has knocked down others 'but never had time to watch whether they went down.' Used to have a job repairing washing machines in Detroit. Entered Army December 24, 1941.

HIS STORY

My first advice to gunners is to take good care of their guns. This is important. They shouldn't depend on anybody else to do it for them.

Every gunner should see that his oil buffer is set right. He should check his electrical equipment before taking off, because it gets cold up there and if his equipment isn't right he'll suffer.

The Germans will try to fool you. They'll come in and attack and then as they pass they'll let out a streak of smoke as if they are going down. Then they'll come back. Also, they try to imitate our escorts. They get where you can hardly see them and unless you watch closely you might think they are your own fighters. Then suddenly they'll break in fast as hell and start shooting. If you have escort you're likely to be less alert than when you don't have them. But if you'll keep alert you'll be okay.

Always watch the other gunners if you can. If you are a waist gunner, watch the other waist gunner. If he needs help, give it to him. He may have attacks coming in and be short of ammunition. If he is, give him some of yours.

Combat crews should never go into combat with the idea that they are not coming back. Those who have that in their minds are the least likely to get through.

It's always a great thrill to get a fighter in your sights and let him have it. I don't know how many I have hit, but I have two confirmed. I'll never forget the day one came in shooting from 5 o'clock. I let him have it and saw my tracers go into his gas tank. He went down. I didn't see the pilot get out.

The Germans are a wild bunch sometimes. On our Bremen raid, the fighters came in bunches of 20 or 30. At the target, the flak started. It was bursting outside the waist windows. I could have reached out and grabbed it. I kept thinking, 'Let's get the hell out of here.' I saw two or three fighters hit by their own flak. It was so thick you could hardly see the ground. The Focke-Wulfs were even bursting through our formation.

You can see the effects of our missions. In England, they used to call St. Nazaire 'Flak City.' The raids have softened it up.

At the waist gun position, you can see what's going on just about anywhere. It's cold, but when you're in flak you warm up. You don't have time to think about being cold. You don't have time to think about being scared either. You might be scared on the way over. You think of all the things that could happen. A lot of funny things run through your mind.

I want to go back as a pilot. I put in for fighter pilot, but if they give me a B-17 I'll take it. I guess it just gets in your blood.

Staff Sergeant Cecil H. Scott, Ball Turret Gunner

Before going into the Army January 12, 1942, Sergeant Scott was a pressman for a rubber company at Bahway, New Jersey. He is 27, oldest member of the crew, wants to be a gunnery officer.

HIS STORY

The ball turret is the best position on the airplane. You see a lot of action in that position, you know what's going on and you are always busy. If the plane catches on fire you know it first because you can see all four engines and you can get out as quickly as anybody else. It isn't too uncomfortable. Of course, a big man shouldn't have the ball turret. I'm small and I get along all right. I was in it seven hours one time and didn't get very tired.

You should get as much practice in the ball turret as possible. Practice using the sight, operating the turret and getting in and out.

The Germans have some tricks that you'll soon know if you are alert. When they attack and come under the ball turret, they turn sideways or clear upside down. They go into a slow roll and they are awfully hard to hit. Sometimes they'll shoot out smoke to make you think they are hit. I have seen ME 109s come out of the clouds and hang on the prop under our ship, probably to try to hit our bombs.

Before the attack, you are usually scared, but when the planes start coming up and attacking you are all right.

I have known fighters to follow us for 15 minutes before attacking. They seem to be looking us over while they circle around, trying to decide where to attack. When you see them start to peel off, you'd better start shooting.

If you can't get a good shot, you might be able to figure out a way to change the position enough to make it possible. For Instance, If you get a plane at the right wing where you can't hit it, you can ask the pilot to lift the wing.

On the Romilly-Sur-Seine raid, about 300 fighters attacked us in relays. The fight lasted a couple of hours, the longest one we had been in. They attacked us as soon as we crossed the coast and circled around us like Indians. Then they started attacking from all directions at once. I thought I got two, but I didn't get credit for them. We kept plugging away at them and somehow got by. Practically all our ammunition was gone when we got back. As many times as they shot at us, we didn't get a single bullet hole in the plane.

Last winter American morale in England got pretty close to the breaking point because we weren't getting any reinforcements. It's good now.

Staff Sergeant Clarence E. Winchell, Waist Gunner

Sergeant Winchell was a chemist for a point company in Chicago before joining the Army in March 1941. He is 26 years old. He wants to be a gunnery officer.

HIS STORY

You can see that Germany is getting desperate. A good example of the things they are trying is dropping bombs on our 'planes from above. It isn't effective, but it's something that bomber crews should watch for.

They seem to be pulling their defenses back into Germany itself. St. Nazaire used to be tough, but it's not so bad now.

Although some of those places in the occupied countries are easier than they used to be, they still are no snap. It's good advice never to sell a target short, because you may get a surprise.

You'll still find stiff fighter opposition. The Germans seem to be trying to feel us out, trying to learn more about our ships and us. They have gone from mass attacks to single attacks and back to mass attacks.

Our crews should have more high altitude training. Bombers and fighters should be in the air at the same time on these training flights so that they can get accustomed to each other and learn what to expect.

The interphone is the most valuable piece of equipment on the ship. Most of the fellows would rather go over with half their guns out than with the interphone out.

Bomber crews must not relax just because they are out of enemy territory. They jumped us once in the middle of the North Sea and damn near shot us down.

There is one incident that stands out in my memory. It was on the Emden raid. We had bombed our target and the fighters were after us. I never saw such crazy flying as they were doing. One Focke-Wulf came in at 9 o'clock and seemed to be concentrating on me personally. I was looking down the barrel of a 20mm. He went over our left wing ship and under us. I don't know yet how he managed to slip through. I was petrified.

The *Memphis Belle* had no better crew than a hell of a lot of other B-17s. If there was anything remarkable about our taking all we did without a casualty, it was a combination of things. We had some luck. We had a good crew and what's just as important, we had absolute confidence in each other.

Contrary to popular belief, *Memphis Belle* was not the first to complete an Eighth Air Force tour, but its twenty-fifth mission, on 17 May 1943 to Lorient, was duly recorded (using a 'stand-in' B-17F) in 16-mm colour, and used to great effect in the documentary. Everyone, it seemed, wanted to meet the famous men of the *Memphis Belle*. On 26 May they were introduced to HM King George VI and Queen Elizabeth at Bassingbourn, and on 9 June General Eaker paid them a visit and then bade them a stateside farewell to take part in a bond tour of US cities. When the tour was completed in December, Bob Morgan got married, not to Margaret Polk, his 'Memphis belle', but to Dotty Johnson, a hometown girl he met on his war bond tour.

The Memphis Belle premiered in Memphis on 5 April 1944, and was released ten days later. Reviewing the film the day after the premiere, Elizabeth Ballenger of the *Memphis Press-Scimitar* said,

It's about as far removed from the movietown pictures of American fighting men and planes as Peter Pan. Without any stars, without any Hollywood, it is one of the most beautiful and thrilling films that has hit the Memphis movie screens ... We have REALLY been on a bombing raid now. Nobody should miss it.

Time magazine:

The *Belle*'s mission takes its crew among prodigious scenes that have seldom been so well recorded. Even the take off into the mild sunlight, has grandeur. As the swift ground shrivels into easy, floating legibility, cinema addicts feel that sudden magical suction in the midriff which the actual experience brings. Climax of this effect: a magnificent close-up of the landing gear as it retracts, flattening like the feet of a bird in flight ... It is one of the few genuinely exciting U.S. documentaries. *Memphis Belle* is a remarkable film.

The *Chicago Daily Tribune*:

Here is one of the most thrilling and beautiful real life air movies ever made. Up 25,000 feet the flyers were, as they swept over the Nazi base. You note the close formations, which are the squadron's greatest protection; you see the streaming, swirling vapor trails, the nasty black shell smoke. You hear the controlled voices of flyers. Commands given and answered. You are in a strange, terrible, beautiful world, like something out of your dreams. Here is a movie that is not to be reviewed, but SEEN.

Liberty magazine:

Your heartbeat is tuned to the roar of motors, the skull shattering vibration of guns. Home at last, you watch the broken bombers limping in, heavy with wounded men. There is nothing faked about this superb Technicolor document; its making took thirteen combat flights and a man's life. If you don't come away dizzy from the indescribable impact of air war, we're sorry for you!

Britons saw the film for the first time in the winter of 1944/5. The colourful and exciting thirty-eight-minute masterpiece gave cinemagoers a timely reminder of the grim reality of the war that was being fought at high altitude in the skies over Europe.

In the spring of 1943, Redding, Leyshon and 'Tex' McCrary were drawn to Bassingbourn, which became famous for attracting press and photographers from London to its portals like a siren. It was more easily accessible from London than were most bases in far-flung East Anglia, with their poor road and rail links. The base, which had been built during the pre-war RAF expansion plan, was relatively easy to reach from London and the permanent facilities had earned for its occupants the nickname the 'Country Club Set'. Centrally heated brick-built barracks, comfortable messes and paved roads beat freezing cold bases any day of the week. Not for them far-flung Nissens reached only by muddy paths in deep, penetrating woods and thickets, often miles from the airfield. When 'Tex' McCrary wanted to hitch a ride aboard a Flying Fortress he normally headed for Bassingbourn.[3] It was the base where McCrary did most of his 'hitch-hiking', as he called it, flying three missions with Captain Oscar O'Neill's crew, and he 'got to know them pretty well'. McCrary flew the 23 June mission to Hüls aboard *Our Gang*, flown by 'Smitty' Smith.

That summer one of America's foremost writers and master storytellers also journeyed from London to Bassingbourn, to write a series of dispatches for the *New York Tribune* and other newspapers. His name was John Steinbeck.

CHAPTER 10

'Somewhere in England', John Steinbeck

'The men are reading a little booklet that has been distributed, telling them how to get along with the English. The book explains language differences. It suggests that in England a closet is not a place to hang clothing, that the word 'bloody' should be avoided, that a garbage can is a dust bin and it warns that the English use many common words with a meaning different from what we assign to them: Many of our men find this very funny and they go about talking a curious gibberish which they imagine is a British accent.'

Somewhere in England, 25 June 1943.[1]

The bomber crew is getting back from London. The men have been on a forty-eight-hour pass. At the station an Army bus is waiting and they pile in with other crews. Then the big bus moves through the narrow streets of the little ancient town and rolls into the pleasant green country. Fields of wheat with hedge-rows between. On the right is one of the huge vegetable gardens all cut into little plots where families raise their own produce. Some men and women are working in the garden now, having ridden out of town on their bicycles.

The Army bus rattles over the rough road and through a patch of woods. In the distance there are a few squat brown buildings and a flagstaff flying the American flag. This is a bomber station. England is littered with them. This is one of the best. There is no mud here and the barracks are permanent and adequate. There is no high concentration of planes in any one field. Probably no more than twenty-five Flying Fortresses live here and they are so spread out that you do not see them at once. A raider might get one of them, but he would not be likely to get more than one.

No attempt is made to camouflage the buildings or the planes – it doesn't work and it's just a lot of work. Air protection and dispersal do work. Barbed wire is strung along the road, coils of it and in front of the administration building there is a gate with a sentry box. The bus pulls to a stop near the gate and the men jump down, adjusting their gas masks at their sides. No one is permitted to leave the place without his gas mask. The men file through the gate, identify themselves and sign in back on the post. The crews walk slowly to their barracks.

The room is long and narrow and unpainted. Against each side wall are iron double-decker bunks, alternating with clothes lockers. A long rack in the middle between the bunks serves as a hangar for winter coats and raincoats. Next to it is the rack of rifles and submachine-guns of the crew.

Each bunk is carefully made and to the foot of each are hung a helmet and a gas mask. On the walls are pin-up girls. But the same girls near each bunk – big-breasted blondes in languorous attitudes, child faces, parted shiny lips and sleepy eyes, which doubtless mean passion, but always the same girls.

The crew of the *Mary Ruth* have their bunks on the right-hand side of the room. They have had these bunks only a few weeks. A Fortress was shot down and the bunks were emptied. It is strange to sleep in the bed of a man who was at breakfast with you and now is dead or a prisoner hundreds of miles away. It is strange and necessary. His clothes are in the locker, to be picked up and put away. His helmet is to be taken off the foot of the bunk and yours put there. You leave his pin-up girls where they are. Why change them? Yours would be the same girls.

This crew did not name or come over in the *Mary Ruth*. On the nose of the ship her name is written and under it Memories of Mobile. But this crew does not know who *Mary Ruth* was, nor what memories are celebrated. She was named when they got her and they would not think of changing her name. In some way it would be bad luck.[2]

A rumour has swept through the airfields that some powerful group in America has protested about the names of the ships and that an order is about to be issued removing these names and substituting the names of towns and rivers. It is to be hoped that this is not true. Some of the best writing of the war has been on the noses of bombers. The names are highly personal things and the ships grow to be people. Change the name of *Bomb Boogie* to St. Louis, or *Mary Ruth* or *Mobile Memories* to Wichita, or the *Volga* [sic, *Vulgar*] *Virgin* to Davenport and you will have injured the ship. The name must be perfect and must be approved by every member of the crew. The names must not be changed. There is enough dullness in the war as it is.[3]

Mary Ruth's crew sit on their bunks and discuss the hard luck of *Bomb Boogie*. *Bomb Boogie* is a hard-luck ship. She never gets to her target. Every mission is an abortion. They bring her in and go over her and test her and take her on test runs. She is perfect and then she starts on an operation flight and her engines get bad or her landing gear gives trouble. Something always happens to *Bomb Boogie*. She never gets to her target. It is something no one can understand. Four days ago she started out and never got as far as the coast of England before one of her engines conked out and she had to return.

One of the waist gunners strolls out, but in a minute he is back. 'We're alerted for tomorrow,' he says. 'I hope it isn't Kiel. There was a hell of a lot of red flak at Kiel.'

'The guy with the red beard is there,' says [Staff Sergeant William R.] Brown, the tail gunner. 'He looked right at me. I drew down on him and my guns jammed.'

'Let's go eat,' the turret gunner says.

*

BOMBER station in England, June 28, 1943 – The days are very long. A combination of summer time and daylight-saving time keeps them light until eleven-thirty. After mess we take the Army bus into town. It is an ancient little city which every American knows about as soon as he can read. The buildings on the narrow streets are Tudor, Stuart, Georgian and even some Norman. The paving stones are worn smooth and the flagstones of the sidewalks are grooved by ages of strollers. It is a town to stroll in. American soldiers, Canadians, Royal Air Force men and many of Great Britain's women soldiers walk through the streets and Britain drafts its women and they are really in the Army, driver-mechanics, dispatch riders, trim and hard in their uniforms.

The crew of the *Mary Ruth* ends up at a little pub, over-crowded and noisy. They edge their way in to the bar, where the barmaids are drawing beer as fast as they can. In a moment this crew has found a table and they have the small glasses of pale yellow fluid in front of them. It is curious beer. Most of the alcohol has been taken out of it to make munitions. It is not cold. It is token beer – a gesture rather than a drink.

The bomber crew is solemn. Men who are alerted for operational missions are usually solemn, but tonight there is some burden on this crew. There is no way of knowing how these things start. All at once a crew will feel fated. Then little things go wrong. Then they are uneasy until they take off for their mission. When the uneasiness is running it is the waiting that hurts.

They sip the flat, tasteless beer. One of them says, 'I saw a paper from home at the Red Cross in London.' It is quiet. The others look at him across their glasses. A mixed group of pilots and ATS girls at the other end of the pub have started a song. It is astonishing how many of the songs are American. 'You'd Be So Nice to Come Home to,' they sing. And, the beat of the song is subtly changed. It has become an English song.

The waist gunner raises his voice to be heard over the singing. 'It seems to me that we are afraid to announce our losses. It seems almost as if the War Department was afraid, that the country couldn't take it. I never saw anything the country couldn't take.'

The ball-turret gunner [Staff Sergeant Henry Maurice Crain] wipes his mouth with the back of his hand. 'We don't hear much' he says; 'it's a funny thing, but the closer you get to action the less you read papers and war news. I remember before I joined up I used to know everything that was happening. I knew what Turkey was doing. I even had maps with pins and I drew out campaigns with coloured pencils. Now I haven't looked at a paper in two weeks.'

The first man went on, 'This paper, I saw had some funny stuff in it. It seemed to think that the war was nearly over.'

'I wish the Jerries thought that,' the tail gunner says, 'I wish you could get Goering's yellow noses and them damned flak gunners convinced of that.'

'Well anyway,' the waist gunner says, 'I looked through that paper pretty close. It seems to me that the folks at home are fighting one war and we're fighting another one. They've got theirs nearly won and we've just got started on ours. I wish they'd get in the same war we're in. I wish they'd print the casualties and tell them what it's like. I think maybe that they'd like to get in the same war we're in if they could get it to do.'

The tail gunner comes from so close to the border of Kentucky he talks like a Kentuckian. 'I read a very nice piece in a magazine about us,' he says. 'This piece says we've got nerves of steel. We never get scared. All we want in the world is just to fly all the time and get a crack at Jerry. I never heard anything so brave as us. I read it three or four times to try and convince myself that I ain't scared.'

'There was almost solid red flak over Bremen last Thursday,' the radio man [T/Sergeant Richard O. Maculley] says. 'Get much more and we can walk home over solid flak. I hate that red flak. We sure took a pasting Thursday.'

'Well, we didn't get any,' says the ball turret gunner. 'We got the nose knocked out of our ship, but that was an accident. One of our gunners in a ship high on ahead tossed out some shell casings and they came right through the nose. They've got her nearly fixed up now.'

'But anyway,' the first man says doggedly, 'I wish they'd tell them at home that the war isn't over and I wish they wouldn't think we're so brave. I don't want to be so brave. Shall we have another beer?'

'What for?' says the tail gunner. 'This stuff hasn't got even enough character for you to dislike it. I'm going back to wipe my guns. Then I won't have to do it in the morning.'

They stand up and file slowly out of the pub. It is still daylight. The pigeons are flying about the tower of an old Gothic church, a kind of architecture especially suited to nesting pigeons.

The hotel taken over by the Red Cross is crowded with men in from the flying fields which dot the countryside. Our bus drives up in front and we pile in. The crew looks automatically at the sky. It is clear, with little puffs of white cloud suspended in the light of a sun that has already gone down.

'Looks like it might be a clear day,' the radio man says.

'That's good for us and it's good for them to get at us.'

The bus rattles back toward the field. The tail gunner muses. 'I hope old Red Beard has got a bad cold,' he says.

'I didn't like the look in his eye last time.'

(Red Beard is an enemy fighter pilot who comes so close that you can almost see his face.)

*

BOMBER station in England, June 30, 1943 – It is a bad night in the barracks, such a night as does not happen very often. It is impossible to know how it starts. Nerves are a little thin and no one is sleepy. The tail gunner of the other outfit in the room gets down from his upper bunk and begins rooting about on the floor.

'What's the matter?' the man on the lower bunk asks.

'I lost my medallion,' the tail gunner says.

No one asks what it was, a St. Christopher or a good-luck piece. The fact of the matter is that it is his medallion and he has lost it. Everyone gets up and looks. They move the double-decker bunk out from the wall. They empty all the shoes. They look behind the steel lockers. They insist that the gunner go through all his pockets. It isn't a good thing for a man to lose his medallion. Perhaps there has been an uneasiness before. This sets it. The uneasiness creeps all through the room. It takes the channel of being funny. They tell jokes; they rag one another. They ask shoe sizes of one another to outrage their uneasiness. 'What size shoes you wear, Brown? I get them if you conk out.' The thing runs bitterly through the room.

And then the jokes stop. There are many little things you do when you go out on a mission. You leave the things that are to be sent home if you have an accident, you leave them under your pillow; your photographs and the letter you wrote; and your ring. They're under your pillow and you don't make up your bunk. That must be left unmade so that you can slip right in when you get back. No one would think of making up a bunk while its owner is on a mission. You go out clean-shaven too, because you are coming back, to keep your date. You project your mind into the future and the things you are going to do then.

In the barracks they tell of presentiments they have heard about. There was the radio man who one morning folded his bedding neatly, on his cot and put his pillow on top. And he folded his clothing into a neat parcel and cleared his locker. He had never done anything like that before. And, sure enough, he was shot down that day.

The tail gunner still hasn't found his medallion. He has gone through his pockets over and over again. The brutal talk goes on until one voice says, 'For God's sake shut up. It's after midnight. We've got to get some sleep.'

The lights are turned out. It is pitch black in the room, for the blackout curtains are drawn tight. A man speaks in the darkness. 'I wish I was in that ship by now.' He knows that he will be all right when the mission starts. It's this time of waiting that hurts and tonight it has been particularly bad.

It is quiet in the room and then there is a step and then a great clatter. A new arrival trying to get to his bunk in the dark has stumbled over the gun rack. The room breaks into loud curses. Everyone curses the new arrival. They tell him where he came from and where they hope he will go. It is a fine, noisy outburst, and the tension goes out of the room. The evil thing has gone.

You are conscious, lying in your bunk, of a droning sound that goes on and on. It is the Royal Air Force going out for the night bombing again. There must be hundreds of them – a big raid. The sound has been going on all evening and it goes on for another hour. Hundreds of Lancasters, with hundreds of tons of bombs. And, when they come back you will go out.

You cannot call the things that happen to bombing crews superstition. Tension and altitude do strange things to a man. At 30,000 feet, the body is living in a condition it was not born to withstand. A man is breathing oxygen from a tube and his eyes and ears are working in the reduced pressure. It is little wonder, then, that he sometimes sees things that are not there and does not see things that are there. Gunners have fired on their own ships and others have poured great bursts into empty air, thinking they saw a swastika. The senses are not trustworthy. And the sky is treacherous with flak. The flak bursts about you and sometimes the fragments come tearing through your ship. The fighters stab past you, flaring with their guns. And, if you happen to see little visions now and then, why, that's bound to happen. And if on your intensified awareness, small incidents are built up with meanings, why, such things always happen under tension. Ghosts have always ridden through skies and if your body and nerves are strained with altitude, too, such things are bound to happen.

The barrack room is very silent. From a corner comes a light snore. Someone is talking in his sleep. First a sentence mumbled and then, 'Helen, let's go in the Ferris wheel now.'

There is secret sound from the far wall and then a tiny clink of metal. The tail gunner is still feeling through his pockets for his medallion.

*

BOMBER station in England, July 1, 1943 – In the barracks, a brilliant white light flashes on, jerking you out of sleep. A sharp voice says, 'All right, get out of it! Briefing at three o'clock, stand-by at four-twenty. Better get out of it now.'

The crew struggles sleepily out of their bunks and into clothes. It is 2.30 a.m. There hasn't been much sleep for anyone.

Outside the daylight is beginning to come. The crew gropes its way through sleepiness and the semidarkness to the guarded door and each goes in as he is recognised by the guard.

Inside there are rows of benches in front of a large white screen, which fills one wall. Some of the crews are already seated. The lights go out and from a projector an aerial photograph is projected on the screen. It is remarkably clear. It shows streets and factories and a winding river and docks and submarine pens. An Intelligence officer stands beside the screen and he holds a long pointer in his hand. He begins without preliminary. 'Here is where you are going,' he says and he names a German city.

'Now this squadron will come in from this direction,' the pointer traces the road, making a black shadow on the screen. The pointer stops at three long, narrow buildings, side by side. 'This is your target. They make small engine parts here. Knock it out.' He mentions times and as he does a sergeant marks the times on a blackboard. 'Standby at such a time, take-off at such a time. You will be over your target at such a time and you should be back here by such a time.' It is all on the minute – 5.52 and 9.43. The incredible job of getting so many ships to a given point at a given time means almost split-second timing.

The Intelligence officer continues: (Next three sentences cut by censor.) 'Good luck and good hunting.' The lights flood on. The pictured city disappears. A chaplain comes to the front of the room. 'All Catholics gather at the back of the room,' he says.

The crews straggle across the way to the mess hall and fill their plates and their cups, stewed fruit and scrambled eggs and bacon and cereal and coffee.

The *Mary Ruth*'s crew is almost gay. It is a reaction to the bad time they had the night before. All of the tension is broken now, for there is work and flying to be done, not waiting. The tail gunner says, 'If anything should happen today, I want to go on record that I had prunes for breakfast.'

They eat hurriedly and then file out, washing their dishes and cups in soapy water and then rinsing them in big caldrons near the door.

Dressing is a long and complicated business. The men strip to the skirt. Next to their skins they put on long light woollen underwear. Over that they slip on what looks like long light-blue-coloured underwear, but these are the heated suits. They come low on the ankles and far down on the wrists and from the waists of these suits protrude electric plugs. The suit, between two layers of fabric, is threaded with electric wires which will carry heat when the plug is connected to the heat outlet on the ship. Over the heated suit goes the brown cover-all. Last come thick, fleece-lined heated boots and gloves which also have plugs for the heat unit. Next goes on the Mae West, the Orange rubber life preserver, which can be inflated in a moment. Then comes the parachute with its heavy canvas straps over the shoulders and between the legs. And last the helmet with the throat, speaker and the earphones attached. Plugged in to the intercommunications system, the man can now communicate with the rest of the crew no matter what noise is going on about him. During the process the men have got bigger and bigger as layer on layer of equipment is put on. They walk stiffly, like artificial men. The lean waist gunner is now a little chubby. They dress very carefully, for an exposed place or a disconnected suit can cause a bad frostbite at 30,000 feet. It is dreadfully cold up there.

It is daylight now and a cold wind is blowing. The men go back to the armament room and pick up their guns. A truck is waiting for them. They stow the guns carefully on the floor and then stiffly hoist themselves in. The truck drives away along the deserted runway. It moves into a side runway. Now you can see the ships set here and there on the field. A little group of men is collected under the wings of each one.

'There she is,' the ball-turret man says. 'I wonder if they got her nose repaired.' It was the *Mary Ruth* that got her nose smashed by cartridge cases from a ship ahead. The truck draws up right under the nose of the great ship. The crew piles out and each man lifts his gun down tenderly. They go into the ship. The guns must be mounted and carefully tested. Ammunition must be checked and the guns loaded. It all takes time. That's why the men were awakened so long before the take-off time. A thousand things must be set before the take-off.

*

BOMBER station in England, July 2, 1943. The ground crew is still working over the *Mary Ruth*. Master Sergeant Pierce, of Oregon, is the crew chief. He has been long in the Army and he knows his engines. They say of him that he owns the *Mary Ruth* but he lends her to the skipper occasionally. If he says a flight is off, it is off. He has been checking the engines a good part of the night.

Corporal Harold is there, too. He has been loading bombs and seeing that the armament of the ship is in condition. The ground crew scurry about like rabbits. Their time is getting short. They have the obscure job, the job without glory and without publicity and the ships could not fly without them. They are dressed in coveralls and baseball caps.

The gunners have mounted their guns by now and are testing the slides. A ground man is polishing the newly mended nose, rubbing every bit of dirt from it, so that the bombardier may have a good sight of his target.

A jeep drives up carrying the officers: [Lieutenant Kenneth L.] Brown, [2nd Lieutenant James H.] Quenin [the co-pilot], [2nd Lieutenant Vincent J.] Bliley and [2nd Lieutenant James P.] Feerick. They spill a number of little square packets on the ground, one for each man. Captain Brown distributes them. They contain money of the countries near the target, concentrated food and maps. Brown says, 'Now, if we should get into any trouble don't go in the direction of — because the people haven't been very friendly there. Go toward — you'll find plenty of help there.' The men take the packets and slip them in pockets below the knees in their coveralls.

The sun is just below the horizon now and there are fine pink puff clouds all over the sky. The captain looks at his watch. 'I guess we better get going,' he says. The other Brown, the tail gunner, runs over. He hands over two rings, a cameo and another. 'I forgot to leave these' he says. 'Will you put them under my pillow?' The crew scramble to their places and the door is slammed and locked. The waist doors are open, of course, with the guns peering out of them, lashed down now, but immediately available. The long scallop of the cartridge belts drapes into each one.

The captain waves from his high perch. His window sits right over the ship's name – Mary Ruth, Memories of Mobile. The engines turn over and catch one at a time and roar as they warm up. And now, from all over the field, come the bursting roars of starting engines. From all over the field the great ships come rumbling from their dispersal points into the main runways. They make a line like giant bugs, a parade of them, moving down to the take-off stretch.

The captain signals and two ground-crew men dart in and pull out the chocks from in front of the wheels and dart out again. The Mary Ruth guns her motors and then slowly crawls out along her entrance and joins the parade. Along the runway the first ship whips out and gathers speed and takes the air and behind her comes another and behind another and behind another, until the flying line of ships stretches away to the north. For a little while the squadron has disappeared, but in a few minutes back they come over the field, but this time they are not in a line. They have gained altitude and are flying in a tight formation. They go roaring over the field and they have hardly passed when another squadron from another field comes over and then another and another. They will rendezvous at a given point, the squadrons from many fields, and when the whole force has gathered there will be perhaps a hundred of the great ships flying in Vs and in Vs of Vs, each protecting itself and the others by its position. And this great flight is going south like geese in the fall.

There is incredible detail to get these missions off. Staff detail of supply and intelligence detail, deciding and briefing the targets, and personnel detail of assigning the crews, and mechanical detail of keeping the engines going. *Bomb Boogie* went out with the others, but in a little while she flutters back with a dead motor. She has conked out again. No one can know why. She sinks dispiritedly to the ground.

When the mission has gone the ground crews stand about looking lonesome. They have watched every bit of the take-off and now they are left to sweat out the day until the ships come home. It is hard to set down the relation of the ground crew to the air crew, but there is something very close between them. This ground crew will be nervous and anxious until the ships come home. And if the *Mary Ruth* should fail to return they will go into a kind of sullen, wordless mourning. They have been working all night. Now they pile on a tractor to ride back to the hangar to get a cup of coffee in the mess hall. Master Sergeant Pierce says, 'That's a good ship. Never did have any trouble with her. She'll come back, unless she's shot to pieces.' In the barracks it is very quiet; the beds are unmade, their blankets hanging over the sides of the iron bunks. The pin-up girls look a little haggard in their sequin gowns. The family pictures are on the tops of the steel lockers. A clock ticking sounds strident. The rings go under Brown's pillow.[4]

*

BOMBER station in England, July 4, 1943 – The field is deserted after the ships have left. The ground crew go into barracks to get some sleep, because they have been working most of the night. The flag hangs limply over the administration building. In the hangars repair crews are working over ships that have been injured. *Bomb Boogie* is brought in to be given another overhaul and *Bomb Boogie*'s crew goes disgustedly back to bed.[5]

The crews own a number of small dogs. These dogs, most of which are of uncertain or, at least, of ambiguous breed, belong to no one man. The ship usually owns each one and the crew is very proud of him. Now these dogs wander disconsolately about the field. The life has gone out of the bomber station. The morning passes slowly. The squadron was due over the target at 9.52. It was due home at 12.43. As 9.50 comes and passes you have the ships in your mind. Now the flak has come up at them. Perhaps now a swarm of fighters has hurled itself at them. The thing happens in your mind. Now, if everything has gone well and there have been no accidents, the bomb bays are open and the ships are running over the target. Now they have turned and are making the run for home, keeping the formation tight, climbing, climbing to avoid the flak. It is 10 o'clock, they should be started back – 10.20, they should be seeing the ocean by now.

The crew last night had told a story of the death of a Fortress, and it comes back to mind.

It was a beautiful day, they said, a picture day with big clouds and a very blue sky. The kind of day you see in advertisements for air travel back at home. The formation was flying toward St. Nazaire and the air was very clear. They could see the little towns on the ground, they said. Then the flak came up, they said, and some Messerschmitts parked off out of range and began to pot at them with their cannon. They didn't see where the Fortress up ahead was hit. Probably in the controls, because they did not see her break up at all.

They all agree that what happened seemed to happen very slowly. The Fortress slowly nosed up and up until she tried to climb vertically and, of course, she couldn't do that. Then she slipped in slow motion, backing like a falling leaf and she balanced for a while and then her nose edged over and she started, nose down, for the ground.

The blue sky and the white clouds made a picture of it. The crew could see the gunner trying to get out and then he did and his parachute fluffed open. And the ball-turret gunner – they could see him flopping about. The bombardier and navigator blossomed out of the nose and the waist gunners followed them. Mary Ruth's crew were yelling, 'Get out, you pilots.' The ship was far down when the ball-turret gunner cleared. They thought the skipper and the co-pilot were lost. They stayed with the ship too long and then the ship was so far down that they could hardly see it. It must have been almost to the ground when two little puffs of white, first one and then the second, shot out of her. And the crew yelled with relief. And then the ship hit the ground and exploded. Only the tail gunner and ball-turret man had seen the end. They explained it over the intercom.

Beside the no. 1 hangar there is a little mound of earth covered with short, heavy grass. At 12.15 the ground men begin to congregate on it and sweat out the home-coming. Rumour comes with the crew chief that they have reported but it is rumour. A small dog, which might be a gray Scottie if his ears didn't hang down and his tail bend the wrong way, comes to sit on the little mound. He stretches out and puts his whiskery muzzle on his outstretched paws. He does not close his eyes and his ears twitch. All the ground crew are there now, waiting for their ships. It is the longest set of minutes imaginable.

Suddenly the little dog raises his head. His body begins to tremble all over. The crew chief has a pair of field glasses. He looks down at the dog and then aims his glasses to the south. 'Can't see anything yet,' he says. The little dog continues to shudder and a high whine comes from him.

And here they come. You can just see the lots far to the south. The formation is good, but one ship flies alone and ahead. 'Can you see her number? Who is she?' The lead ship drops altitude and comes in straight for the field. From her side two little rockets break, a red one and a white one. The ambulance – they call it the meat wagon – starts down the runway. There is a hurt man on that ship.

The main formation comes over the field and each ship peels to circle for a landing, but the lone ship drops and the wheels strike the ground and the Fortress lands like a great bug on the runway. But the moment her wheels are on the ground there is a sharp, crying bark and a streak of grey. The little dog seems hardly to touch the ground. He streaks across the field toward the landed ship. He knows his own ship. One by one the Fortresses land and the ground crews check off the numbers as they land. *Mary Ruth* is there; only one ship is missing and she landed farther south, with short fuel tanks. There is a great sigh of relief on the mound. The mission is over.[6]

CHAPTER 11

Double Strike

'In August 1943 the assault against the German Air Force continued. Airfields in France were bombed again. Twenty-nine enemy fighters were claimed destroyed when the Fortresses made a daylight attack on targets in the Ruhr. But the most grievous wounds suffered by the Luftwaffe came on August 17; one year to the day after the VIII Bomber Command had begun operations over Europe. On that day, in perfect weather, the largest armada of Fortresses ever assembled was dispatched against two high-priority industrial targets deep inside Germany. Two aerial task forces struck the factories at Schweinfurt which produced approximately half of Germany's total output of ball bearings. A third, fighting its way through fighter opposition of unparalleled ferocity, paralyzed the Nazis' second-largest Messerschmitt factory at Regensburg and flew straight on to Africa.'

Full Stride, Target: Germany: The US Army Air Forces' Official Story of the VIII Bomber Command's First Year over Europe.

On 24 July 1943, the Eighth Air Force mounted the long-awaited succession of attacks that would become known as 'Blitz Week'. Crews flew four missions in five days until, on 31 July, groups were told to stand down. Crews had flown themselves almost to a standstill, and in a week of sustained combat operations 8th Bomber Command had lost around a hundred aircraft and ninety combat crews. This reduced its combat strength to under 200 heavies ready for combat. However, losses were made good and Major-General Ira C. Eaker, Chief of 8th Bomber Command, kept up the pressure on the enemy as he sent his bombers daily to targets in the Reich.

On 12 August, 330 bombers hit targets in the Ruhr. Three days later, 8th Bomber Command participated in the 'Starkey' deception plan, which was created to make the enemy believe that an invasion of the French coast was imminent, to help relieve some of the pressure on Russia and halt troop movements to Italy. Strikes against enemy airfields in France and the Low Countries continued on 16 August, then early that evening base operations staff throughout eastern England waited for their orders for the morrow, the anniversary mission of the Eighth Air Force. Throughout the east of England, staff waited in anticipation, none more so than those at Grafton Underwood, where Budd Peaslee's 384th had a special interest. Speculation had been rife on the base ever since late July, when the group had received an order from higher headquarters. Colonel Peaslee explains:

> It said 'Select one of the best of your lead crews, stand them down. Send them to headquarters, 8th Bomber Command for special briefing, thereafter they will not leave the base nor communicate with other crews. They will fly practice flights daily and practise high-altitude bombing on the Irish Sea bombing range whenever possible.'

Crews knew something special would be in the offing for the anniversary mission, but what? They had laid bets that the subterfuge was part of the preparations for the first ever American air raid on Berlin; for others, an attack on Hitler's mountain retreat at Berchtesgaden was most likely. In fact Eaker and his planners had conceived a most ambitious and daring plan to attack, simultaneously, aircraft plants at Schweinfurt and Regensburg. The selection of Regensburg and Schweinfurt as the targets for the anniversary mission of 8th Bomber Command came at a time when the Luftwaffe's operational fighter strength on the Western Front was showing a significant increase. Regensburg was the second-largest aircraft plant of its kind in

Europe – the largest was at Wiener Neustadt near Vienna – and it was estimated that the total destruction of the plant would cause a nine-month delay in production. Immediate results would be felt in operational strength, it was hoped, in between one-and-a-half and two months. Crews were told that production at Regensburg was estimated at 200 Me-109s a month, or approximately 25 to 30 per cent of Germany's single-engine aircraft production.

Few doubted the importance of mounting a mission against the plants, but hitherto the campaign against the German aircraft industry had been waged within reasonable striking distance from the British mainland. The original plan to bomb all three plants on one day, 7 August, had been disrupted by bad weather, so the plan had been modified to bomb each target when the opportunity arose. On 13 August Wiener Neustadt was bombed by B-24s of 8th Bomber Command, and on 14 August by B-24s of the 9th Air Force, both forces flying from North Africa. Not enough 1st Wing Fortresses were equipped with 'Tokyo tanks', so they could not make the 725-mile trip, but now preparations were almost complete for the daring double strike. Such was the importance that the 'top brass' would lead the heavies deep in to southern Germany. Even the loss of an eye in a bombing raid while he watched the Battle of Britain as an American observer was not enough to deter Brigadier-General Robert Williams, commander of the 1st Wing, and he would lead his force to Schweinfurt while Col Curtis E. LeMay led the 4th Wing to Regensburg.

To minimise attacks from enemy fighters, it was decided that LeMay's B-17s would fly on to North Africa after the target. The 1st Wing, meanwhile, would fly a parallel course to Schweinfurt to further confuse the enemy defences, and then return to England after the raid. Despite this, crews remained sceptical, as Howard E. Hernan, a gunner in the 303rd Bomb Group at Molesworth, explains: 'We had been briefed for this one three weeks before, so naturally the Germans knew we were coming. Since the previous mission had been scrubbed we were called in every day and told not to mention the target area. Intelligence seemed to think there were a lot of spies in Great Britain.' Crews realised the risks better than anyone and were made aware how important the targets were. Claude Campbell, Hernan's pilot on the mission, wrote,

> Our target was the ball-bearing factory, or rather I should say the elimination of Schweinfurt and all its inhabitants. It is predicted that this is the strike that will break Hitler's back. We were told that within three months from this date Hitler will feel the blow so acutely that he will throw in the towel.

Despite the planning, Eaker and his subordinates were under no illusions. They knew the B-17 crews would have a running fight on their hands, but hoped that the P-47 fighter escort would keep losses down.

At Thorpe Abbotts, home of the 100th Bomb Group, part of the 4th Wing strike force, officers and men sat through the briefing. Among them was Lieutenant Colonel Beirne Lay Jr, who, as a captain, had been one of Eaker's original 'seven' senior officers who had flown to England with the general in 1942. Lay had spent the early part of the war 'flying a desk' but had clamoured for action and had now got his wish. Lay would fly with the 100th as a special observer. His account, *I Saw Regensburg Destroyed*, first published in the *Saturday Evening Post*, is one of the classical passages in the history of air warfare:

> In the briefing room, the intelligence officer pulled a cloth screen away from a huge wall map. Each of the 240 sleepy-eyed combat crew members in the crowded room leaned forward. There were low whistles. I felt a sting of anticipation as I stared at the red string on the map that stretched from our base in England to a pinpoint deep in southern Germany, then south across the Alps, through the Brenner Pass to the coast of Italy, then past Corsica and Sardinia and south over the Mediterranean to a desert airdrome in North Africa. You could have heard an oxygen mask drop. 'Your primary', said the intelligence officer 'is Regensburg. Your aiming point is the centre of the Messerschmitt 109 aircraft and assembly shops. This is the most vital target we've ever gone after. If you destroy it, you destroy

thirty per cent of the Luftwaffe's single-engine fighter production. You fellows know what that means to you personally.' There were a few hollow laughs.

After the briefing, I climbed aboard a jeep bound for the operations office to check up on my Fortress assignment. The stars were dimly visible through the chilly mist that covered our blacked-out bomber station, but the weather forecast for a deep penetration over the Continent was good. In the office I looked at the crew sheet, where the line-up of the lead, low and high squadrons of the group is plotted for each mission. I was listed for a co-pilot's seat. While I stood there and on the chance suggestion of one of the squadron commanders who was looking over the list, the operations officer erased my name and shifted me to the high squadron as co-pilot in the crew of a steady Irishman named Lieutenant Thomas E. Murphy [a commercial airline pilot from Waltham, Massachusetts], with whom I had flown before. Neither of us knew it but that operations officer saved my life right there with a piece of rubber on the end of a pencil.

At 0530 hours, fifteen minutes before taxi time, a jeep drove around the five-mile perimeter track in the semi-darkness, pausing at each dispersal point long enough to notify the waiting crews that poor local visibility would postpone the take-off for an hour and a half. I was sitting with Murphy and the rest of our crew near the *Piccadilly Lily*. She looked sinister and complacent, squatting on her fat tyres with scarcely a hole in her skin to show for the twelve raids behind her. The postponement tightened, rather than relaxed, the tension. Once more I checked over my life vest, oxygen mask and parachute, not perfunctorily, but the way you check something you're going to have to use. I made sure my escape kit was pinned securely in the knee pocket of my flying suit, where it couldn't fall out in a scramble to abandon ship. I slid a hunting knife between my shoe and my flying boot as I looked again through my extra equipment for this mission; water canteen, mess kit, blankets and English pounds for use in the Algerian desert, where we would sleep on the ground and might be on our own from a forced landing. Murphy restlessly gave the *Piccadilly Lily* another once over, inspecting ammunition belts, bomb bay, tyres and oxygen pressure at each crew station. Especially the oxygen. It's human fuel, as important as gasoline up where we operate. Gunners field-stripped their .50 calibres again and oiled the bolts. Our top turret gunner lay in the grass with his head on his parachute, feigning sleep, sweating out this thirteenth start.

We shared a common knowledge which grimly enhanced the normal excitement before a mission. Of approximately 150 Fortresses who were hitting Regensburg, our group was the last and lowest, at a base altitude of 17,000 feet. That's well within the range of accuracy for heavy flak. Our course would take us over plenty of it. It was a cinch also that our group would be the softest touch for the enemy fighters, being last man through the gauntlet. Furthermore, the *Piccadilly Lily* was leading the last three ships of the high squadron – the tip of the tail end of the whole shebang. We didn't relish it much. Who wants a Purple Heart?

The minute hand of my wristwatch dragged. I caught myself thinking about the day, exactly one year ago, on 17 August 1942, when I watched a pitifully small force of twelve B-17s take-off on the first raid of the 8th Air Force to make a shallow penetration mission against Rouen. On that day it was our maximum effort. Today, on our first anniversary, we were putting thirty times that number of heavies in the air – half the force on Regensburg and half the force on Schweinfurt, both situated inside the interior of the German Reich. For a year and a half, as a staff officer, I had watched the 8th Air Force grow under Major-General Ira C. Eaker. That's a long time to watch from behind a desk. Only ten days ago I had asked for and received orders to combat duty. Those ten days had been full of the swift action of participating in four combat missions and checking out for the first time as a four-engine pilot. Now I knew that it was easier to be shot at than to be telephoned at. Staff officers at an Air Force headquarters are the unsung heroes of this war. And yet I found myself reminiscing just a little affectionately about that desk, wondering if there wasn't a touch of suicide in store for our group. One thing was sure; headquarters had dreamed up the biggest air operation to date to celebrate its birthday in the biggest league of aerial warfare.

The 147 bombers of the 4th Wing could not be delayed for more than ninety minutes if they were to reach North Africa in daylight, and for a time it looked as if their participation was at an end. Thankfully, the mist diminished slightly and the roar of over 500 Wright-Cyclones was heard throughout East Anglia as the Fortresses thundered in to the overcast. That they got off at all was due entirely to the fact that Curtis LeMay's groups had been practising take-offs on instruments for the past few weeks. Colonel LeMay took off from Snetterton Heath at the head of the 96th Bomb Group formation, which would lead the mission. Behind came the 388th and 390th Bomb Groups in the low and high positions, followed by the 94th and 385th making up the Second Combat Wing. Bringing up the rear of the formation were the 95th and 100th Bomb Groups, flying lead and low respectively, each carrying 250-lb incendiaries to stoke up the fires created by the leading groups. Beirne Lay continues,

At 0730 hours we broke out of the cloud tops into the glare of the rising sun. Beneath our B-17 lay English fields, still blanketed in the thick mist from which we had just emerged. We continued to climb slowly, our broad wings shouldering a heavy load of incendiary bombs in the belly and a burden of fuel in the main and wing-tip 'Tokyo tanks' that would keep the Fortress afloat in the thin upper altitudes for eleven hours.

From my co-pilot's seat on the right-hand-side, I watched the white surface of the overcast, where B-17s in clusters of six to the squadron were puncturing the cloud deck all about us, rising clear of the mist with their glass noses slanted upwards for the long climb to base altitude. We tacked on to one of these clutches of six. Now the sky over England was heavy with the weight of thousands of tons of bombs, fuel and men being lifted four miles straight up on a giant aerial hoist to the western terminus of a 20,000 foot, elevated highway that led east to Regensburg. At intervals I saw the arc of a spluttering red, green or yellow flare being fired from the cabin roof of a group leader's airplane to identify the lead squadron to the high and low squadrons of each group. Assembly takes longer when you come up through an overcast. For nearly an hour, still over southern England, we climbed, nursing the straining Cyclone engines in a 300-foot-per-minute ascent, forming three squadrons gradually into compact group stagger formations, low squadron down to the left and high squadron up to the right of the lead squadron, groups assembling into looser combat wings of two to three groups each along the combat wing assembly line, homing over predetermined points with radio compass and finally cruising along the air division assembly line to allow the combat wings to fall into place in trail behind Col Curtis E. LeMay in the lead group of the air division.

Formed at last, each flanking group in position 1,000 feet above or below its lead group, our fifteen-mile parade moved east towards Lowestoft – point of departure from the friendly coast – unwieldy but dangerous to fool with. From my perch in the high squadron in the last element of the whole procession, the air division looked like huge, anvil-shaped swarms of locusts – not on dress parade like the bombers of the Luftwaffe that died like flies over Britain in 1940 but deployed to uncover every gun and permit manoeuvrability. Our formation was basically that worked out for the Air Corps by Brigadier-General Hugh Knerr twenty years ago with 85 mph bombers, plus refinements devised by Colonel LeMay from experience in the European theatre of war. The English Channel and the North Sea glittered bright in the clear visibility as we left the bulge of East Anglia behind us. Up ahead we knew that we were already registering on the German RDF screen and that the sector controllers of the Luftwaffe's fighter belt in Western Europe were busy alerting their Staffeln of Focke Wulfs and Messerschmitts. I stole a last look back at cloud-covered England, where I could see a dozen spare B-17s, who had accompanied us to fill in for any abortives from mechanical failure in the hard climb, gliding disappointedly home to base.

Four P-47 groups were scheduled to escort the Regensburg force but only one group rendezvoused with the bombers as scheduled. The overburdened Thunderbolts could not possibly hope to protect all seven groups in the 4th Wing. The long, straggling formation stretched for 15 miles and presented the fighter pilots with an awesome responsibility. Fortresses in the rear of the formation were left without protection at all and the bomber crews' worst fears were about to be realised. Beirne Lay braced himself for the battle that lay ahead:

> I fastened my oxygen mask a little tighter and looked at the little ball in a glass tube on the instrument panel that indicates proper oxygen flow. It was moving up and down, like a visual heartbeat, as I breathed, registering normal.
>
> Already the gunners were searching. Occasionally the ship shivered as guns were tested in short bursts. I could see puffs of blue smoke from the group close ahead and 1,000 feet above us, as each gunner satisfied himself that he had lead poisoning at his trigger tips. The coast of Holland appeared in sharp black outline. I drew a deep breath of oxygen. A few miles in front of us were German boys in single-seaters who were probably going to react to us in the same way our boys would react, emotionally speaking, if German bombers were heading for the Pratt & Whitney engine factory at Hartford or the Liberator plant at Willow Run. In the making was a death struggle between the unstoppable object and the immovable defence, every possible defence at the disposal of the Reich, for this was a deadly penetration to a hitherto inaccessible and critically important arsenal of the 'Vaterland'.
>
> At 1008 hours we crossed the coast of Holland, south of the Hague, with our group of Fortresses tucked in tightly and within handy supporting distance of the group above us, at 18,000 feet. But our long, loose-linked column looked too long and the gaps between the combat wings too wide. As I squinted into the sun, gauging the distance to the barely visible specks of the lead group, I had a recurrence of that sinking feeling before the take-off – the lonesome foreboding that might come to the last man about to run a gauntlet line with spiked clubs. The premonition was well-founded.

The Luftwaffe began its attacks as the formation entered enemy territory. Lieutenant Richard H. Perry, co-pilot aboard *Betty Boop*, *the Pistol Packin' Mama*, flown by Lieutenant Jim Geary in the 390th Bomb Group, recalls:

> Just after we reached the Dutch coast we were attacked by several FW 190s. A .30 mm calibre armour piercing shell entered the waist gun area and went right through the steel helmet of Sergeant Leonard A. Baumgartner and struck him in the head. The shell also shattered a rudder control cable which made our landing in North Africa very difficult later. I went to the back of the airplane to administer to him. Baumgartner took his last breath in my arms.

At 1017 hours near Woensdrecht, Lieutenant Colonel Lay saw

> the first flak blossom out in our vicinity, light and accurate. A few minutes later, at approximately 1025 hours, a gunner called 'Fighters at two o'clock low.' I saw them, climbing above the horizon ahead of us to the right – a pair of them. For a moment I hoped they were P-47 Thunderbolts from the fighter escort that was supposed to be in our vicinity but I didn't hope long. The two FW 190s turned and whizzed through the formation ahead of us in a frontal attack, nicking two B-17s in the wings and breaking away in half rolls right over our group. By craning my neck and back, I glimpsed one of them through the roof glass in the cabin, flashing past at a 600 mile-an-hour rate of closure, his yellow nose smoking and small pieces flying off near the wing root. The guns of our group were in action. The pungent smell of burnt cordite filled the cockpit and the B-17 trembled to the recoil of nose and ball turret guns. Smoke immediately trailed from the hit B-17s but they held their stations. Here was early fighter reaction. The members of the crew sensed trouble. There was something desperate about the way those two fighters came in fast right out of their climb, without any preliminaries. Apparently, our own fighters were busy somewhere farther up the procession. The interphone was active for a few seconds with brief admonitions: 'Lead 'em more …'; 'Short bursts'; 'Don't throw rounds away'; 'Bombardier to left waist gunner, don't yell. Talk slow.'

Three minutes later the gunners reported fighters climbing up from all around the clock, singly and in pairs, both FW 190s and Me 109Gs. The fighters I could see on my side looked too many for sound health. No friendly Thunderbolts were visible. From now on we were in mortal danger. My mouth dried up and my buttocks pulled together. A co-ordinated attack began, with the head-on fighters coming in from slightly above, the nine and three o'clock attackers approaching from about level and the rear attackers from slightly below. The guns from every B-17 in the group ahead were firing simultaneously, lashing the sky with ropes of orange tracers to match the chain-puff bursts squirting from the 20mm cannon muzzles in the wings of the Jerry single-seaters. I noted with alarm that a lot of our fire was falling astern of the target – particularly from our hand-held nose and waist guns.

Nevertheless, both sides got hurt in this clash, with the entire second element of three B-17s from our low squadron and one B-17 from the 95th falling out of formation on fire, with crews baling out and several fighters heading for the deck in flames or with their pilots lingering behind under the dirty yellow canopies that distinguished some of their parachutes from ours. Major John Kidd, our twenty-four-year-old group leader, flying only his third combat mission, pulled us up even closer to the 95th Group for mutual support.

As we swung slightly outside with our squadron, in mild evasive action, I got a good look at that gap in the low squadron where three B-17s had been. Suddenly, I bit my lip hard. The lead ship [*Alice From Dallas*, of that element had pulled out on fire and exploded before anyone baled out. It was the ship to which I had originally been assigned.

Alice From Dallas, piloted by Roy Claytor, who was leading the second element of the low squadron, was shot down by flak bursts at 1020 hours while over eastern Belgium. The B-17 erupted in flames and eight men managed to bail out safely. Edward Musante's – the right waist gunner – parachute fouled the horizontal stabiliser, and he was killed when the aircraft exploded. The ball turret gunner was also killed after failing to get clear in time. For most of the crew it was only their tenth mission.

Both of Claytor's wingmen, Thomas Hummel and Ronald Braley's *Tweedle o'Twill* were shot down by a combination of flak and fighters. A B-17 in the 95th Bomb Group was also shot down. In addition, *Picklepuss*, piloted by Lieutenant Robert Knox in the lead squadron, was hit by fighters and knocked out of formation soon after crossing the River Moselle. A second attack inflicted more damage, and *Picklepuss* became separated from the rest of the group. The crew were faced with a decision: should they try to make Switzerland or fly back to England? Ernest Warsaw, the navigator, persuaded them that they should try to get back to Thorpe Abbotts, so Knox headed for the German border. Just south of Aachen three Bf 110s from St Trond, who had been detailed to pick off any returning cripples, attacked the ailing bomber. Two of the fighters, which attacked from the rear, were shot down, but the third, which attacked head-on, succeeded in shooting the B-17's right wing off with cannon fire. Warsaw, Walter Paulsen, the radio operator, and Clover Barney, the engineer, managed to bail out before the rapid descent pinned the crew to the inside of the spiralling bomber. A fourth man, Edwin Tobin, the bombardier, was saved when he was blown out in the explosion before the bomber hit the ground. Tobin knew nothing of his descent and only came round in a German hospital.

Lay continues,

I glanced over at Murphy. It was cold in the cockpit but sweat was running from his forehead and over his oxygen mask from the exertion of holding his element in tight formation and the strain of the warnings that hummed over the interphone and what he could see out of the corners of his eyes. He caught my glance and turned the controls over to me for a while. It was an enormous relief to concentrate on flying instead of sitting there watching fighters aiming between your eyes. Somehow the attacks from the rear, although I could see them through my ears via the interphone, didn't bother me. I guess it was because there was a slab of armour plate behind my back and I couldn't watch them anyway. I knew that we were in a lively fight. Every alarm bell in my brain and heart was ringing a high-pitched warning. But my nerves were steady and my brain working. The fear was unpleasant but it was bearable. I knew that I was going to die and so were a lot of others. What I didn't know was that the real fight, the 'Anschluss' of Luftwaffe 20mm cannon shells, hadn't really begun. The largest and most savage fighter resistance of any war in history was rising to stop us at any cost and our group was the most vulnerable target.

We absorbed the first wave of a hailstorm of individual fighter attacks that were to engulf us clear to the target in such a blizzard of bullets and shells that a chronological account is difficult. It was 1041 hours, over Eupen, that I looked out of the windows after a minute's lull and saw two whole squadrons, twelve Me 109s and eleven FW190s, climbing parallel to us as though they were on a steep escalator. The first squadron had reached our level and was pulling ahead to turn into us. The second was not far behind. Several thousand feet below us were many more fighters, their noses cocked up in maximum climb. Over the interphone came reports of an equal number of enemy aircraft deploying on the other side of the formation. For the first time I noticed an Me 110 sitting out of range on our level out to the right. He was to stay with us all the way to the target, apparently radioing our position and weak spots to fresh 'Staffeln' waiting farther down the road. At the sight of all these fighters, I had the distinct feeling of being trapped – that the Hun had been tipped off or at least had guessed our destination and was set for us. We were already through the German fighter belt. Obviously, they had moved a lot of squadrons back in a fluid defence in depth and they must have been saving up some outfits for the inner defence that we didn't know about. The life expectancy of our group seemed definitely limited, since it had already appeared that the fighters, instead of wasting fuel trying to overhaul the preceding groups, were glad to take a cut at us.

Swinging their yellow noses around in a wide U-turn, the twelve-ship squadron of Me 109s came in from twelve to two o'clock in pairs. The main event was on. I fought an impulse to close my eyes and overcame it. A shining silver rectangle of metal sailed past over our right wing. I recognised it as a main exit door. Seconds later, a black lump came hurtling through the formation, barely missing several propellers. It was a man, clasping his knees to his head, revolving like a diver in a triple somersault, shooting by us so close that I saw a piece of paper blow out of his leather jacket. He was evidently making a delayed jump, for I didn't see his parachute open.

A B-17 [*The WAAC Hunter*, piloted by 2nd Lieutenant Henry P. Shotland, whose crew were on their first mission] turned gradually out of the formation to the right, maintaining altitude. In a split-second it completely vanished in a brilliant explosion, from which the only remains were four balls of fire, the fuel tanks, which were quickly consumed as they fell earthwards.[1]

I saw red-, yellow- and aluminium-coloured fighters. Their tactics were running fairly true to form, with frontal attacks hitting the low squadron and rear attackers going for the lead and high squadrons. Some of the Jerries shot at us with rockets and an attempt at air-to-air bombing was made with little black time-fuse sticks, dropped from above, which exploded in small grey puffs off to one side of the formation. Several of the FWs did some nice deflection shooting on side attacks from 500 yards at the high group, then raked the low group on the breakaway at closer range with their noses cocked in a side slip, to keep the formation in their sights longer in the turn. External tanks were visible under the bellies or wings of at least two squadrons, shedding uncomfortable light on the mystery of their ability to tail us so far from their bases. The manner of the assaults indicated the pilots knew where we were going and were inspired with a fanatical determination to stop us before we got there. Many pressed attacks home to 250 yards or less, or bolted right through the formation wide out, firing long, twenty-second bursts, often presenting point-blank targets on the breakaway. Some committed the fatal error of pulling up instead of going down and out. More experienced pilots came in on frontal attacks with a noticeably slower rate of closure, apparently throttled back, obtaining greater accuracy. But no tactics could halt the close-knit juggernauts of our Fortresses, or save the single-seaters from paying a terrible price.

Our airplane was endangered by various debris. Emergency hatches, exit doors, prematurely opened parachutes, bodies and assorted fragments of B-17s and Hun fighters breezed past us in the slip stream. I watched two fighters explode not far beneath and disappear in sheets of orange flame; B-17s dropping out in every stage of distress, from engines on fire to controls shot away; friendly and enemy parachutes floating down and, on the green carpet far below us, funeral pyres of smoke from fallen fighters marking our trail.

On we flew through the cluttered wake of a desperate air battle, where disintegrating aircraft were commonplace and the white dots of sixty parachutes in the air at one time were hardly worth a second look. The spectacle registering on my eyes became so fantastic that my brain turned numb to the actuality of death and destruction all around us. Had it not been for the squeezing in my stomach, which was trying to purge itself, I might easily have been watching an animated cartoon in a movie theatre.

The minutes dragged on into an hour and still the fighters came. Our gunners called coolly and briefly to one another, dividing up their targets, fighting for their lives and ours with every round of ammunition. The tail gunner called that he was out of ammunition. We sent another belt back to him. Here was a new hazard. We might run out of .50 calibre slugs before we reached the target. I looked to both sides of us. Our two wingmen were gone. So was the element in front of us – all three ships. We moved up into position behind the lead element of the high squadron. I looked out again on my side and saw a cripple, with one prop feathered, struggle up behind our right wing with his bad engine funnelling smoke into the slipstream. He dropped back. Now our tail gunner had a clear view. There were no more B-17s behind us. We were the last men.

I took the controls for a while. The first thing I saw when Murphy resumed flying was a B-17 [*Escape Kit*, piloted by Lieutenant Curtis Biddick] turning slowly out to the right, its cockpit a mass of flames. Richard Snyder, the co-pilot, crawled out of his window, held on with one hand, reached back for his parachute, buckled it on, let go and was whisked back into the horizontal stabiliser of the tail. I believe the impact killed him. His parachute didn't open.[2]

I looked forward and almost ducked as I watched the tail gunner of a B-17 ahead of us take a bead right on our windshield and cut loose with a stream of tracers that missed us by a few feet as he fired on a fighter attacking us from six o'clock low. I almost ducked again when our own top turret gunner's twin muzzles pounded away a foot above my head in the full forward position, giving a realistic imitation of cannon shells exploding in the cockpit, while I gave a better imitation of a man jumping six inches out of his seat.

Still no let up. The fighters queued up like a bread line and let us have it. Each second of time had a cannon shell in it. The strain of being a clay duck in the wrong end of that aerial shooting gallery became almost intolerable. Our *Piccadilly Lily* shook steadily with the fire of its .50s and the air inside was wispy with smoke. I checked the engine instruments for the thousandth time. Normal. No injured crew members yet. Maybe we'd get to that target, even with our reduced firepower. Seven Fortresses from our group had already gone down and many of the rest of us were badly shot up and short-handed because of wounded crew members. Almost disinterestedly I observed a B-17 pull out from the preceding 95th Bomb Group and drop back to a position about 200 feet from our right wing tip. His right 'Tokyo tanks' were on fire and had been for a half-hour. Now the smoke was thicker. Flames were licking through the blackened skin of the wing. While the pilot held her steady, I saw four crew members drop out the bomb bay and execute delayed jumps. Another baled out from the nose, opened his parachute prematurely and nearly fouled the tail. Another went out of the left waist gun opening, delaying his opening for a safe interval. The tail gunner dropped out of his hatch, apparently pulling the ripcord before he was clear of the ship. His parachute opened instantaneously, barely missing the tail and jerked him so hard that both his shoes came off. He hung limp in the harness, whereas the others had shown immediate signs of life, shifting around in their harness. The Fortress then dropped back in a medium spiral and I did not see the pilots leave. I saw the ship though, just before it trailed from view, belly to the sky, its wing a solid sheet of yellow flame.

Now that we had been under constant attack for more than an hour, it appeared certain that our group was faced with extinction. The sky was still mottled with rising fighters. Target time was thirty-five minutes away. I doubt if a man in the group visualised the possibility of our getting much farther without 100 per cent loss. I know that I had long since mentally accepted the fact of death and that it was simply a question of the next second or next minute. I learned first-hand that a man can resign himself to the certainty of death without becoming panicky. Our group firepower was reduced to thirty-five per cent and ammunition was running low. Our tail guns had to be replenished from another gun station. Gunners were becoming exhausted and nerve-tortured from the nagging strain – the strain that sends gunners and pilots to the rest homes. There was an awareness on everybody's part that something must have gone wrong. We had been the aiming point for what looked like most of the Luftwaffe. It looked as though we might find the rest of it primed for us at the target.

At this hopeless point, a young squadron commander [Major Gale Cleven, flying with Captain Norman Scott in *Phartzac*] down in the low squadron, was living through his finest hour. The 350th squadron had lost its second element of three ships early in the fight, south of Antwerp, yet he had consistently maintained his vulnerable and exposed position in the formation rigidly, in order to keep the guns of his three remaining ships well uncovered to protect the belly of the formation. Now, nearing the target, battle damage was catching up with him fast. A 20mm cannon shell penetrated the right side of his airplane and exploded beneath him, damaging the electrical system and cutting James Parks, the top turret gunner, in the leg. A second 20mm shell entered the radio compartment, killing Norman Smith, the radio operator, who bled to death with his legs severed above the knees. A third 20mm shell entered the left side of the nose, tearing out a section about two feet square and tore away the right-hand nose gun installations, injuring Norris Norman, the bombardier, in the head and shoulder. A fourth 20mm shell penetrated the right wing into the fuselage and shattered the hydraulic system, releasing fluid all over the cockpit. A fifth 20mm shell punctured the cabin roof and severed the rudder cables to one side of the rudder. A sixth 20mm shell exploded in the no. 3 engine, destroying all controls to the engine. The engine caught fire and lost its power, but eventually I saw the fire go out. Confronted with structural damage, partial loss of control, fire in the air and serious injuries to personnel and faced with fresh waves of fighters still rising to the attack, this commander was justified in abandoning ship. His crew, some of them comparatively inexperienced youngsters, were preparing to bale out. The co-pilot pleaded repeatedly with him to bale out. His reply at this critical juncture was blunt. His words were heard over the interphone and had a magical effect on the crew. They stuck to their guns. The B-17 kept on.

Fighter tactics were running fairly true to form. Frontal attacks hit the low and lead squadrons, while rear attackers went for the high. The manner of their attacks showed that some pilots were old-timers, some amateurs and that all knew pretty definitely where we were going and were inspired with a fanatical determination to stop us before we got there. The old-timers came in on frontal attacks with a noticeably slower rate of closure, apparently throttled back, obtaining greater accuracy than those that bolted through us wide open. They did some nice shooting at ranges of 500 or more yards and in many cases seemed able to time their thrusts to catch the top and ball turret gunners engaged with rear and side attacks. Less experienced pilots were pressing attacks home to 250 yards and less to get hits, offering point-blank targets on the break-away, firing long bursts of twenty seconds and in some cases actually pulling up instead of going down and out. Several Focke Wulf pilots pulled off some first-rate deflection shooting on side attacks against the high group, then raked the low group on the breakaway out of a sideslip, keeping the nose cocked up in the turn to prolong the period the formation was in their sights. I observed what I believe was an attempt at air-to-air bombing, although I didn't see the bombs dropped. A patch of seventy-five to a hundred grey-white bursts, smaller than flak bursts, appeared simultaneously at our level, off to one side.

Near the Initial Point, at 1150 hours, one hour and a half after the first of at least 200 individual fighter attacks, the pressure eased off, although hostiles were still in the vicinity. A curious sensation came over me. I was still alive. It was possible to think of the target. Of North Africa. Of returning to England. Almost idly, I watched a crippled B-17 pull over to the kerb and drop its wheels and open its bomb bay, jettisoning its bombs. Three Me 109s circled it closely but held their fire while the crew baled out. I remembered now that a little while back I had seen other Hun fighters hold their fire, even when being shot at by a B-17 from which the crew was baling. But I doubt if sportsmanship had anything to do with it. They hoped to get a B-17 down fairly intact. We turned at the IP at 1154 hours with fourteen B-17s left, two of which were badly crippled. They dropped out after bombing and headed for Switzerland. The no. 4 engine on one of them [*Oh Nausea*] was afire but the plane was not out of control. Major William Veal, leader of the high squadron [in *Torchy 2nd*], received a cannon shell in his no. 3 engine just before the start of the bombing run but went into the target with the prop feathered.[3]

In the one and a half hours preceding the bomb run, seventeen Fortresses altogether were shot down. The 385th Bomb Group lost three bombers while others, so badly shot up, would barely make it over the treacherous snow-covered Alps. Aubrey 'Bart' Bartholomew, a young Canadian-born ball turret gunner in *Raunchy Wolf*, was almost blown out of his turret at 19,000 feet after persistent attacks during the bomb run. Bart's turret door blew off as a result of an ill-fitting door hinge, and only the toe of his left flying boot hooked under the range pedal of his guns saved him from being sucked out. Oxygen and interphone cables were severed and he lost contact with the rest of the crew. Somehow he managed to pull himself back in to his turret and attract the attention of a crewman, who cranked him back into the B-17.

The bombing was extremely accurate and might well have had something to do with the presence of Colonel LeMay, exponent of high-level bombing techniques, in the first wave. The 390th had placed 58 per cent of its bombs within 1,000 feet of the MPI, and 94 per cent within 2,000 feet. *Rick O'Shay*, flown by Captain Gerald F. Ritcher, circled Regensburg after the bombing and the crew could see smoke towering up to almost 10,000 feet. It was a sight to cheer all the crews in the surviving 128 ships in the 4th Wing as LeMay led them off the target. The 2nd Combat Wing was forced to swing around in a 360° turn, and make another bomb run after the target had been obscured by smoke from the leading wing's bombs. Then it was the turn of the last two groups over the target, the 95th and 100th, to add their incendiary clusters to the conflagration.

Beirne Lay wrote,

And then our weary, battered column, short of twenty-four bombers but still holding the close formation that had brought the remainder through by sheer air discipline and gunnery, turned in to the target. I knew our bombardiers were grim as death while they synchronised their sights on the great Me 109 shops lying below us in a curve of the winding blue Danube, close to the outskirts of Regensburg. Our B-17 gave a slight lift and a red light went out on the instrument panel. Our bombs were away. We turned from the target towards the snow-capped Alps. I looked back and saw a beautiful sight – a rectangular pillar of smoke from the Me 109 plant. Only one burst was over and into the town. Even from this great height I could see that we had smeared the objective. The price? Cheap. 200 airmen.

Six main workshops were hit, five being severely damaged. A hangar was partially destroyed, and storerooms and administrative buildings wrecked. Thirty-seven Me 109s at dispersal were at least damaged, if not wrecked, and all production at the plant came to an abrupt halt. Although unknown at the time, by way of a bonus the bombing had destroyed the fuselage jigs for a secret jet fighter, the Me 262. Two of the 390th Group's Fortresses had been shot down in the target area, and a third, out of fuel, headed for Spain. It crash-landed near Toulon in France, and the crew were made prisoners of war. The surviving 128 B-17s, some flying on three engines and many trailing smoke, were

attacked by a few fighters on the way to the Alps. LeMay circled his
formation over Lake Garda near Verona to give the cripples a chance to
rejoin the Wing, but two smoking B-17s – one in the 390th and the other,
the 100th, *High Life* in the 100th Bomb Group, flown by Lieutenant
Donald Oakes – glided down towards the safety of Switzerland, about
40 miles distant. Oakes landed wheels-up at Dubendorf, a military
airfield near Zurich, to become the first B-17 to land in Switzerland.
Flak Happy in the 100th Bomb Group, piloted by Ronald Hollenbeck,
which had been hit in the bomb bay shortly before the target and had
jettisoned its bombs, tried to make for Switzerland with two engines
out, but the crew were forced to bail out over Italy.

Among the survivors in the 100th Bomb Group who headed for
North Africa was Beirne Lay:

We approached the Mediterranean in a gradual descent, conserving
fuel. Out over the water we flew at low altitude, unmolested by
fighters from Sardinia or Corsica, waiting for hours through the
long hot afternoon for the first sight of the North African coastline.
The prospect of ditching, out of gasoline and the sight of other B-
17s falling into the drink seemed trivial matters after the vicious
nightmare of the long trail across southern Germany. We had walked
through a high valley of the shadows of death, not expecting to see
another sunset and now I could fear no evil. Eventually, at dusk, with
red lights showing on all of the fuel tanks in my ship, the seven B-
17s of the group still in formation circled over Bertoux and landed
in the dust after eleven hours in the air. Our crew was unscratched.
Sole damage to the airplane – a bit of ventilation round the tail
from flak and 20mm shells. We slept on the hard ground under the
wings of our B-17 but the good earth felt softer than a silk pillow
and, waking occasionally, we stared up at the stars. My radio headset
was back in the ship. And yet I could hear the deep chords of great
music.[4]

Red lights were showing on all four fuel tanks in every ship, and it
was a ragged collection of survivors that landed at intervals up to 50
miles along the North African coast. Among the fourteen survivors

in the 390th Bomb Group, which had set out from Framlingham with twenty B-17s, was *Rick O'Shay*, piloted by Captain Gerald F. Ritcher and Wilfred W. Alfred. After the target, *Rick O'Shay* fought a running battle with the fighters, and a 20-mm shell exploded in the tail position, severely wounding the gunner in the chest and arms. Ritcher nursed the ailing bomber over the Alps with his oxygen system shot out, and headed for the Mediterranean. The crew were weary from lack of oxygen and from beating off fighter attacks. The Luftwaffe had attacked their B-17 in tens and twenties until they couldn't count them anymore. Apart from a six-minute respite over the target, it seemed they had been under attack for the greater part of the eleven-hour flight. Now the calm blue waters of the Mediterranean were in sight. No pilot in the group was certain he would make Africa, and several aircraft commanders knew they would not. Ritcher wrote later,

> One by one they started slipping out of formation and headed down to the water. I saw three splash in before I realised that we'd have to go too. The crew threw everything overboard to lighten the aircraft. Guns, tools, ammunition, helmets, camera and everything they could tear loose went over the side before we settled down to ditch.

Ritcher watched the waves, looking for a trough to set the B-17 in, when Alfred spotted the African coast straight ahead. Ritcher pulled up the nose, prayed a little and gunned the engines. *Rick O'Shay* made it, landing on a dry lake bottom. The pilots turned to taxi off to the side and the engines quit – out of fuel!

In the 100th Bomb Group, *Oh Nausea*, flown by Lieutenant Glen S. Van Noy, was also forced to land on the sea. Van Noy put the B-17 down about 90 miles north of Sicily, which crews had been briefed would be in Allied hands by the end of the day. The bomber floated for an hour and half, and gave the crew ample time to get in to their dinghies. All were taken prisoner. The loss of *Oh Nausea* brought the 100th Bomb Group's total losses to nine; the highest loss in the 4th Wing, which had lost twenty-four bombers in total. Although they did not yet know it, the 4th Wing had encountered so many fighters en route because the 1st Wing had been delayed by thick inland mists for three-and-a-half hours after the 4th Wing had taken off, and this had effectively prevented a two-pronged assault which might have split the opposing fighter force. The delay gave the Luftwaffe time to refuel and rearm after dealing with the Regensburg force, and deal now with the Schweinfurt force.

The 91st Bomb Group from Bassingbourn led the 1st Wing to Schweinfurt with Lieutenant Colonel Clemens L. Wurzbach, the CO, and Col Cross of Wing headquarters flying lead in *Oklahoma Oakie*. Brigadier General Robert B. Williams, the task force commander, also flew in the 91st formation. The 381st Bomb Group from Ridgewell flew low group. Following close on their heels was the 103rd Provisional Combat Wing, led by Colonel Maurice 'Mo' Preston, CO of the 379th Bomb Group:

I was positioned towards the front of the column and the 303rd from Molesworth flew the low box. The top box was a composite furnished by the 303rd and the 379th. The 379th provided the top element of six airplanes in this composite box. We began to encounter enemy fighters when we were about halfway to the target and had them almost constantly with us from there until we left the target area on the way out. There was every indication that the Germans were throwing at us just about everything they had in their inventory. We saw everything we had ever seen among those identification models we had hanging up back in our briefing room and some we just couldn't identify. Certainly, there were FW 190s, Me 109s and 110s, Heinkels, Dorniers and at times I thought I saw even a Stuka or two. And the planes apparently came from many different branches of aviation.

Probably they had interceptor units, tactical air (ground support) units and even training units. You name it; they were all there. Probably as a result of introducing units that were not combat-seasoned, the tactics employed were most unusual. The fighters queued up as usual out to the right front and up high but then instead of turn-diving down for attack on the lower elements, they turned in more sharply and delivered diving attacks on the topmost elements – woe be it to that 379th element in the composite box. That entire element of six aircraft was left in central Germany that day. This was the only time I ever saw the Germans employ such a technique and it may have been limited to the particular force that attacked my part of their formation. I don't know, but it was certainly unusual. Even so, it was effective, as our losses will attest. Here again I must say that although I had a box-seat for the whole show – riding up front where I was – I saw those bombers go down but I didn't witness the destruction of a single fighter.

The 303rd Bomb Group flying in the low box also had its problems, as Howard Hernan, in *The Old Squaw*, piloted by Claude Campbell, recalls:

On the way over we had two abortives from our squadron, leaving it under-strength. It looked bad. We had a P-47 escort part of the way in and they were to pick us up on the way back. By this time they were using belly tanks and pilots would tell crews over the intercom when the fighters were due to leave. Quite a long while before we reached the target there were a lot of Me 110s. The P-47s were supposed to leave us about ten minutes previously. Out on the right of us flying out about 2,000 yards were six Me 110s, flying in a stacked-up formation with the lead ship low. Occasionally, there would be a German fighter calling out our altitude to the ground for the flak gunners, but I'm sure these were not doing that. All the time I was watching these Me 110s and then I suddenly saw the sun glint off four wings of planes above us. Right at that moment I couldn't identify them so I kept my eye on them. When they got above these Me 110s they dived down and I could see that they were four P-47s that were supposed to have been gone ten minutes before. Flying a finger-four to the right, they came down at a seventy or eighty degree angle, made one pass and got all six Me 110s. They were just sitting-ducks. The rear gunner in the last Me 110 evidently spotted the P-47s commencing their dive and baled out!

Immediately afterwards three enemy fighters came in at us from about one o'clock. A FW 190 was in the lead and right behind him came two P-47s on his tail. The FW 190 was making his turn to attack us and all six turrets were pointed at him. I'm sorry to say we got the FW 190 and the first P-47. The other Thunderbolt peeled off and headed for home. We felt bad about it and I doubt whether the P-47 pilot realised he was so close to the bomber formation. There was little flak from the target, which was battered from the bombs of other B-17s. We loosed our incendiaries into the middle of the town and, as we left, huge fires were burning. The trip out was a long one and fighters were many.

The coast of England was a welcome sight for the survivors, but not all the Fortresses were able to land back at their home bases. Lieutenant David Williams, lead navigator aboard the 91st lead ship, *Oklahoma Oakie*, recalls,

Our group had lost ten aircraft and we were one of only two aircraft which were able to make it back to Bassingbourn without an intermediate landing. At that, we had part of our left wing shot off from a 20mm frontal attack which resulted in our left wingman being completely shot out of the air. We discovered after landing that we also had an unexploded 20mm in our left main wing tank. A bullet of unknown calibre (I hope it was not a .50) came through the top of the nose, passed through my British right-hand glove, through my left pant leg and British flying boot without so much as breaking the skin, then out through the floor. It paid to be skinny at the time!

At bases throughout eastern England, anxious watchers counted in the returning Fortresses. Eighteen had taken off from Grafton Underwood, but the watchers in the control tower had no need to count further than thirteen. At Molesworth things were a little different, as Claude Campbell explains:

For some unknown reason there were no losses from the 303rd. The lead bombardier was hit in the stomach forty-five seconds from the target and the waist gunner was killed and the other wounded. It was the longest, most impressive, toughest and the most important raid of the war. We got a bullet hole through our left aileron and one through the fuselage which went under Miller's [the co-pilot's] seat and a fragment struck my hand. Following the raid the 8th got the biggest let-down of the war by the RAF. The British night bombers were to follow us and do most of the damage. Our job was merely to start fires so they could saturate the area with blockbusters. But they assumed the target was hit and enough damage done so they failed to follow. It was discovered later that Schweinfurt was not hit as terrifically as supposed. We sacrificed 600 men, sixty planes and many injured men to start those fires.

Colonel 'Mo' Preston concludes.

The first Schweinfurt was a matching of excessive efforts. We, for our part, put up a maximum all-out effort in an attempt to deal the Hun a telling blow and at the same time prove to one and all the decisive nature and the viability of the daylight programme. The Germans, on the other hand, felt themselves pricked at their sensitive heartland with their major industries threatened and the morale of their population in the balance. So they put up everything they had to stop the Yankee thrust and make it so costly it would not be repeated. The result was a mixed bag. Our effort fell far short of expectations but nonetheless achieved some of its purposes. But the losses suffered were certainly unbearable and could not be borne by us on a sustained basis.

8th Bomber Command lost thirty-six Fortresses on the Schweinfurt raid, with a further twenty-four being lost on the Regensburg strike, making sixty lost in combat (almost three times as high as the previous highest, on 13 June, when twenty-six bombers were lost).

The worst hit were the 381st and 91st Bomb Groups, which lost eleven and ten B-17s respectively. Twenty-seven B-17s in the 1st Wing were so badly damaged that they never flew again. The third-highest loss of the day went to the 100th Bomb Group in the 4th Wing, which lost nine Fortresses. Sixty Fortresses had to be left in North Africa pending repairs, so in the final analysis the 8th had actually lost 147 bombers to all causes on 17 August. The almost non-existent maintenance facilities in North Africa ruled out any further shuttle missions, but General LeMay and the 4th Wing earned the following accolade from General Frederick L. Anderson at Wing headquarters, Elveden Hall: 'Congratulations on the completion of an epoch in aerial warfare. I am sure the 4th Bombardment Wing has continued to make history. The Hun now has no place to hide.'

CHAPTER 12

'The Ugly Duckling Loses Its Label', Captain John R. 'Tex' McCrary

'The Marauder is a beautiful piece of machinery, but it will never take the place of the airplane.'

This is a story about the Marauders and the kids who fly and fight in them. The Marauder has had some rough going over here in the Big League. A lot of people had to be sold on it.

Arthur Brisbane once said: 'God thought up the best advertisement – the rainbow. And he was smart enough to reserve the best space for it.'

Airpower over here in Britain has sold itself in the same space. Day after day and night after night, you hear the roar of bombers and fighters over London, reminding all the men who make decisions in high places that no city is safe from air power. Great advertising.

Air power has sold itself by performance. That's the only way an individual plane, like the Marauder, can sell itself. The Marauder should have had a head start – the name of the maker has been a byword that dates back nearly to Kittyhawk. But it ran into sales resistance none the less.

The bombers Glenn Martin makes are the heroes of this story. The B-26 Martin Marauder, medium bomber, came to this front several months ago. They used them first on low-level stuff. The first job was a sweet one; no losses. Twelve of them hit a power station in Holland early in May. Then they went out once more to hit another target in Holland. But this time they got the hell knocked out of them. They just got shot down. That was all. Period. And it was period, too, for the Marauders.

There were a couple of rough jokes being told on Fortress stations about the plane:'Have you heard about the wire they sent to the Martin plant?

'You've got a fine plane, but we suggest one modification: Put four silver handles on it like a proper coffin should have.'

Another one was aimed at the Marauder's lack of wing span. They called them the Baltimore vagrants – no visible means of support. And the most cutting crack of all was this one: 'The Marauder is a beautiful piece of machinery, but it will never take the place of the airplane.'

They had just about buried the Marauders when a stubborn guy named Thatcher, from Maryland, came over with a new group.[1] They tell me he flew the first B-26 off the line. He was convinced the Marauder was a good plane for this theatre and his was the group that first proved it.

Tactics were shifted; instead of hedge-hopping, they went out at medium altitudes and bombed in formation like their big-brother Forts. Spits covered their raids, as they had covered the first of the Fortress jobs. The Marauders flew 4,000 sorties – that means that a total of 4,000 planes went out – on a total of 75 raids between the end of May and the end of September. The total loss was only 13 – only one shot down by fighters, the rest bagged by flak. The 'Ugly Duckling' had lost its label.

Main target of the Marauders was the Nazi airfields in France, the fields from which Nazi fighter planes would fly to stop an invasion. The Marauder tactics were dress rehearsal for the Big Push.

One of the boys who rides the Marauders has linked the Jap and German fronts with his story – Captain Fred Kappeler, from Alameda, California. He's the Group Navigator for Colonel Thatcher's outfit. Before he came here, he was in one of the Mitchells that followed Doolittle to Tokyo. It's tough to make Fred talk about that trip.

'What the hell – I just rode.'

But sometimes the kids in the outfit will get him to tell the story, about how it all started:

'They asked for volunteers, but we didn't really have a chance to volunteer. I was out playing golf one afternoon when the order came in. Our CO didn't even ask us if we wanted to go. He just said okay for all of us and he didn't even know what the job was. But that was fine with us. We would have been sore if he hadn't grabbed the chance. All we knew at first was that it was to be a dangerous and important job somewhere in the Pacific. Most of us that first night guessed where it was and how we would have to do the job, but we didn't have to wait long to find out the whole story. We got told the next day. We trained for two months and then we went to sea, eighteen days at sea before we took off. Guess you saw it in the movies. Pretty bad day, but we had to do it when we did, or miss the chance. There were sixteen different targets, one for each plane.

'Mine was a refinery. We didn't get the one we were supposed to, but we did get another one, with 2,000 pounds of incendiaries.

'We got jumped by 5 fighters – didn't have much firepower on the Mitchell then. Just one gun in the nose and two in the turret and in the tail we had two black broomsticks to make the Japs think we had a sting. We got 2 of the Japs that came after us and then the others turned back.

'We got over the place where we were supposed to have landed – but it was at eleven o'clock at night. So when we had only about a half hour of gas left, we all bailed out and that's all there was to it.'

It's almost impossible to get any more out of him than that. There is a saying that 'every hero winds up a bore.' Not this one. But on one point, I did get a rise out of him. I slyly hinted that the Ploesti raid had been a far tougher job: 'Well, maybe so – but we were in the air even longer than the fourteen hours it took the Libs to get to Ploesti and back.'

He went on up into China after that job and fought with Chennault's outfit[2] for a while. The most B-25s we ever got in the air at one time was about 15.

And then he got serious, very serious: 'You know the kind of a job I'd like to get? I'd like to get a job planning deals like Ploesti and Tokyo. The kind of jobs that just can't be done, but we figure out a way to do them.

'You know the best way to get a job done in the Air Forces? Just tell the boys it's dangerous and act like you don't think they can pull it off. That's all you got to do.'

That's sort of the way the Marauders got started, too. And it must be the right way. Today they've become the foundation of the whole 9th Air Force.

CHAPTER 13

ASR

'The "Dixie Demo" dropped back to cover a crippled Fort – the "Fitin-Bitin's" always do that. It's not healthy, but the "Fitin-Bitin's" don't give a damn. They don't like to lose their own ships, but they don't like to see any other Forts go down either. And so the Dixie Demo *dropped back to cover a pal. Skipper of the 'Demo' was Lt. Alphonse Maresh, from Ennis, Texas. His ship got hit hard, gas tanks drilled – but he'd done his job. The ship he covered got away okay. Then the fight began, to get his own ship back across the Channel. He had to save The Record. The crew tossed out everything they could, chopped loose the fixtures and tossed them out too. But they couldn't quite make it. The shores of England were only a few hundred yards ahead when the "Demo" had to ditch. She hit in shallow water and when the crew piled out, they only got wet to their waists. They felt pretty silly, sitting in their rubber dinghies, paddling ashore, with a thousand and more people cheering for them. They felt silly and sad, because they'd killed The Record by not getting their ship home. But next day an Air Service Command Mobile Repair Unit fished the "Dixie Demo" out of the drink and brought her home. Once more The Record was saved.'*

'Two from Hollywood', *First of the Many* by Captain John R. 'Tex' McClary

The claims and losses on the Double Strike mission – 288 enemy fighters claimed destroyed, sixty B-17s missing – were both an indication of the scope of the fiercest air combats since the Battle of Britain and a warning of what lay ahead before the back of the Luftwaffe could be finally broken. In a Fortress named X *Virgin*, a waist gunner was killed. Four men deliberately bailed out so that remaining crew members would have enough oxygen to take the ship over the target. When the bomb-release mechanism failed to work, a wounded gunner loosened the shackles with a screwdriver, then jumped on the bombs until they fell free. In a Fortress named *My Prayer*, fire broke out and the ship went in to a dive. All crew members bailed out except the pilot, co-pilot and the top turret gunner, whose chute was so damaged by flames that he was unable to jump. The pilot finally brought the bomber out of its dive, and the gunner, painfully wounded by a shell fragment in the leg, managed to smother the blaze with the help of the co-pilot. The gunner then took over the nose guns, the co-pilot the waist guns and they held off enemy fighters until the Fortress was down to housetop altitude and the fighters gave up the chase:

> We came home at 210 mph, buzzing cities, factories and airfields in Germany. It was the first legal buzzing I've ever done. We drew some fire, but I did evasive action and we escaped further damage: The people in Germany scattered and fell to the ground when they saw us coming, but in Belgium the people waved and saluted us.

Over Belgium, the co-pilot started jettisoning everything that could be spared. He came across a pair of shoes and, seeing a Belgian standing in a field cheering enthusiastically, tied the laces together and dropped the shoes to him. Running low on gas and without a navigator to guide them, the three men brought their plane across the Channel and landed it safely on an RAF aerodrome.

Equally harrowing was the trip of *Pregnant Portia*, a Fortress in the task force that bombed Regensburg. Again a life raft became dislodged and tangled itself in the elevators. In vain, members of the crew tried to shoot it off; one gunner from Texas even tried to rope it. Enemy fighters, seeing that the Fortress was in trouble, gave it their best attention: 'We could see the Alps in the distance by this time. Since we expected our tail to flop off any minute, we looked longingly at those mountains and prayed harder than we had ever prayed before...'

Portia made it over the Alps, but halfway across the Mediterranean it became evident that her gasoline would not be sufficient. Other Fortresses were having similar trouble. One pulled out of formation, on the advice of the Group leader, and struggled to a crash landing in Spain. *Portia* flew until the fourth engine sputtered and went dead. The ditching was smoothly executed, but there was only one five-man dinghy for a crew of ten men. The other was still wrapped around *Portia*'s tail; it was the last thing the crew saw as their ship sank:

> She seemed to hate as much to leave us as we did to lose her. Honestly, the way she lunged and settled in the water, it looked as though she were a human thing, wanting to go along with us ... I never want to spend another night like that. Five of us sat in the dinghy and five hung on outside. Don't let anyone tell you about the warm Mediterranean seas. It ain't so. The night got blacker and we got gloomier. When trails of daylight finally came up we were all half dead. With the sun, though, our spirits rose again and we took stock of ourselves. During the night everything we had – even the stuff in our pockets – had floated away. At eleven o'clock the little automatic radio transmitter we had went out and that is when we started praying in earnest. Incidentally, the following Sunday we attended church en masse!
>
> Anyway, as the afternoon came on a B-26 sighted us and stayed right over us until one of those British Air-Sea Rescue launches came out and picked us up. We thought we were as hard as nails after all, we were a combat crew. But right then we felt like ninety-year-old men.

The anniversary raids were studded with similar incidents. One pilot who had flown on the first mission one year before was forced down in the North Sea. A British seaplane landed beside him and picked up the entire crew. Unable to take off with such a load, it taxied all night toward the coast of England and was finally met by a rescue launch.

On the landing field from which the initial raid had been launched, a group of newspapermen held their collective breath as a crippled fortress named *Rationed Passion* slanted in for a belly landing. It skidded safely along the runway and stopped a few feet from an old weather-beaten bomber used only for towing targets and other utility work. One of the newsmen, glancing at the faded name on the nose of the old Fort, recognised *Alabama Exterminator*, one of the twelve original Fortresses that flew against Rouen.

The pilot who had flown on the first mission one year before, 1st Lieutenant Eugene M. Lockhart, now in the 91st Bomb Group, was forced down in the North Sea on the Schweinfurt raid.

'What a hell of a way to celebrate an anniversary,' 1st Lieutenant Eugene M. Lockhart moaned as he swam away from his sinking bomber and climbed in to an inflated rubber dinghy. Exactly one year before, Lockhart, a blonde, twenty-five-year old boy from Hilsboro, North Carolina, had flown to Rouen as a pilot on the first Flying Fortress raid over Europe. There were only twelve B-17s and three enemy fighters that day. Since his injury on his fourth mission, he had been forced to abandon combat until mid-June. Schweinfurt was his nineteenth raid, and he was piloting *Hitler's Gremlin* when he ran into trouble on the way to the target. A 20-mm cannon shell hit the left wing tip and blew that to pieces. There was a large hole in the right stabiliser, and then another cannon shell hit number three engine in the intake manifold. The pilots did not feather the prop but let the motor windmill and trusted to luck that it would not get hot and start burning. A feathered prop was always an invitation to enemy fighters. Lockhart managed to keep the ship near the formation and flew over the target. On the way home they were hit again by swarms of fighters, which they successfully beat off without further damage. Staff sergeants Chester W. Raphoon of Clarksburg, West Virginia, and John Husick of Broadtop, Pennsylvania, the two waist gunners, claimed they destroyed an enemy fighter.

When the *Gremlin* reached the Belgian coast, number one engine 'conked out for lack of gas,' recalled engineer, twenty-six-year old Tech Sergeant Ted Cetnarowski of Milwaukee, Wisconsin. 'By luck the fighters left us. We feathered the props on the two bad engines and started a long power glide toward England from five miles up. I guess we had about a hundred miles of water to cross.'

Cetnarowski, Lockhart and co-pilot 2nd Lieutenant Clive M. Woodbury of Fresno, California, knew that they were not yet out of danger. They had been watching the fuel gauge and knew that their efforts to keep the damaged bomber in formation had used too much gasoline and that they would not be able to make England.

Captain Lockhart had us throwing out guns, ammunition and unnecessary radio equipment to lighten the ship, our radio operator was calling the English monitor stations so that they could get a location 'fix' on us. Slowly we came down to 2,000 feet and held her there for a time over the North Sea. Our two overworked engines were fading. All the crew, except the pilot and co pilot, were in the radio room huddled and braced against the forward bulkhead.

Soon the two good engines sputtered and stopped – out of gas. They prepared to ditch. Up to this point the radio operator, Tech Sergeant William C. Dardon of Rotan, Texas, had stayed at his desk sending out the distress signal. 'Lockhart made a nice landing; first our tail hit,' continues Cetnarowski.

Then the ball turret sent out a shower of spray. We were skimming beautifully until we hit the front side of a swell and came up short. The radio room door broke under the impact and two of us landed in the bomb bay. The bomb bay doors were smashed inward and the ocean was pouring in. My Mae West was inflated and held me up. I looked up through the radio door and saw the rest of the crew scrambling out the radio hatch. We got two back into the radio room and I pulled the release handle for the two dinghies.

Husick, Cetnarowski and the bombardier, 2nd Lieutenant Robert Sherwin, of 570 Park Avenue, New York, were thrown through the closed door of the radio room in to the bomb bay where they found themselves in water shoulder deep. By pushing and pulling each other, the four managed to get out of the open hatch in the radio room ceiling before the big bomber sank a few seconds later. When Ted Cetnarowski got outside, one dinghy came floating by: 'I grabbed on to it and it pulled me along through the water. The Fort was sinking. The dinghy got caught under the sinking tail and I was pulled under with the dinghy. The crew got into the dinghies okay.'

The ten-man crew piled in to two dinghies, where they sat for three hours before being sighted by a Spitfire. Earlier they had shot a flare to attract a group of 'planes', which turned out to be a flock of birds. Within an hour, guided by a searching Spitfire, a Walrus flying boat landed alongside, took the men aboard and began taxiing toward England, unable to take off because of the load. It was not exactly a smooth ride. By this time it was dark, and when a rescue launch arrived they thought at first that it was a German *E-boat*. Three of the men were transferred to the launch, with difficulty due to the high sea. The others stayed with the Walrus, taxiing for nine hours and reaching England early the next morning. They were taken to British Air-Sea Rescue headquarters and given tea, brandy, cigarettes and dry clothing.

Cetnarowski must at one stage have begun to doubt the value of the good luck charms he always carried. 'I had several,' he recalled.

I carried a Rosary given me by Chaplain Regan at the base. Then I carried a St. Christopher medallion given me by my sister, Marty. When we ditched, the chain broke. Hours later, when I changed to dry clothing, I found the medallion plastered to my wet skin. Another funny thing was that when I got back to base I found a white scarf waiting for me at the mail room. It had arrived before I had taken off the day before. But I was too busy getting ready for the raid to go to the mail room. It was from the folks and written in it in ink was 'happy landings' and their seven autographs. I've had happy landings ever since.

On New Year's Eve, Cetnarowski flew his twenty-fifth combat mission:

That Schweinfurt mission absolutely was my roughest. In the seven months I was over the Continent I saw the Eighth Air Force grow from a small group of 50 or 70 Fortresses until this winter we were punching Hitler with hundreds of bombers. A fellow sees a heck of a lot on a mission. You don't look forward to making the trip, but you go because it is a job to be done. When you get back to your English base, you just forget about what happened that day. You go to your barracks, clean up, loaf around and write a letter home. The day's impressions are on the other side of a curtain, one just doesn't think about them and you josh the folks in your letter that you are learning to drink English tea.

It was on 9 October 1942 that the first rescue of Americans by their Allies took place, after Lieutenant Donald M. Swenson, pilot of a 301st Bomb Group Fortress, fell in the drink about a mile from North Foreland. Swenson told the story:

The fun began as we started home. We were getting plenty of heavy flak and were under constant attack by enemy fighters. We seemed to be getting away with things very nicely until a Focke Wulf 190 winged us with an explosive cannon shell, slightly wounding the bombardier. Then we started to get other hits. One went into our outboard engine, which started smoking badly. The generators were knocked out and the intercom system went dead. The co-pilot and I found that we couldn't hold our altitude. We were losing about 1,500 feet a minute and the English coast was a long way off. After discovering I couldn't talk to the crew on the interphone I turned the controls over to the co-pilot and went aft. We had only about 5,000 feet at this point and there wasn't any time to waste. I got hold of the top turret gunner and told him to get the rest of the gunners together in the radio compartment. Then I climbed down the nose to call the bombardier and the navigator. Then I went back to the controls and got ready to 'ditch' the ship. We had had ditching practice just the day before, so everyone knew what he had to do. We jettisoned the waist guns and adjusted our parachutes and Mae Wests. The water looked cold and I remember thinking it also looked hard. There were waves and I had heard that when you land on water and hit a wave the effect is very much like flying into a stone wall.

It was. We laid her in a belly landing, as slowly as we could, with the tail well down. But even at that we hit so hard that it threw the crew all over the ship. A couple of them were stunned for a moment. The navigator was flung from the radio compartment into the bomb bay and knocked unconscious. The top turret gunner had a Very pistol in his lap. It flew up and cut his head. I think all of us were more or less dazed momentarily. The men tried to launch the rubber rafts; but they had been so damaged that, with the exception of one which could be only partially inflated, they were entirely useless to us. Then came another problem. When the men started dropping into the cold water, they realised that the heavy winter equipment some of them were wearing was too heavy for their Mae Wests to support. Splashing around in the icy water, the ones in lighter clothing managed somehow to hold the others up while they got out of their leather jackets, trousers and flying boots and struggled into their life preservers again. The co-pilot had been hurt in the landing and I saw him float out of a window and drift under the wing of the ship. I swam after him and managed to grab him and drag him over to the partially inflated dinghy. Then the navigator's log floated past, so I retrieved that. About then everything began to seem perfectly logical, it's funny but I was doing some very careful reasoning. The trouble was I didn't always get the right answer. The ship went down in about a minute and a half, I imagine. Land-planes always sink fast when you 'ditch' them. I ordered some of the men into the partially inflated boat. The rest held on to the edges of it. One of the gunners was bent, bound and determined that we were going to let him sink. He'd go down and then come up and spit seawater and then go down again; but he kept trying to make us let him go. It took a direct order to make him behave. He thought he was hurting our chances of survival.

Then came the worst part – waiting for help to get there and wondering if any help was going to come. What we didn't know was that we were as good as rescued – already. Some time before our ship hit the water the machinery of HM Air-Sea Service started to roll. The lead plane in our Spitfire escort had told them that we were going down over the Channel and gave them our position. Soon a small boat with a rescue crew already on deck came foaming up to us.

Right here a strange thing happened. The men on the boat made no sound and scowled at us with cold and gloomy faces. I didn't get it, until one of my men in the water called out something to them. Then one of the rescue crew yelled, 'Hell, they're Yanks!' and after that everybody grinned at us and started calling, 'Hold on, Maties! We'll have you out of there in half a mo'!' We found out later why they had been scowling at us. They thought we were Germans because of the powder-blue colour of the electrically heated jumpers that a couple of the gunners wore. It seems that they pick up Germans too but somehow they can't develop any wild enthusiasm about the job. Our rescue constituted a special occasion for this crew because, they told us, the crew of various Air-Sea Rescue boats had organized a pool to be won by the first crew to pick up some Americans.[1]

On 21 May 1943 the major drama of the day unfolded in and around a 423rd Bomb Squadron B-17 in the 306th Bomb Group at Thurleigh, when the target for the seventh time was the U-boat pens at Wilhelmshaven. *Dearly Beloved*, flown by Lieutenant Robert H. Smith from La Mesa, Texas, and his co-pilot, 2nd Lieutenant Robert McCallum, was flying in the low element of the low squadron of the low group, 'the hottest spot there is'. The young pilot was immortalised in a chapter called 'Double Trouble' in *First of the Many* by 'Tex' McCrary:

You've got to start training a kid at fourteen for what he's got to stand in modern air war. Take the case of a baby-faced boy named Bob McCallum. In a half dozen missions, he had enough things happen to him to crack the mind of a man of thirty. His youth, plus his long training, absorbed the shock.

Bob was born in Scotland, went to America with his folks when he was two, grew up all through the Middle West and went to school in Omaha. He was in the ROTC in high school.

He was headed for medical school when the urge to fly started wrestling with him and finally won. His mother argued and lost. He took a CPT course and then came to England via the Clayton Knight Committee, after training with a bunch of guys that included:

'a technical engineer, a radio commentator from Cleveland, a fellow with eight years in college studying chemistry, an instructor in flying and a guy who had a rating from the Boeing School, but wanted to fly fighters. And there was a Hollywood producer, too. The Eagles were getting a lot of publicity about that time; I guess that's what decided a lot of us.'

Bob had tried to get into our own Air Forces, but it seems that when he was in college, 'there was a collie dog chasing a cat one morning and they both ran between my legs and I landed on my elbow and I've never been able to get my arm straight since then. Something always happens to me.'

Besides that, he was born in Scotland. So he was just about to go on Ops with the Lancasters in the RAF, when everybody started transferring into the Eighth US Air Force. Bob came over into the Eighth in January, when things were bad...

Dearly Beloved was hit by flak and fighters at the initial point of the bomb run. The fighters flew alongside out of range, not singly but in eighteens. They pulled on ahead and turned together, and then peeled off and hit the group 'company front' to divide the Fortress firepower. The squadron leader went down in flames before they reached the targets. That jumbled the formation, which didn't help. Then the Forts dropped their bombs and made their turn for home and that was when *Dearly Beloved* got it. The B-17 stopped a burst right at the roots of the left wing, and the superchargers on engines 3 and 4 were knocked out. The manifold pressure dropped down and down on the left side, and the ship dropped back, out of the group. The engines were not burning, there was just a lack of power. Then the fighters came in again. A 20-mm burst on the nose of engine 4. The oil pressure dropped to 0. Then she started throwing oil. Had to feather it. One gone and three to go. About the same time, Staff Sergeant Arthur 'Art' R. Adrian from Milwaukee sent a Bf 109 diving into the water with his ball turret guns. A couple of rounds holed the ball turret but did not hit the gunner.

The crippled Fort was just about over the German coast, at 18,000 feet. Another burst of cannon fire knocked out the oxygen system all over the ship and scrambled the intercom, too. The cowling of engine

2 was shredded and disappeared. The engine kept turning over, naked in the gale, but very little power. Then it was hit again and the prop ran away. Then there was fire, first in the engine, then back in the radio compartment, as another shell exploded in the bomb bay. By sheer determination and flying skill, Smith managed to keep his plane in the air. He put the Fortress into a steep dive to shake off the fighters. Staff Sergeant Billy Lamb, tail gunner, from Belton, Texas, had used up all his ammunition; he crawled forward for more from the nose. Then the crew forward threw out everything they could to lighten the ship – waist guns and ammunition and radio. Everything that wasn't bolted down went out the window to help the staggering Fort keep flying.

Staff Sergeant Wayne J. Gray, from Coraopolis, Pennsylvania, flying in the nose as togglier, got the second kill, and the flaming enemy plane almost hit *Dearly Beloved*. The next attacker went to Tech Sergeant Hendrick Kate from Manchester, New Hampshire, who downed an FW 190 that had also been fired at by the engineer, Tech Sergeant Bennett F. Buchanan from Fort Worth. Fifteen German fighters swarmed on the plane at 17,000 feet as it was gliding downward with two engines feathered and a third streaming oil. Smith and McCallum fought desperately to control the plane.

The next attacking fighter went to Buchanan, then Gray got his second. By now cannon shells were starting fires in the plane, and Staff Sergeant Clarence W. 'Bull' Durham from Chattanooga had to leave his waist gun for firefighting duties. He controlled three separate blazes, turned back to his own guns and got a 109 just as Adrian was claiming his second from the ball turret.[2] Perhaps the strangest event of the day, and one of those happenings long talked about, was in part the handiwork of Staff Sergeant Billy Lamb. He was firing alternately at two attacking planes, one level and the other high, and was scoring hits on both. The two pilots, intent on the attack, failed to see each other, collided and both plummeted in to the sea. Score two for Lamb!

Adrian got his third, an FW 190, as the Fort was settling closer to the water, still pointed toward a distant England. Smith ordered his crew to prepare for ditching, even though a lone fighter was still trailing them. He told Bob McCallum to get up in the vacated top turret and 'try to swat down a couple of the black-bellied bastards'. Bob climbed up, switched on his gun buttons and swung the turret through a half circle, just in time to see a Ju 88 creeping right down over the rear elevator, getting cocked for the kill. The Ju 88 swung wide for a raking shot. He filled the turret sights and slopped over the edges, he was in so close. McCallam squeezed hard on the trigger handles, and fired and fired until the guns would fire no more. The fighter seemed to stand still in the air, then he jumped and then climbed straight up and over, 'smoking like a locomotive'. McCallam crawled out of the turret and back into his seat, grinned at Smith and yelled, 'Reckon I scared him away.' McCallum became the only co-pilot in Eighth AF history credited with shooting down a German fighter. They had gone over the target at 12.40; Bob fired his last shot at exactly 14.10. That was a good hour and a half of steady fighting; and the fight was not over yet. They had one good engine left and that was coughing. The airspeed sank down and down: 120–115–110–100. Smith dropped the flaps a third to hold the B-17 off the water, trying to nurse *Dearly Beloved* home. They were only thirty-five minutes from the English coast. Then the airspeed dropped to 95 and *Dearly Beloved* headed for the 'drink'. At 14.21 *Dearly Beloved* hit with a 'helluva thump', threw Smith and McCallum against their safety belts, and knocked out two of the crew, cold. The B-17 settled onto the long swells of the North Sea. The surface was almost glassy smooth, which eased the touchdown considerably, but seawater spewed all over the place, rushing in through flak holes and up through the crushed bomb bay. The radio hatch had been jettisoned, and, as the Fortress slowed in the water, the crew scrambled out on to the wings and in to the dinghies, neither of which had been damaged in their compartments atop either side of the fuselage. The pilots fought their way out of the side windows and Smith disappeared into the water. 'Listen, if that hole had been only six inches square, I'd a gotten out anyhow!' Lieutenant Daniel Barberis, the bombardier from Bergen, New Jersey, reached in, grabbed Smith's jacket and pulled him back on to the wing.

The record of seven enemy planes downed on a single mission, set in November 1942 by Lieutenant 'Wild Bill' Casey's crew, was surpassed, and the new record now became eleven by Smith's crew. The survivors talked about their turkey shoot while in the rafts, but that was not their immediate concern. As they floated away from the plane, they lashed the two rafts together and, under Smith's leadership, completed the prescribed procedures for ditching and leaving the plane, which went down quickly. *Dearly Beloved* disappeared forever at 14.23. According to 'Tex' McClary,

they crawled up on the right wing; the rest of the crew was already there. One dinghy was out, the other one stuck. They yanked it loose and inflated it. They were all pretty happy to be alive – they had gone down in the right tradition, fighting. The gunners had knocked down 11 Jerries – a record that beat the previous high set by Captain Martini and his 'Cocktail Kids' in April.

They were all out there in the two dinghies, laughing. When a Fort circled them, with the whole crew waving out the waist gun windows, they said: 'Hell, this is a cinch. We'll wait out here until Air Sea Rescue picks us up and then we'll get a week in the rest home. Pretty soft.'

Wrong again. They watched their ditched Fort poke one wing into the air, then its tail, then dive out of sight. They settled down and waited to be picked up. And waited. And waited.

Darkness brought anxiety and anxiety brought fear. It was cold. This was May, in the North Sea. All of them were pretty wet by now. It rained. They heard a plane about 1315, fired flares and yelled, but heard the plane no more. They huddled close to keep warm. Next morning, they had to comb scrambled ice out of their hair; everything was white with frost. There was no cheerfulness now. There was dense fog. You could scarcely see from one dinghy to the other – they were tied together. They paddled. Pretty pitiful, paddling with something the size of a fly swatter, out in the middle of the North Sea...

'We didn't have much food, but we rationed what there was,' says Barberis. 'Our main energy went into cranking the Gibson Girl emergency radio.'[3] The Gibson Girl antenna was carried aloft by a balloon and during the moonlit night it caused some visual problems for the exhausted fliers; it appeared to be the same size as the moon and for a time was located right next to it. The SOS signals were heard in England, but no one was able to establish an accurate fix. The men remained awake all night, endeavouring to keep each other warm for the rescue which they 'knew' was imminent.

The hours ticked on and during the second day the waves came up and a dense fog settled in. By afternoon spirits were beginning to sag and rescue seemed more and more remote to the stricken airmen. But the search was continuing and British crews were about, working in areas of limited visibility. Three times during the day, they heard the sound of engines. They fired flares wildly and blew their whistles and yelled. But yelling only made them jumpier. And then the rain came again and their spirits touched bottom. It was night again. Nobody said 'Christ, we're finished' but everybody felt it. Suddenly, one of the boys jumped up and yelled: 'There's a boat. Look, a big goddamn boat. Right there.' And he pointed straight ahead. One of the boys started to clip him on the jaw to shut him up, thought he had gone off his nut. But another one jumped up and yelled: 'Sure, he's right. There it *is*!' This time, he pointed up, not out and sure enough, there it was. Bob McCallum stood up and looked and gasped: 'My Gawd, it's a battleship!'

At about 7 p.m. the Royal Navy minesweeper almost ran over them. Frantic signals were exchanged and the ship hove to and quickly pulled the ten wet airmen aboard. They were ninety-two miles off England when they were picked up, drifting the wrong way. Everyone had been drenched during the ditching when water poured in through the open radio hatch. 'No matter how we tried, we just could not get dried out,' says Barberis.

While combat wounds were minor, remembers Gray, the real problem facing all of the men was hives created by the mixture of salt water with wool clothing. This only eased with treatment and rest. Once aboard the minesweeper, each of the men was given a ration of rum and all promptly went to sleep on the long trip in to port. Their adventure in the water had begun only sixty miles off the coast of Germany and concluded in England.

When Smith's men arrived at the Air-Sea Rescue Station, Major John Lambert was waiting with a plane to take the newest heroes back to Thurleigh where they 'boosted the morale of the group about 200 per cent,' wrote Major Shuller, the group surgeon. All were bundled off to rest homes for a week of complete relaxation, the officers to Stanbridge Earls at Romsey and the enlisted men to Moulsford Manor, Berkshire.[4]

And after a week in the rest home – 'The first damn day we came back, we were alerted for a mission. We went to the briefing and what do you think was the target? Bremen! Like I told you, they never give me an easy one. Smitty was scheduled to be sent home, but they sent him to Bremen instead. He was plenty mad. And the whole crew, except three of the gunners, we all went along with him. Sure it was rough – we got three flak holes in our new ship. But the fighters didn't bother us this time. We didn't have anything painted on the nose of the new Fort. Not even a name.'

This was the mission where the new wing went to Kiel and the old boys hit Bremen. Coming home from Kiel, the 'first of the new' got careless; the gunners all took their guns out, started cleaning them on the way back across the North Sea. Half way home, a flock of Ju 88s jumped them. Total losses of the Eighth that day were 26 Forts – 22 were the 'new boys.'

In the Battle of Germany, the fighting doesn't stop when you step out of the ring.[5]

On 13 June 1943 the 1st Wing was assigned Bremen, while the 4th Wing went to Kiel for another raid on the U-boat yards. *Shackeroo!*, flown by Major Lewis G. Thorup, had its left stabiliser shot away and three engines put out of action. *Shackeroo!* staggered over the sea for a further 30 miles on the one remaining engine before Thorup ditched the crippled Fortress in the water. 'Pappy' Colby's crew dropped a life raft and a radio, but both broke up as they hit the sea. ASR finally rescued Thorup's crew after eleven hours in the water.

On 22 June 1943, the Eighth Air Force carried out its first large-scale attack on the Ruhr, with a raid by just over 230 Fortresses on the Hüls chemical and synthetic rubber plant near Recklinghausen, the most heavily defended target in the *Reich* at this time. *Old Ironsides*, flown by Lieutenant Buster Peek, ditched in the North Sea with the tail gunner dead.[6] Next day, 180 Forts were sent to the Villacoublay and Bernay-St-Martin airfields in France, but all were recalled. After a day's

rest, 197 Fortresses were dispatched to bomb Hamburg, but cloudy
weather broke up the formations and made formation flying very
difficult. The 167 Forts that made it across the enemy coast attacked
convoys and targets of opportunity. Fifteen B-17s, including six in the
379th and five in the 91st, were shot down. At Molesworth, three Forts
of the 360th Squadron in the 'Hell's Angels' were missing also. There
was no sign of *The Wiche's Tit* and Lieutenant Dave Mack's crew; *The
Avenger* and Lieutenant Joseph F. Palmer's crew; or *Qui-Nine Bitter
Dose*. *The Witche's Tit* was famous for the broom-riding hag with
pasty orange flesh, green-and-black-striped stockings and black-and-
white teeth that adorned the nose. *Qui-Nine Bitter Dose*, whose name
was partly made up with a pair of dice – one showing five and the
other four – had sundry patches from earlier trips over the Continent.
The pilot, Captain George V. Stallings, was a big man from Rowayton,
Connecticut, weighing almost 250 lbs. He was accustomed to urinate in
flight without crawling through the bomb bay to the relief tube, simply
opening his side-sliding window and letting go. The resultant steam in
the below-zero upper air had led to false reports about *Qui-Nine* being
on fire over the target. *Qui-Nine* was leading the high squadron, but
Stallings could see nothing further because of the solid cloud building
continuously as the mission went on. At the target, *The Witche's Tit*
was hit by flak and it went down, smoke streaming from the radio
compartment hatch. Stallings could see chutes coming out and knew
that his close friend Dave Mack was still alive. Mack and eight of his
crew were taken prisoner. Then enemy fighters attacked *The Avenger*;
only four men got out, and seven of the crew, including Palmer, who
was dead in his seat, were killed.

Qui-Nine was the next victim. Dick Jones, the radio operator, was
hit in the chest by a 20-mm shell and he died instantly. One of the
gunners was hit in the knee, and a 20-mm, which exploded by the nose,
ripped through the outer skin, popping and spewing out fragments
that shredded navigator James Ford Kelly's maps. Then a cannon shell
exploded under the table, throwing fragments into his leg. As they
crossed the coast near Emden, *Qui-Nine* took more flak hits. Down
below, Stallings could see a smokescreen covering Emden. Perhaps the
Germans thought that this was a big raid and not a badly damaged

B-17 staggering out to the North Sea. Despite taking more hits from fighters over Emden, Stallings and his co-pilot Joe Bradbury kept the shattered Fort in the air. Kelly brought them in right over the Norfolk coast, but damage to the B-17 was such that Stallings decided not to risk attempting a crash-landing, and he ordered the crew to bail out in the vicinity of RAF Coltishall at 5,000 feet. However, as they prepared to bail out, the escape door and the bomb bay doors were jammed. Finally the crew jumped on them and out they went. Stallings took *Qui-Nine* back out to sea, and, just as the plane crossed the shoreline near Waxham, he put on his parachute and bailed out. Hanging in his harness, Stallings looked back at the Fortress. All that was left of the tail was about 6 feet of spars, and all along the fuselage were chinks of light coming through holes. *Qui-Nine* circled once and then hit the sea in a cloud of spray and steam.

At 1200 hours the coastguard telephoned Caister lifeboat station to report that an airman had landed in the sea by parachute 500 yards south-west of Waxham. The coxswain and several other crewmen were away, so the ex-coxswain, seventy-three-year old Charles Laycock, took charge. He put together a scratch crew, which included three soldiers, and launched the Caister boat *Jose Neville* at 1220 hours. The Fortress had already sunk; the crew of the lifeboat could see the B-17 under the water, and reported its position to a Royal Navy rescue launch. A fresh north-westerly wind was blowing, and the sea was choppy. The wind caught Stallings' chute as he hit the sea, and it dragged him about ½ mile before he unbuckled the harness and began swimming toward the shore. A few people had gathered to warn him that the beach was mined. Finally Stallings was led to a small cottage, where a little old lady took a bottle with about an inch of rum in it from her mantelpiece and offered it to Stallings. He felt that he could not take it and politely declined, but the lady insisted. 'I've been saving it for just such an occasion,' she said.[7]

On 17 July, a record 332 bombers, including the 385th and 388th Bomb Groups, which were flying their first missions as part of the 4th Wing, were despatched early in the morning to Hannover. At 9.55, after the bombers had crossed the Dutch coast, the mission was recalled owing to bad weather, which had prevented the combat wings from forming up properly. Twenty-one heavies bombed Amsterdam with poor results, and thirty-four others bombed targets of opportunity. Fortunately for the unescorted bombers, the widely dispersed formations prevented the German fighter controllers from concentrating their fighters in any one area, and encounters were few. Luftwaffe pilots claimed thirteen bombers shot down. One of these was *Snowball*, of the famed 'Ball Boys' Squadron in the 351st Bomb Group, which caught the brunt of a head-on attack. After a twenty-minute air battle, 1st Lieutenant William Peters, who was flying his thirteenth mission, ditched the plane in the North Sea, midway between Amsterdam and England:

> The nine of us who survived to climb into life rafts were later found by the pilot of an Anson, picked up by the crews of two Walruses and transferred to two naval launches. Three hours and several bottles of Johnny Walker later, we staggered happily onto the wharf at Great Yarmouth, more inebriated than hurt. Ambulances took us to a Roman Catholic hospital in town where we spent the night. The last thing we wanted to see the next morning was fish but at breakfast we were confronted by kippers![8]

A total of 101 RAF and USAAF airmen were rescued from the North Sea in just fifty hours from 25 July to 1930 hours on 27 July 1943, when nineteen Fortresses were reported missing. The first SOS from one of these B-17s was received by a Coastal Command Group flying control officer in the late afternoon of 25 July, when the 4th Bomb Wing headed for Warnemünde on the north German coast, before clouds obscuring the target forced the Fortresses to make for the submarine-construction yards at Kiel. About thirty fighters attacked the 94th Bomb Group near the target. Lieutenant John P. Keelan, pilot of 42-230206 *Happy Daze*, recalls,

> When the fighters hit us, the wing swelled up like a balloon and then burst into flames and we went into a dive. I didn't give the order to bail out because I thought we might pull out of it. I got it under control only 150 feet from the water, just in time to ditch, about 60 miles off the coast. [Getting into a life raft one of the gunners fell

into the water, breaking the strap on his Mae West and he could not swim! He was never seen again.] We tied our dinghies together and then started worrying. We were a long way from home and closer to Germany than any other land. We were afraid that the Germans might pick us up. We not only watched Kiel burning that night but we actually sat out there in the water and had a grandstand view of the RAF bombing of the German coast. We could see the flak bursting and the fires started by the RAF blockbusters.

That evening when the first of a mounting flood of ditched aircraft reports began flowing in to the Coastal Command Group flying control centre, the senior FC officer remarked,

I've never known anything like it before. On the second afternoon alone we had as many as 50 reports about dinghies which had been sighted. Positions poured in – from the ditching aircraft, from aircraft flying over the North Sea, from radio stations, launches, RAF stations and commands.

HSLs, Walrus and Hudson aircraft, lifeboats, trawlers, fishing smacks and Royal Navy vessels searched for survivors, while airborne lifeboats carried by ASR aircraft were twice dropped in one day and once more for located dinghies 200 miles apart. At one period, more than seventy search aircraft were in the air at the same time, and immediate reliefs for these were required as each reached the limits of its endurance.

More than 200 aircraft of Bomber, Fighter and Coastal Commands of the RAF, as well as bombers of the USAAF, took part in the day-and-night search operations. Most were over 100 miles from the English coast, almost halfway across the North Sea; a few air crews were spotted by the Royal Observer Corps and were rescued relatively close to shore, but one crew of nine Americans was saved 200 miles out – only 60 miles from the Dutch coast – by the dropping of an airborne lifeboat.[9]

About noon on 26 July, a Halifax spotted the crew of *Happy Daze*. It was known that the area was heavily mined and therefore dangerous for surface vessels to attempt a rescue. Two Hudsons, coded 'O' and

'W', of 279 Squadron at Bircham Newton on the North Norfolk coast, headed out to the Frisians in perfect weather to find the survivors. When 35 miles north-east of Cromer, they unexpectedly sighted 1st Lieutenant Paul S. Casey Jr's crew of Fortress 42-22981/K of the 92nd Bomb Group. This had only just ditched, and all ten crew were in the process of transferring from the wings to two dinghies, so 'W', piloted by Wing Commander B. G. Corry DFC, dropped its lifeboat, which came down 100 yards from the crew and was quickly boarded. At 1505 hours the first dinghy load had successfully transferred to the lifeboat, which they paddled over to the second dinghy. Ten minutes later the Fortress sank. Simultaneously 'W' was able to signal to an MTB that a lifeboat had been dropped to the survivors. Corry recalled,

> The crew had clambered out on to the wings and were getting into two dinghies. Three men were in one dinghy and another was in the water. When the dinghies started drifting apart I decided to drop the lifeboat. Down it went, landing like a leaf on the water, between one of the dinghies and the sinking aircraft. The air crew quickly boarded it and as I left, it was chugging back to land, with another aircraft providing air cover. The survivors couldn't have been in the water for more than a few minutes.

Corry left Flight Lieutenant Pedersen circling the survivors in 'O'. While circling, Pedersen's gunner tried to sink one of the empty dinghies but only succeeded in deflating it. At 1806 hours, the lifeboat signalled 'Send boat, motors...' 'O' replied, 'Motors under hatch.' The lifeboat responded, 'Motors u/s.' 'O' then signalled, 'Launch on way,' and continued to circle the survivors. The American crew had some difficulty before the motors were started, but soon stopped as the chokes were left partly closed. Sails were set on a course of 220°. At 1915 hours, after having sailed for 20 miles, HSL 2551 of 24 Air Sea Rescue Unit was sighted 6 miles to the south-west, and it was guided to the lifeboat. At dawn next morning more aircraft were sent to locate this lifeboat and escort it home. They soon found it, and launches were despatched to meet it, while relief aircraft dropped extra supplies of fuel to the seaborne crew. The HSL took Casey's crew in tow to Great Yarmouth.[10]

Wing Commander Corry, who had returned earlier, sent out another lifeboat-equipped Hudson to the original search area. Flight Lieutenant E. Fitchew in 'U', and Sergeant G. Curtis in 'V', were already airborne before Corry landed, and they flew to the position off Ameland. On the way, 16 miles north-north-east of Cromer two dinghies were sighted, tied together and containing eight US airmen. They had been sighted earlier by the crew of Anson EG496, which had dropped a smoke float and a Lindholme-type dinghy. Fitchew decided that Curtis should stay with these survivors, who were from B-17G *Destiny's Tot* in the 322nd Bomb Squadron, 91st Bomb Group at Bassingbourn in Cambridgeshire, flown by 2nd Lieutenant Jack A. Hargis. Two of the crew – Lieutenant William H. 'Bill' Turcotte, navigator and bombardier, and Lieutenant Capen R. Simons – were replacements from a new crew split to fly first missions with experienced crews. Turcotte and Simons' crew had left Grand Island, Nebraska, on 1 July, and then made orientation and training flights over East Anglia. 'The first combat mission is always memorable and no exception when we were assigned to the Jack A. Hargis aircrew on 26 July,' says Turcotte.

The Hargis crew was assigned as a spare ship to fill in any position aborted for mechanical or other reasons. After assembly at altitude and leaving the coastline there were no aborts in our squadron or group. The pilot, having completed several missions, elected to fill a slot in another group heading to Hanover, target a synthetic rubber factory. Over enemy territory and guns were test-fired; there were reports over the intercom of 'bogeys' – two B-17s going down – the IP or turn on bomb run, flak barrage, 'bombs away' and we were out of it. With a 'mouth full of cotton' and the enemy coastline in view, fear turned to exhilaration and excitement over the North Sea, but not for long. We had left formation and descending when we heard over the intercom, 'Prepare for ditching'. Looking down, I could see the pattern of waves and the sea was fairly calm. Taking up our positions seated on the floor of the radio room and backs to the bulkhead wall, we soon felt a jolt as the ball turret hit the water, then jam-up together as the ship hit the water and ploughed to a stop. We were out the radio room hatch and pilots out the cabin windows and launched the two dinghies, five in each off the wingtips and watched as *Destiny's Tot* sank slowly, then broke at the radio hatch making crunching sounds and went under, its 'triangle A' group mark and tail gun the last to go. My first reaction? 'There go my Luckies and Zippo under the compass cover.'

Within minutes, *Destiny's Tot* had sunk to the point where the tail plane was beneath the water surface. The weight of the engines and of the water above the tail plane soon caused the aircraft to break its back and then sink rapidly. 'May Day' by the radio operator before ditching, along with a hand-cranked radio signal, soon brought two Spitfires of 118 Squadron circling low, and then a large dinghy was dropped, almost a bullseye between the two dinghies. Two Walruses of 278 Squadron, call signs Quicksand 6 and 8, were vectored to the location while the Anson continued to circle the survivors in their dinghies. At 1850 hours, in thick haze with visibility of about 1½ miles, the first Walrus (K8549), crewed by Flying Officer William Land and Flying Officer Scott, landed in a moderate swell. As the pilot water taxied his Walrus to the dinghies, he found ten men huddled up in sleeping bags, which had been dropped by the Anson in the Lindholme container, uninjured and in good spirits. With the aid of the boathook on the Walrus, Scott transferred five men into their aircraft before a take-off was attempted along the swell. Walrus L2307, crewed by Warrant Officer George Reeder and Flight Sergeant Cyril Rolls, taxied up, and the five other Americans were loaded in to the amphibian. 'They were plainly overloaded, like sardines packed in a can,' recalled Bill Turcotte.

We never saw the other Walrus after it taxied away.

The sea now had whitecaps and swells. The pilot and co-pilot wireless operator made a takeoff run, the waves had whitecaps and swells were rough and jolting as we bounced along and came to a jarring stop. The wireless operator had a fainting spell and passed out. We pulled him into the hatch and stuffed a rag between his teeth, thinking he was having a seizure. Within a few minutes, he came out of it and the pilot tried another takeoff run riding a swell until we ploughed under a wall of water that momentarily submerged us. It broke off part of the horizontal tail plane. We taxied for hours over rough sea until a high-speed ASR motor launch picked us up along with the rest of the crew. The other Walrus (affectionately called 'Shagbats' by the British) took off back to base after unloading. Ours taxied behind until it took on water that caused an electrical short and had to be towed.

From time to time, Land throttled back to listen for any outside activity. It was a dark moonless night, and on the horizon they could see a line of searchlights dipping from the vertical to a horizontal position indicating the direction of Great Yarmouth. They could hear aircraft in the distance; however, being close to the shipping lane known as 'E Boat Alley', they dare not make any visual signals. At about 0330 hours, just as first light was dawning, a High Speed Launch out of Great Yarmouth intercepted the Walrus. The five rescued crewmen were transferred to the launch and the Walrus placed in tow. The tow itself proved as awkward to control as with the aircraft moving under its own power. It was decided to slip the tow a few miles from the coast and follow the lights of the launch under the power of the Pegasus engine, which had behaved faultlessly throughout the whole episode. Curtis climbed to get a fix after dropping his Lindholme containers, which the survivors reported to have landed 'almost a bulls-eye between our two dinghies'. They managed to reach them and climb in. At 1845 hours a Walrus appeared and picked up some of the survivors. This was followed a short time later by another Walrus, which collected the remainder. Sergeant Douglas Whittaker, the observer, recalled, 'We dropped some smoke floats and a Lindholme dinghy into which all eight piled and then we called for help and circled for two hours until an amphibious Walrus picked them up. Felt elated.'

Meanwhile, Fitchew continued toward Ameland. At 1829 hours he sighted a Halifax in the evening light and followed it for several minutes until he found five dinghies tied together, containing the nine survivors of *Happy Daze* 60 miles north of Borkum. A second Halifax was circling the dinghies. Three sets of Lindholme gear had been dropped by the two Halifaxes that had originally sighted them. 'He dropped three big dinghies,' recalled John Keelan, 'and then hung around to protect us from possible attack by a Ju 88 that hovered in the distance. Soon another RAF plane joined him.' Fitchew dropped his airborne lifeboat within 30 yards of the survivors and two of them paddled their dinghy over to it and climbed aboard. They then returned to pick up the other survivors and were successfully underway by 1916 hours. Fitchew said later, 'We dropped the lifeboat without difficulty and the American boys scrambled aboard it. There were nine of them and we stayed to give them air protection until darkness came.' Keelan recalled, 'It was a sight to see that boat come parachuting down, settling right beside us. It was all closed with hatches sealed, we opened it up and there were sleeping bags, food, water, gasoline and directions for running the thing.'

At 2006 hours, the two Halifaxes and the Hudson were joined by a third Halifax, and shortly after that by three Fortresses. 'It looked like the combined Allied air force above us,' Keelan said. Unfortunately the Americans had not shipped the rudder correctly on the boat and so the tiller broke; resourcefully, they took it aboard, bored a hole in the blade with the boat's knife, rigged steering cords and proceeded towards England. 'I had an idea that I might get the boys to head for New York,' Keelan said.

They sailed the boat 120 miles until 0730 hours, at which point the Danish fishing vessel *Betty* was sighted, and they were taken aboard. At the time, it was reported that the boat set course for Denmark and that a burst of fire across the bow by a searching Halifax brought a 180° change of course, but it was later revealed that this report was issued to protect the Danes' families. The Danes had agreed to take the crew to England and, instead of returning to Denmark, decided to join the Free Danish Navy operating from the British Isles. The search for the lifeboat, meanwhile, had continued, first by Flying Officer Pederson, then by Wing Commander Corry, who found the fishing vessel and homed HSLs to it. Sometime later, two HSLs intercepted the boat, and after a bottle of rum had been consumed the Danes continued towards the East Coast shore. *Betty* entered Great Yarmouth at 2245 hours, its journey closely escorted by RAF fighters.[11]

On 26 July the Royal Observer Corps sighted two crews a few miles off the Norfolk coast, and signalled out the Cromer lifeboat, *H F Bailey*, which rescued the ten-man American crew and a five-man

RAF Wellington crew. Some of the drama for the day was saved for the English coastline by *Dixie Demo II* (41-24417) of the 306th Bomb Group, piloted by Lieutenant Alphonse H. Maresh, who ditched 500 yards off Cromer beach. As they had begun their climb that morning, Maresh had found that he had three erratic superchargers, especially number 2. He was running with too much power, and burning fuel at a high rate. Just before the target, the B-17 was hit hard by flak, especially in the number 1 fuel tank and in the bomb bay; the tail gunner, Tech Sergeant Reaford G. Watkins, was cut on the face and had a tooth knocked out. Now, with number 1 feathered, Maresh managed to keep the plane with the formation until the bombs were dropped, and 'from that point on it was just a question of getting back on the gas we had,' said the pilot. With their power and fuel problems, they were downhill all the way home. When they hit 6,000 feet, about forty-five minutes from England, they lost a second engine and began letting down again. Nearing Cromer at 15.04, they were down to 500 feet and close to shore when both number 3 and number 4 engines quit. Maresh and 2nd Lieutenant Robert J. Hoyt, co-pilot, made a dead stick landing in the water. Lifeboats put out from shore and picked up all the crew within minutes.[12]

Another ROC post saw a Fortress and signalled a nearby fishing vessel to the spot quickly. It was a 92nd Bomb Group B-17, flown by Captain Blair G. Belongia, which, after sustaining an attack by seven FW 190s just after entering the enemy coast, suffered the loss of two engines and lagged behind the formation. Bombs were salvoed south of Hannover, and the ship was put into a slow, shallow dive and the shortest route taken for home, with every possible care taken to avoid the heavily defended areas. However, flak was encountered at Ashendorf, and to avoid it the aircraft dropped down to 50 feet, narrowly missing some of the buildings of the town. Over Emden Bay, heavy fire was encountered, but the enemy smokescreen helped immeasurably. Limping along over the sea at about 200 feet, the aircraft was attacked by a Bf 109. Belongia dropped down to about 25 feet, and the fighter, unable to dive under the ship, nosed up to the right, where Staff Sergeant Joseph M. Walsh, the tail gunner, fired a burst into its belly. The enemy crashed into the sea. With fuel running low, Belongia ordered everything removable to be jettisoned. Over the English coast, the No. 1 engine went dry. When no suitable landing field was sighted, Belongia turned the aircraft back out to sea and ordered the crew to take their positions in the radio room for ditching. The plane was brought down on the water about 2 miles from shore near Sheringham; the crew abandoned ship safely and piled into one dinghy. An hour later they were picked up by the fishing boat and landed on the coast.[13]

Walrus L2307, containing the crew of *Destiny's Tot*, was taxied in to the Royal Naval Base at Gorleston by Warrant Officer George Reeder and Flight Sergeant Cyril Rolls; the undercarriage was lowered and the aircraft run up on to the beach. The time was 0425 hours. It was estimated that the aircraft had been taxiing for eight hours, at an average speed of about 6 knots, over a distance of about 50 miles. For the latter part of the journey, the Walrus had 18 inches of water in the hull. 'After a 25-mile taxi ride at 6 knots and 15 more aboard the launch and "Shagbat" following our stern light, we reached Yarmouth at 0400,' concludes Bill Turcotte. 'The Walrus was beached and 18 inches of water drained. After repairs, it flew back to Coltishall base. After the engine was taken down, the cylinders were caked with salt. Some craft!'

After being presented with a very welcome open bottle of whiskey by the Base Commodore, the crew and their passengers were taken to the mess. In addition to their own Fortress crew, there were two further B-17 crews of about twenty men that had been picked up by the launches the previous day. With the Walrus crew being transported back to base, a maintenance crew from Coltishall arrived to drain the aircraft and repair the tail plane. In spite of a few problems with the engine on start-up, the aircraft was floated and flown back to Coltishall without any further mishap.[14]

'About mid-morning after a short nap,' continues Bill Turcotte,

there was a sort of celebration by rescued and rescuers and the Hargis crew signed their names on a 50-franc note from our escape kit. A stripped-down B-17 picked us up at a nearby B-26 base. Back at the Group, we had our picture taken and a week of R & R at 'Flak-city' near the Channel coast – customary for ditched crews at the time.

A few weeks later, when the 322nd Squadron led the 91st Group on the first Schweinfurt mission, on 17 August, Bill Turcotte was flying his fourth mission with all his original crew:

> Me 109s and FW 190s attacked head on, wings blazing, peeling off belly up below us. Repeated passes wing to wing and the Hargis aircrew on our left wing in *Dame Satan* (42 2990) were hit by a 109 that came barely over our left wing. I watched as it left formation. Over the ball-bearing factories at Schweinfurt, bombs raked the target area and great columns of brown smoke and dust were rising. I hardly noticed the flak in the absence of fighters. They met us again and again on the way out. All ammunition in the nose was expended. Hot cartridge cases were three inches deep and burned your ankles. We made it, but four of the 322nd crews went down, including *Dame Satan*.

Hargis and Sergeant Tucker, the ball turret gunner, were killed when their parachutes failed to open. Four men evaded capture; four other crew were taken prisoner.

> We had 20mm shrapnel damage, a direct hit at the waist window, the gunner with shrapnel leg wounds and a gaping hole in the left wing from flak. The mission cost 65 B-17s, 11 from the 91st Group. It was the first great air battle of the war. We were just scared and glad to be back, as we watched a B-17 land safely with wounded aboard. We learned that Lt. James A. Judy had been shot down and pulled out of a slow spin, ordered the crew to bail out, then hedge-hopped the crippled ship with only his badly wounded engineer aboard to crash land at Manston airfield in *My Prayer*.

One of the B-17s that failed to return to Molesworth was *Jersey Bounce Jr* in the 'Hell's Angels' Group, which was damaged by flak and was ditched east of Cromer. A 20-mm shell exploded in the radio room while twenty year old Tech Sergeant Forrest L. 'Woody' Vosler, the radio operator, was firing his .50-calibre machine gun at the enemy. He was hit by splinters, which lodged in his face and chest, and he was partly blinded by blood streaming down the retina inside his eyes. He believed he was going to die, and the fear became so intense that he went completely berserk; and then he became calm. He was ready to die, but he remained at his post and clung to life. Vosler even managed to repair his radio by touch. Then he lapsed into unconsciousness, and when he came round he sent an SOS to Air-Sea Rescue. His duty done, Vosler asked the crew to lower him out of the aircraft without a parachute to help lighten the plane, but they refused. After the ditching, Vosler scrambled out on to a wing unaided, and prevented another wounded crewman from drowning. The crew were finally rescued by a passing Norwegian coaster and put ashore at Great Yarmouth. Vosler, who for a year had worked as a drill press operator in Livonia, New York, before enlisting in 1942, was awarded the Medal of Honor for his actions. He received the award the following August, when President Roosevelt pinned the medal on his chest in a ceremony at the White House. Vosler was discharged from the service after ten months in hospitals.

Why Worry? in the 728th Squadron, piloted by 2nd Lieutenant Milton M. Mard of Jersey City, was attacked by a horde of FW 190s and Bf 109s. The right waist gunner, Sergeant Joseph L. Soucy, recalled,

> A lot of things happened fast. A very sickening sight I saw was a guy who had bailed out, but pulled his ripcord too soon and his chute got tangled in the prop of a plane below his and ripped his chute right off his back. All there was left was a few pieces of cord waving in the breeze and there he was looking back at it on his way down. We were getting hit by then, they were shooting at us and us at them.

On the first pass, enemy machine-gun fire put two of *Why Worry?*'s engines out of operation. On the second pass, the rudder and horizontal and vertical stabilisers were nearly severed, and the oxygen system was knocked out. A 20-mm shell exploded in the left waist and wounded the gunner. His left hand, shoulder and right eye were bleeding profusely. Another shell struck Joseph Soucy. He was hit in the neck, upper right arm and left leg. Although in great pain, he said nothing about his wounds so that he would cause no anxiety to the rest of the crew. Instead, he remained at his gun, firing with his one good hand, and blew up one enemy fighter and probably destroyed another. Tearing through the tail section, another shell exploded in the ammunition box and set off a belt of rounds. 'It scared the hell out of me,' joked the tail gunner, Sergeant Martin A. Smith. 'I almost thought it was good old American 4th of July'.

Joseph L. Soucy continues,

A 20mm shell hit the left waist gunner's machine gun, exploded and a chunk of steel went up his arm between the two bones of his forearm. He then went to the radio room and was using that gun with his good hand. I was still at my gun trying to keep off the Bandits. It was then I found out that we had only two engines running and one of them wasn't running too well. The word was passed to use up all our ammo and to drop the ball turret. It seemed that everyone was too nervous to do anything so with just my good left hand, I dropped the ball turret. I was later told that by dropping the ball turret, the plane gained 15 mph speed, just enough to get us to the English Channel. There we ditched our plane, hitting the water with a crash. Since my right arm was of no use, I didn't think I could pull myself out of the top escape hatch in the radio room. The plane being torn open, I just walked right out through the side, hanging on. Then I pulled the cord on my Mae West but unknown to me, the thing was full of holes and just fizzled. Someone yelled that the plane was rolling over on me and to get away from it. I let go and went down. Being fully dressed and with only one good arm, I could not manage to stay up so Martin Smith jumped into the water to help me stay afloat until a dingy could be found to keep me up.[15]

While the radio operator, Private Royce E. Heath, was administering first aid, the third engine went out. 'When that one went out' stated the bombardier, 2nd Lieutenant William D. Blades, 'my heart seemed to stop. We had only one engine to crawl back home on.' Because of the inoperative oxygen system, the crew took turns sniffing from two emergency oxygen bottles for the remainder of the hectic trip. During this time the ship started to constantly nose up, causing additional trouble. *Why Worry?* dropped its bombs on the target and left the formation for her home base. A P-47 drew up close and escorted the limping Fort. 'The P-47 was a wonderful creature,' commented the navigator, 2nd Lieutenant Thomas J. McDonald, 'it made us feel like we were in mother's arms.'

In sight of the English coast, the ship could no longer limp, and Mard announced that they were going to ditch in the Channel. 'We skipped along on the water like a toboggan on a toboggan run,' recalled the top turret gunner, Staff Sergeant George Boyce. *Why Worry?* nosed down and then hit the water. The right waist gunner, weighing over 200 lbs, floundered around in the water and, although wounded, tried to inflate his Mae West preserver. It failed him, for it had been peppered with the 20-mm exploding shell. Tail gunner Smith made a dash for the drowning gunner and held him afloat in the icy waters for about fifteen minutes. 'We paddled one of our dinghies around and picked them both up,' said Sergeant Edward Koster. 'It was a great thing for Sergeant Smith to do,' commented Koster, 'for he is a little fellow, weighing only about 150 pounds.' The crew was picked up by Air-Sea Rescue and rushed to a hospital on reaching the English coast. By ditching in the Channel, it qualified the entire crew as members of the 'Gold Fish Club', an exclusive club reserved for crewmen who have to ditch in the water or bail out and land in the 'drink'.

On 31 March 1945 a 280 Squadron Warwick took off from Beccles to help a PBY5 Catalina that had landed off the Dutch coast to pick up the pilot of a Mustang, and, after damage, could neither taxi to the man nor take off again in the heavy seas. 'Z' found the amphibian and dropped a lifeboat at 9.00 on 1 April, but the Catalina rammed it when attempting to come alongside on one engine. Then some Me 262 jets came on the scene and shot up the PBY5, severing its tail, and as it started to sink the crew took to their life rafts. Warwick 'Y' dropped a second lifeboat when the coast was clear, but it landed some way off and was half capsized and sinking when the amphibian's survivors reached it, so they remained in their dinghies. At 17.48 Fortress *Teamwork 78* made the first recorded operational USAAF I-A lifeboat drop; the boat was eventually boarded, and got under way by 16.20. When the weather came down, contact was lost. Wind speed was estimated at 40 knots, with 20-foot waves and very low cloud. Not until the weather cleared a little on 3 April was contact re-established, when Warwick 'K' homed onto a radio SOS and found the lifeboat drifting helplessly. 'K' dropped its own lifeboat and spare petrol, but both were ignored. Later that day, Warwick 'E' dropped a fifth lifeboat to them, but it was not recovered, although spare petrol was. The late Patrick Troughton, who became a well-known actor, took up the tale:

> When our unit of RMLs had searched until short of fuel they returned to HMS *Midge* at Great Yarmouth and I, as Senior Officer, took out RMLs 514 and 498 into full North Sea Gale conditions being promised that aircraft would guide us to the Americans. It was dark by the time we reached the given position within 20 miles of Heligoland, but could find nothing in the heavy seas so we stopped engines and drifted with wind and tide through the night. At dawn on 4 April we began searching again and soon sighted flares which led us to the lifeboat; 498 picked up the crew whilst we sank the lifeboat by gunfire and proceeded back to base, some two hundred miles away, reaching there early on the 5th.

The actual USAAF reports vary considerably in content, some almost completely ignoring the efforts of the RAF, but one, and a letter from the rescued men, gives very generous praise for the Royal Air Force and Royal Navy.[16]

Notes

1. Yankee Doodle Goes to Town

1. Charles Kegelman rose rapidly in promotion. In April 1943 he was a lieutenant colonel in command of the 48th Fighter Group at William Northern Field, Tennessee, and he remained in this post until 8 November. On 12 November he assumed command of the 337th Fighter Group at Sarasota, Florida, as a full colonel. On 16 November 1944 he assumed command of the 42nd Bomb Group at Sansapor, New Guinea, which by March 1945 were operating North American B-25 Mitchells from Moratai. On 10 March, Kegelman's aircraft was involved in a mid-air collision with his wingman and he was killed. Kegelman Airfield (near Cherokee, Oklahoma) is named in his memory and is used for touch-and-go landings by T-37s and T-38s from Vance AFB.

3. The Forts Fly High, 'Bruce Sanders'

1. Leonard R. Gribble, a thriller writer of such works as *The Scarlet Widow*, wrote *Bombers Fly East* for the Air Ministry in 1942, using his pen name, 'Bruce Sanders'. (Chorley.)
2. *Dry Martini* and *Boom Town* were both assigned to the 305th Bomb Group at Chelveston.
3. Baird-Smith was shot down flying a Lancaster on 7 Squadron on the night of 20/21 January 1944 when it exploded near Doberitz. He survived and was taken prisoner. Five of his crew died.

4. 1st Lieutenant Jack Mathis, twenty-two-year-old lead bombardier on the *Duchess*, piloted by Captain Harold L. Stouse, was posthumously awarded the Medal of Honor, America's highest military award, for completing his bomb run despite being mortally wounded.

5. Lieutenant General Frank Maxwell Andrews was killed on 4 May 1943 when the Liberator in which he was flying, piloted by Captain Robert 'Shine' Shannon of the 93rd BG, crashed into a bleak Icelandic mountain on the way home to the USA. Only Sgt George Eisel, tail gunner, survived, after being trapped in the wreckage for fourteen hours. Shannon, son of the editor of a small daily paper in Washington, Iowa, with the crew of *Hot Stuff* were the first at Hardwick to complete a tour. Andrews Field was so named in memory of the general.

6. *Boom Town* (41-24533), which was part of the original complement of the 305th Bomb Group, was lost with Lieutenant John J. Hall and crew on 22 June on the mission to Hüls. It crashed at Valburg in Holland with the loss of four men KIA. Six men were taken prisoner.

7. *Boom Town Jr.* was lost with Lieutenant Don W. Moore's crew on 27 August 1943 when the Fortress was hit by flak over France. Four crew were KIA, six became PoWs.

8. On 17 April, a record 111 Fortresses and Liberators set out for the Focke-Wulf factory at Bremen. The Thurleigh group lost ten of its sixteen Fortresses dispatched, and it was 'stood down' indefinitely after this devastating mission. In total, sixteen B-17s were lost. Forty-six more were damaged. Gunners claimed sixty-three fighters shot down. Post-war German records reveal ten Luftwaffe fighters were lost. At least the reference to the target being 'smothered' with bombs was accurate. Focke-Wulf Flugzeugbau had been hit by a good proportion of the 531 x 1,000-lb bombs dropped, and according to a German estimate half the factory was destroyed. However, FW 190 assembly had stopped six months earlier under a production dispersal plan. (*The Mighty Eighth* by Roger A. Freeman.)

9. Captain Pervis Youree in the 306th Bomb Group got *Old Faithful* back to Thurleigh but it was a mystery to him how they made it.

10. 91st Bomb Group at Bassingbourn.

11. In the 305th Bomb Group at Chelveston.

4. The Old One-Two

1. Of the sixty airmen shot down in enemy territory, twenty-two
    survived as PoWs. When a prisoner in Stalag Luft III, Colonel
    Stillman surmised that the mission was a disaster, and that one
    factor had contributed to its failure. When Captain Stephens
    aborted at the start of the mission, he climbed to 1,000 feet.
    Stillman did not blame him for this, as it was standard operating
    procedure for the B-26 in order to allow the crew to bail out if
    necessary. However, Stillman was convinced that, in so doing,
    Stephens had unwittingly exposed his aircraft to enemy radar,
    thus alerting the Germans to the presence of the rest of the
    force. As a result of the 17 May disaster, the 322nd Bomb Group
    was stood down, and it was deemed suicidal to fly the Martin
    Marauder at low level, so tactics were rethought and the B-26
    was used at medium level and from bases in Essex so that fighter
    cover for them could be improved. On Sunday 13 June, when
    102 B-17s of the 1st Wing were assigned Bremen while the 4th
    Wing went to Kiel for another raid on the U-boat yards, the 94th,
    95th and 96th Bomb Groups took off from their bases at Earls
    Colne in Essex, Framlingham in Suffolk and Andrews Field in
    Essex for the last time. On their return from the raid they touched
    down at the former B-26B/C Marauder bases at Bury St Edmunds
    (Rougham), Horham in Suffolk and Snetterton Heath in Norfolk
    respectively, and the 322nd, 323rd and 386th Medium Bomb
    Groups transferred to airfields in Essex, where they joined the
    387th at Chipping Ongar. The 322nd Bomb Group moved to
    Andrews Field near Braintree to resume operations on 31 July
    1943. Colonel Glen C. Nye, the man who had nursed the 322nd
    Bomb Group in the early days of its existence, before Colonel
    Stillman, took command.

5. The Log of the Liberators

1. *Target: Germany: The US Army Air Forces' Official Story of the
    VIII Bomber Command's First Year over Europe*, 1944.
2. On 17 May 1943, thirty-six-year-old Lieutenant Colonel Addison
    T. Baker replaced Colonel Ted Timberlake as CO of the 93rd
    Travelling Circus when Timberlake assumed command of the
    201st Provisional Combat Wing. When elevated to brigadier-
    general in August 1943, aged thirty-three, Ted Timberlake became

the youngest American general officer since the Civil War. Baker was born in Chicago on New Year's Day 1907. He left school in 1927 and worked as a motor mechanic in Akron, Ohio. He enlisted in the AAF in 1929, earning his wings the following year, and was commissioned as a 2nd Lieutenant in the Air Reserve. Assigned inactive status between 1932 and 1940, Baker ran his own service station in Detroit, Michigan, and worked for a graphite bronze company in Cleveland, Ohio. He had joined the National Guard in Michigan in 1936 and later transferred to the Buckeye State's 112th Observation Squadron before it was called in to federal service in 1940. In February 1942 he was assigned to the 98th Bomb Group at Barksdale Field, Louisiana, for B-24 pilot training, and the following month was assigned as CO of the 328th Squadron in the 93rd. Before taking over the Group, he held the post of Operations Officer. Under Baker, 'Ted's Travelling Circus' became simply the 'Travelling Circus'.

3. Colonel Addison Baker flew *Hell's Wench*, leading twenty-one B-24s to the Group's target at White II, Concordia Vega. In the co-pilot's seat beside him was Major John 'The Jerk' Jerstad, the Operations Officer from Davenport, Iowa. Jerstad had graduated with a Bachelor of Science degree at Northwestern University in Illinois in 1940, and taught in a high school in St. Louis, Missouri, before he enlisted as an aviation cadet in July 1941. It was said that he was worshiped by the young pilots of new crews and was, according to Captain John R. 'Tex' McCrary, 'as tough as a mule-skinner and tender as your grandmother'.

4. Like John M. Redding and Captain Harold Leyshon, Captain John R. 'Tex' McCrary was a war reporter (as well as a Photographic Officer) for Eighth Air Force Public Relations. He had once worked on the *New York Mirror*, which always specialised in 'rape, riot and ruin'. Born John Reagan McCrary in 1910 in Calvert, Texas, the son of a cotton farmer hurt by the Depression, he later attended Phillips Exeter Academy and Yale, where he was a member of Skull and Bones. He started in journalism as a copy boy at the *New York World-Telegram*. He left to join the *Daily Mirror*, later becoming its chief editorial writer. After divorcing his first wife in 1939, McCrary began writing the column 'Only Human', and in 1941 met Jinx Falkenburg. When he interviewed her, she was starring in Broadway tuner *Hold on to Your Hats* with Al Jolson.

5. Lieutenant Colonel Joseph S. Tate Jr, from St Augustine, Florida, and West Point '41, who was flying *Ball of Fire Jr*.

6. Twelve o'Clock High

1. Between October 1942 and August 1943, the 367th suffered the heaviest losses in 8th Bomber Command.
2. Lanford later flew in the 483rd Bomb Group, 15th Air Force, and was shot down on his seventeenth mission, finishing the war as a PoW in Stalag Luft III.
3. Wütz Galland was shot down and KIA, 17 August 1943, in an engagement with a 56th Fighter Group P-47.
4. Colonel Charles T. Phillips, with whom Eaker and Longfellow had gone to the Philippines in July 1919, was given the 4th Bomb Wing. Phillips was KIA in North Africa on 15 December 1942.

7. Battles of the Bomb Groups

1. 'NUMBER ONE PRIORITY' from *Skyways to Berlin*, Major John M. Redding and Captain Harold Leyshon (Bobbs Merrill, 1943).
2. 1st lieutenants Robert H. McPhillamey and Wilbur E. Wockenfuss and seven others survived to be taken prisoner. Robert Perkins Post was among the dead.
3. Twenty years to the day, at an Air Force Association dinner in New York City, Walter Cronkite, Gladwin Hill and Paul Manning were awarded a special citation for their participation in the raid. Paul Manning, twice nominated for a Pulitzer Prize, went on to cover the B-29 missions over Japan.
4. The hydraulic and power lines in the tail turret were shot out, as were the primers, intakes, carburettors, oil coolers and oxygen regulators. The undercarriages wouldn't work. The tyres were punctured. There was a 15-inch hole in the right tail-flap. There were forty-seven .30-calibre holes and five 20mm holes in the rear fuselage; sixteen .30s and four cannon in the left fin; five .30s and one cannon in the stabilisers; nine .30s and four cannon in the right wing; three .30s in the right aileron; twelve .30s in the top fuselage; thirty-six .30s in the left wing and twenty-seven .30s in the bomb-bay doors. And all gun barrels were 'burned out'.
5. Either Unteroffizier Heinz Hanke of 9./JG1, in a FW 190, or Unteroffizier Wennekers of 2./JG1, in a Bf 109, had claimed the

apparently doomed B-24 as their first victory. Captain Beattie H. 'Bud' Fleenor and crew were lost with *Missouri Sue* in the Bay of Biscay on 16 April 1943. All except the bombardier, who had bailed out over France, perished.

8. *Phyllis Had the Stuff*, Charles W. Paine

1. The 352nd Bomb Squadron, 301st Bomb Group at Chelveston.
2. Thirty B-17s of the 97th and 301st were involved. More than 400 fighter escorts provided cover. The 15th Bomb Squadron (Light) flew a diversionary sweep along the enemy coast.
3. Sixteen cannon shell and over 200 bullet holes were later counted in the aircraft.
4. *Memphis Belle – Dispelling the Myths* by Graham Simons and Harry Friedman (GMS 2008). Although the 301st Bomb Group (and the 97th Bomb Group) would continue to fly missions from England until mid-November, on 14 September they were, on paper at least, assigned to the Twelfth Air Force, which was activated in Washington DC on 20 August. Both the 97th and the 301st, along with four fighter groups, left for North Africa in November 1942 and earned undying fame with raids from the desert and later from Italy. The remaining groups in England still had to prove that high-altitude missions in daylight, often without escort, could justify further B-17 and B-24 groups being sent to the ETO.

9. Twenty-Five Missions: The Story of the *Memphis Belle*

1. Correspondence between Ben Grant and Harry Friedman, co-author of *Memphis Belle – Dispelling the Myths* by Graham Simons and Harry Friedman (GMS Enterprises 2008).
2. Robert Knight Morgan was born on 31 July 1918. He enlisted as an Aviation Cadet at Richmond, Virginia, and in February 1941 he received his orders to report for basic training. Though he was a maniac for speed, Morgan became a bomber pilot, and by May 1942 he was part of the 29th Bombardment Group. By 1942 he was twice married, having divorced each time. Morgan became known as 'Floorboard Freddie' because he wore out more brakes than any pilot in his group. He landed his Fortress hot and always said that he would rather run out of runway at the other end than

not make the runway on the touchdown. During crew training at Walla Walla, Washington Morgan, not yet a 1st Lieutenant, began romancing Margaret Polk of Memphis, Tennessee, who was visiting her sister in Walla Walla. Legend has it that Margaret inspired the name *Memphis Belle*, which Morgan had painted on both sides of the fuselage of his B-17 at Bangor, Maine, in September 1942 before leaving for Bassingbourn. However, Morgan's co-pilot, Jim Verinis, recalled that he and Morgan went to see the movie *Lady for a Night*, starring Joan Blondell and John Wayne. In the movie there is a Mississippi River gambling boat, and Verinis remembered that either Miss Blondell or the boat was called the *Memphis Belle*. The romance between Morgan and the Memphis girl would flourish for a time, and in England Morgan flew over the French sub pens and German dockyards in a sweater knitted by Margaret. A Hollywood scriptwriter would have had them married and flying off into the sunset, but war was no respecter of tradition, and Morgan and Margaret later married other partners. The legendary artwork, though, remained indelibly painted on the nose of the B-17 through thick and thin.

3. *Luck Is No Lady, First of the Many* (1944). In 1945, he was one of the first Americans to visit Hiroshima after the atomic bomb was dropped. He advised journalists not to write about what they had seen because he did not think Americans could stand to know 'what we've done here'. After John Hersey published his account in the *New Yorker*, McCrary said, 'I covered it up and John Hersey uncovered it. That's the difference between a PR man and a reporter.' After the war, McCrary edited the American *Mercury* magazine. He soon renewed his friendship with Jinx Falkenburg, who had become a star under contract at MGM and was one of the nation's highest-paid models. They were married in June 1945. Although they were separated years later, they never divorced. McCrary and his wife had two radio talk shows, *Hi Jinx* and *Meet Tex and Jinx*, and a TV show, sometimes broadcasting from Gotham's Waldorf-Astoria Hotel, where they could nab celebs as they stopped to pick up their room keys. McCrary died aged ninety-two in New York.

10. 'Somewhere in England', John Steinbeck

1. Born in Salinas, California, in 1902, John Steinbeck grew up in a fertile agricultural valley about 25 miles from the Pacific Coast;

both valley and coast would serve as settings for some of his best fiction. In 1919 he went to Stanford University, where he intermittently enrolled in literature and writing classes until he left in 1925 without taking a degree. During the next five years, he supported himself as a labourer and journalist in New York City, and then as a caretaker for a Lake Tahoe estate, all the time working on his first novel, *Cup of Gold*, which was published in 1929. After marriage and a move to Pacific Grove, California, he published two California fictions and worked on short stories. Popular success and financial security came only with *Tortilla Flat* in 1935, stories about Monterey's *paisanos*, and *Of Mice and Men* (1937) and *The Grapes of Wrath*, the book considered by many his finest, in 1939. He devoted his services to the war, writing, in 1942, *Bombs Away* and the controversial play-novelette *The Moon Is Down*. He died in 1968, having won a Nobel Prize for Literature in 1962.

2. Arriving by the Southern Ferry Route via Marrakesh, this Boeing B-17F was officially assigned to the 91st Bomb Group on 19 April 1943. *Plane Names & Fancy Noses* by Ray Bowden (Design Oracle Partnership, London 1993).

3. The *Vulgar Virgin* FTR on 13 May 1943.

4. Lieutenant Kenneth Brown's crew and *Mary Ruth, Memories of Mobile* FTR on 22 June 1943 when it was attacked by fighters and exploded over the target at Hüls. T/Sergeant Richard O. Maculley, S/Sergeant Raymond Litzo and S/Sergeant William G. Allen were KIA. The others survived to be taken into captivity. Litzo was flying in the tail gun position normally occupied by William R. Brown, who flew as one of the waist gunners and survived, as did Kenneth Brown, Quenin, Bliley, Feerick, Crain, and T/Sergeant James O. Akers, the top turret gunner. The crew had flown the *Mary Ruth* on each of its seven missions from Bassingbourn.

5. *Bomb Boogie* FTR on 6 September 1943.

6. *Mary Ruth* FTR on 27 June 1943.

11. Double Strike

1. Nine of the crew managed to bail out before the B-17 exploded; they were made PoWs. The body of the tail gunner, Foster Compton, who was wounded in the attack, was recovered from the wreckage at Roxheim, 5 kilometres south of Worms.

2. Sergeant Lawrence Godbey, the engineer, died from wounds

sustained by a 20-mm shell which hit him in the shoulder and hip. Dan Mackay, the bombardier, and John Dennis, the navigator, both badly burned, survived the bail-out and were treated in Frankfurt hospital for several weeks before being sent to a PoW camp. Biddick and Robert DeKay, the radio operator, were also killed. Snyder's remains were discovered months later, hanging from his parachute in a tree.

3. Despite the fire and an oxygen failure, *Torchy 2nd* successfully bombed the target, and the crew extinguished the fire and managed to reach North Africa safely.

4. On 28 February 1944 Lieutenant Colonel Lay took command of the 487th Bomb Group, which flew B-24s. He was shot down over France on 11 May 1944, but bailed out safely, and evaded capture. Captain Thomas Murphy and five of his crew were killed on 8 October 1943, when *Piccadilly Lily* exploded and crashed at Bremen. Five crew survived and were taken into captivity. Beirne Lay, who also adapted *Twelve O'Clock High* for the TV series of the same name, died on 26 May 1982.

12. 'The Ugly Duckling Loses Its Label', Captain John R. 'Tex' McCrary

1. The 323rd Bombardment Group (M), commanded by Colonel Herbert B. Thatcher and based at Horham, later Earls Colne. They flew their first mission on 16 July 1943. The 323rd, the 322nd, 386th and 387th Marauder Groups were assigned to the Ninth Air Force, 9th Bomber Command on 16 October 1943.

2. Claire Chennault's American Volunteer Group, which was known as the 'Flying Tigers'.

13. ASR

1. *Target Germany: The US Army Air Forces Official Story of the VIII Bomber Command's First Year over Europe* (1944).

2. The other waist gunner was Sergeant Aygmund Warminski, from Hamtramck, Michigan.

3. The term 'Gibson Girl' is associated with this radio because of its 'hourglass' shape, which was attributed to the personification of the feminine ideal in the satirical pen-and-ink illustrated stories created by Charles Dana Gibson, over more than eighteen years spanning the late nineteenth and

early twentieth centuries. The unit was developed for use in case of forced landings on water. It was designed to be held between the knees while being hand cranked, at which time a continuous tone went out, so that ground stations could establish its position.

4. *First over Germany: A History of the 306th Bombardment Group* by Russell A. Strong (Hunter Publishing Co., 1982)/*First of the Many* by 'Tex' McClary.

5. *First of the Many* by 'Tex' McClary.

6. Nine men aboard B-17F 42-29797 *Old Ironsides* returned. Peek was KIA on 31 August 1943 flying *Eager Beaver*, when he was again forced to ditch in the sea. This time only the tail gunner survived.

7. Captain Stallings was awarded both the British and US DFC. 1st Lieutenant James Ford Kelly, waist gunner Staff Sergeant Joseph S. Klasnick, and engineer Tech Sergeant James A. Watson received the Silver Star for their actions during the mission.

8. The victory was one of four claimed by pilots in the Third *Gruppe* JG 26 at Nordholz, who attacked the incoming bombers west of Heligoland. Finally, the *Abschuss* was awarded to Unteroffizier Rudolf David. The three other claims were not upheld. See *The JG 26 War Diary Vol. 2* by Donald Caldwell (Grub Street, London 1998). Fifty-two bombers were damaged. Luftwaffe losses were twenty fighters damaged or destroyed.

9. 'On Sunday, May 30th 1943 the story of the airborne lifeboat was released to the public. It was the latest development in the sphere of air-sea rescue. For more than two years, since its inauguration in February 1941, the Directorate of Air-Sea Rescue had been attending with ever-growing success to the task of rescuing British and Allied and even enemy pilots whose aircraft had been forced down in the sea. The airborne lifeboat was a logical development of the service rendered for many months by ASR squadrons of Walrus and Lysander aircraft and by the RAF high-speed launches. The new lifeboat was designed to help shipwrecked mariners and air-crews who had come down in the drink, to use one of their own graphic terms, too far from British shores and too near the enemy coast-line to make rescue, by ASR launch or plane reasonably possible. The eventual production of the airborne lifeboat was largely due

to the research and experimental work undertaken by Group Captain E. F. Waring DFC AFC the Deputy Director of ASR. The airborne lifeboat is a compact motor-boat, which can be carried under the fuselage of an ASR aircraft. It is dropped by parachute, which opens when the lifeboat is released and allows the craft to drift down wind towards a bomber crew in their dinghy at the same rate of fall as an airman who has baled out. The lifeboat can be so accurately aimed by an experienced pilot that it strikes the sea within a very few feet of a dinghy's occupants. Provision is made for rough seas and freakish winds in that, no matter at what angle the boat hits the water, it automatically rights itself and floats right way up. It is fitted with special buoyancy tanks, which keep it afloat and uncapsizable in the roughest weather. In weather-protected compartments are two specially converted engines, with stores of clothes, medical equipment, food, and the various kinds of air-sea rescue signalling apparatus. Finally the fuel-tanks hold enough petrol to enable the lifeboat to travel a considerable distance. For emergency use are a portable radio-transmitting set, sails and oars.' *Bombers Fly East.*

10. On 12 August 1943, 1st Lieutenant Paul Casey and his crew were lost over the Netherlands. Two men were KIA, eight were taken prisoner.

11. See *Dinghy Drop: 279 Squadron RAF 1941–46* by Tom Docherty (Pen & Sword 2007).

12. *First Over Germany: A History of the 306th Bombardment Group* by Russell A. Strong (Hunter Publishing 1982).

13. *The Route As Briefed* by John Sloan (Argus Press 1976). The crew of *Yo' Brother* in the 92nd Bomb Group, piloted by Lieutenant Alan E. Hermance, which also ditched in the North Sea, were not as fortunate as Belongia's and Casey's crews. All ten men perished. Captain Belongia was forced to ditch again in the North Sea on 6 September. He and his crew were rescued.

14. Of the 101 crew members rescued during 25–7 July, fifty-nine (forty-nine of these Americans) were picked up by HSLs of the RAF and RN; twenty by RNLI lifeboats from Sheringham and Cromer; thirteen by Walrus aircraft; and nine by various trawlers.

15. Lieutenant Milton Mard was awarded the Soldier's Medal for his efforts in saving the crew. For his heroic action on this mission

and shooting down one enemy aircraft, and probably destroying another, Sergeant Soucy was awarded the Silver Star.

16. *Airborne Lifeboats* by Stephen Brewster Daniels, author of *Rescue from the Skies*, writing in *Wingspan Magazine*.